D0760059

Cities for Sale

LEONIE SANDERCOCK

Cities for Sale

*Property, politics
and urban planning in Australia*

MELBOURNE UNIVERSITY PRESS
1977

First published 1975
Paperback edition 1977

Printed in Hong Kong by
Silex Enterprise & Printing Co. for
Melbourne University Press, Carlton, Victoria 3053
U.S.A. and Canada: International Scholarly Book Services, Inc.,
Box 555, Forest Grove, Oregon 97116
Great Britain, Europe, the Middle East, Africa and the Caribbean:
International Book Distributors Ltd (Prentice-Hall International),
66 Wood Lane End, Hemel Hempstead, Hertfordshire HP2 4RG, England

National Library of Australia Cataloguing in Publication data

Sandercock, Leonie, 1949– .
    Cities for sale: property, politics
    and urban planning in Australia/[by]
    Leonie Sandercock.—Carlton, Vic.:
    Melbourne University Press, 1975.
    Index.
    Bibliography.
    "Revised version of research done
    originally for a doctoral thesis in the
    Urban Research Unit at the Australian
    National University."
    ISBN 0 522 84140 6 paperback

    1. Cities and towns—Planning—
    Australia—History. I. Title.
711.40994

*To Mum and Dad, the quarter-acre block,
and the Ancient Person of my Heart*

Contents

List of Maps

Preface

In the following pages I have tried to explain the failure of urban planning in Australia's three leading cities in the twentieth century. Since the Labor Party won the 1972 federal election a determined national effort has been made for the first time since the 1940s to reform and improve our cities in various ways. Those efforts ought to be based on an understanding of the processes and ideologies behind past failures. Hence the haste with which this book has gone to press.

This is a revised version of research done originally for a doctoral thesis in the Urban Research Unit at the Australian National University. That thesis wandered between two worlds of advice, encouragement and influence—the energetic optimism of Pat Troy and the painful pragmatism of Peter Harrison. Discussions with them have been invaluable. I have also learnt much from my history supervisors, Barry Smith and Bob Gollan, my fellow-student Peter Spearritt, and my undergraduate teacher Hugh Stretton, who first aroused my interest in urban problems, and from comments on the completed thesis by H. J. Dyos, Ian Turner and Max Neutze. Their influence will be apparent.

I warmly thank my friends Owen and Helen Donald, Betty Smith and Dave Walker in Canberra for their support, June Harries for her typing endurance, and all those friends and colleagues in Adelaide, Melbourne and Sydney who gave me their help, especially Ben Hills, Mike Duigan, Jack Mundey, Ruth and Maurie Crow, and Ian Turner.

My greatest debt is to David Donnison for his prompt reading and constructive criticisms of the revised manuscript and for his unflagging enthusiasm.

Preface to paperback edition

Three years on, our cities are still for sale. The structure of political power is still protecting and enriching property owners and pampering rural interests. Accordingly, such planning as is being attempted is still hampered at every level by private property interests exerting influence on public authorities and on politicians. Take three recent cases, in Melbourne alone, for example.

In September 1974 the federal government offered the Victorian government $20 million for the Geelong growth centre on condition that the state government introduce legislation giving the Geelong Regional Authority development powers. State cabinet rejected draft legislation aimed at giving the authority those powers, after intense intra-party lobbying by Geelong members of parliament representing the interests of rural landowners around Geelong. So the federal money lapsed and nothing happened until the state government introduced new legislation in December 1976, providing that land to be acquired for development must first be rezoned for its development use and then bought at the new urban price. The profits of the rezoning would then go to the rural landowners rather than to the growth centre. The money for the purchase of the rezoned land would of course be provided by public funds allocated to the development of Geelong as a growth centre. Public exposure of the effects of this proposed legislation caused the state government to withdraw those clauses concerned with rezoning, much to the annoyance of the Geelong landowners' pressure group.

In February 1977 the state government approved the development of a new satellite city at Mount Ridley. The land for the project is in a corridor approved by the government as non-urban. One company, Lensworth Finance (Vic.) Pty Ltd, stands to win a $9·2 million profit when the land is rezoned for development.

In May 1977 it was revealed that the same company had made a $1·5 million profit on a land sale to the Victorian Housing Commission in December 1973, after owning the land for just twenty days. The land, in the Sunbury area, is zoned for general farming by the Melbourne and Metropolitan Board of Works, but the price paid by the Housing Commission was equivalent to the prices then being paid for land zoned for future subdivision. A consultant's report prepared for the Melton-Sunbury Interim Co-ordination Committee argues that there are a number of major planning reasons which do not favour residential development of that land.

More examples could be given, but these three should suffice to illustrate the continuity of the national hobby of land speculation, the curious methods involved, and the costs in terms of public funds, rational planning, and the welfare of ordinary people. What chance is there of bringing this costly rip-off to a halt?

Any piece of writing about contemporary society and any predictions about its future are based on an amalgam of social values and estimated political possibilities. This book, researched and written in the euphoric 1972–4 period of the Whitlam Labor government, was clearly influenced by the optimism of that milieu in its assessment of the likelihood of making real headway with our urban problems. My analysis of past failure has been reinforced by recent events, but my predictions about the future need some sober reassessment in the light of the events of November–December 1975. Like many Australians, I was outraged and deeply disappointed by those events.

The dismissal of the Labor government by the governor-general on 11 November 1975 proved (for those who still needed convincing) that a dimension of power exists above and beyond the parliamentary process that is available to the capitalist class if and when they feel that their interests are under significant threat.

The election results of December 1975 were a triumph for the forces of materialism and conservatism in Australian society. As Manning Clark has written. election day 13 December 1975 'may be the day which proved once and for all just how hopelessly wedded we. as Australians. are to the petit-bourgeois values—to that very sickness which the progressive part of the world is shedding and destroying'.

My comments in chapter 5 on the election results of December 1949, the last defeat of a federal Labor government, are strangely relevant to the events of December 1975. 'There is no doubt that much of what occurred was the result of capitalist manipulation . . . but it would have been impossible for this to occur if the general political climate had been adverse to such happenings, if the majority of Australians had not wanted precisely the sorts of things they thought those capitalists could deliver. Much of what happened and failed to happen in urban planning in the fifties and sixties can only be understood by keeping this in mind.'

To that time-span of historical failure to improve our cities we must now add the seventies, and probably the eighties. After that, the resource/energy crisis will change most of the parameters, and who knows what might happen then?

L.S.
Melbourne
June 1977

Conversion Factors

(to two decimal places)

1 foot	0.30	metre
1 yard	0.91	metre
1 mile	1.61	kilometres
1 square foot	0.10	square metre
1 square mile	2.59	square kilometres
1 acre	0.40	hectare
£1	$2	
1s	10c	
1d	0.83c	

Introduction

Inequality, City Planning and Income Redistribution

This book is about failure. City planning in Australia this century has failed to improve the welfare of our city dwellers and unless we understand why, our urban planners will continue to devise counter-productive land-use plans and our urban policy-makers will perpetuate the series of income transfers from the poor to the rich which has accompanied the urban planning process in the past.

To the extent that the planning movement has been concerned with redistributive social justice, it has been frustrated since its emergence by the established power structures and ideology of Australia's urban, industrial, bureaucratic society—by the old property-based power holders, by the more recent influence of the technocrats and by the dominant doctrine of modern Western societies that continuing economic growth, based on industrial expansion and the spread of technology, is not only inevitable but also highly desirable. Our urban problems are the spatial expression of the inequalities of a capitalist economy. But that is not the whole story.

The origins of this book lie in my concern with the political, economic and social causes and manifestations of inequality that exist in Australia, particularly as they affect the quality of life in Australian cities. My interest in urban planning stems from the traditional concern of the town planning movement since the turn of the century with social reform—that is, with many of the policies (housing, health, recreation) that could contribute to a more egalitarian society. This tradition was summarized by the New South Wales minister for local government in 1945 in his introduction of the Local Government (Town and Country) Bill:

> The principles of town and country planning may be stated simply as an attempt to regulate in advance the orderly arrangement and use of land ... so as to promote, for the greatest good of the greatest number, the improvement of community life and of the environment in which our people live; to enable the people to enjoy the benefits of social security, good health, safety, education, recreation, employment and shelter, good communications, public utilities and amenities.[1]

1

While town planning ideas encompassed these very broad aims, it has never been within the power of the town planning techniques of zoning and subdivision control to achieve this breadth of intention.

The great historical irony of land use or statutory planning has been that planners have lacked control over that fundamental resource, land. Some of the undesirable economic and social effects of this have been land speculation, often employing land-use plans as 'speculators guides', land shortages, shortages of development funds, and the restriction of planning to an essentially negative role of responding to planning applications and to major private developments rather than initiating and directing urban development for the public benefit.

Hugh Stretton's pioneering study of Australian cities argues that 'very big cities are both physical and psychological devices for quietly shifting resources from poorer to richer and for excusing or concealing —with a baffled but complacent air—the increasing deprivation of the poor.'[2] Apart from Stretton's work, there has been a general neglect, in planning schools and in the social sciences, of empirical research into the equity or distributional aspects of large cities, or of research into ways in which city planning could tackle the problem of the income transfers from poor to rich that occur in the process of indefinite, single-centred growth of cities.[3] Even the academic Left, traditionally concerned with class and power, has failed to see the relevance of the history, politics and economics of urban growth and planning for their analyses of Australian society, yet it provides an excellent case study of ruling-class operations and capitalism at work in Australia.

Urban growth does have significant effects on income distribution, whether deliberate or accidental. If we define 'real income' as command over resources, it is clear that real income is a function of locational accessibility—how close you live to employment opportunities, schools, beaches, welfare services. Access to these can only be obtained at a cost—the cost of overcoming distance, using time, or of buying housing in accessible locations. Poorer households have a very limited choice of locations. As the spatial form of a city is changed (by developing or relocating housing, transport routes, employment, sources of pollution), so also is the cost of access to different things for a household at a given location and hence both the distribution of real income and property values in different locations. Some services are located by public action (for example, educational and health services, open spaces), others by private enterprise. The redistributive aspects of general governmental functions is therefore far from trivial, and increases with city size.[4] No matter who the decision-maker, the very act of locational choice has distributional significance, and since the location of public services could be an important means of income distribution in our economy, more attention ought to be paid to the policies that govern decisions about the location of jobs, services and amenities.

Much of what happens in a city, particularly in the political arena, can be interpreted as an attempt to influence the locational choices of public and private organizations in order to gain income and wealth advantages. City planning could be used to influence the redistribution of income by changing the location of jobs and housing, the value of property rights, the price of goods and services to the consumer. Different groups seek to control these mechanisms through the exercise of political power.

It is in this area, the politics of city planning, that the central thrust of this work lies. Crudely put, who wins and who loses in the distribution of goods, services and property values which are influenced by planning decisions? Have planners themselves been aware of the equity effects of their plans? Does the redistributive potential of city planning explain some of the opposition to its introduction and operation over the last seventy years? What does this tell us about the structure of class and power in Australian society? In theory, city planning *could* become one means of increasing equality in the distribution of real income. Whether it does so in practice depends on both the objectives of the planning authorities and the extent to which they are supported politically by local, state and federal governments. The reasons for the absence of this political support in the past are a large part of the following story.

Chapter 1 begins with an examination of the formative ideas and British origins of the early town planning movement in Australia. It looks at the extent to which the early 'planners' were aware of equity issues and establishes the view of society on which their ideas were based. Consistent with the middle-class backgrounds of most members of the planning movement was the desire to have a non-partisan appeal, the aim of ameliorating class differences and promoting social harmony, and hence the insistence on the technical rather than the political nature of planning. Chapters 2, 3 and 4 move from the world of planning ideas to the practical arena of politics and explain why efforts to introduce planning legislation in Adelaide, Melbourne and Sydney between the two world wars met with so much resistance.

During and after World War II a federal (Labor) government became interested for the first time in the problems of the cities and recognized the connections between physical planning and national economic and social planning. Chapter 5 discusses the conflict between the reformist ideology of the Labor government and the more radical implications of some of its urban planning ideas such as land nationalization, regional planning and citizen participation, and suggests areas of similarity and difference between the Labor government of the 1940s and that elected in 1972. Chapters 6–8 return to the three states and deal with post-war efforts to implement city planning, with the nature of the opposition to it and with the metropolitan land-use and transportation plans eventually produced for each city. Here I argue that the business and property interests that had originally opposed planning legislation have been able, in the post-war period, to manipulate the planning process for private gain. The political power of business and property interests has militated against political support for a radical city planning programme and has forced planning authorities into the role of responding to private developments rather than initiating and controlling city growth and change. But both major political parties have been reluctant to support purposeful planning because both have viewed any controls that could impede economic growth as undesirable.

By way of conclusion the final chapter summarizes the problems of applying a redistributive approach to urban planning in a property-owning democracy and assesses the likelihood of future radical change. Some of the areas from which change can be expected range from a shifting set of interests with the capitalist class to an emerging middle-class concern with environmental amenity and a radical building union's concern with the future of the city and the opportunities for the working class within it. The most powerful initiative for change is that of the new Department of Urban and Regional Development established in December 1972 by the newly elected federal Labor government. The old problems of class power and property ownership that confronts the efforts of this new department, particularly in the sphere of land policy, complete the story.

The issues dealt with in the following pages—the property-power nexus of capitalist society, the growth ideology, conservation and public participation in planning—present a series of dilemmas on a local and national scale: whether a Marxist model provides a comprehensive explanation of the present structure of Australian society; whether popular immediate solutions to planning problems are to be preferred to long-term more expert ones, whether a combination of popular movements and representative institutions can outweigh entrenched power groups, and whether more participatory and redistributive policies will in the end enhance overall human welfare.

Part I

Laissez-faire in the Cities
1900–1945

1

Emergence of the
Town Planning Movement 1900–1920

> On the grounds of public health and well-being absolute freedom to lay out a town anywhere and in any fashion should be limited.
>
> John Sulman 1890

> Town planning covers almost everything that makes for the commercial and industrial expansion of cities and the convenience and health of their dwellers.
>
> John Sulman 1921

Urbanization in Australian History

It may seem strange to write a book about the efforts to give some order to the process of urbanization in Australia when no comprehensive account of the process itself has yet been given. It is even stranger that no such account exists. For Australia has been for the last hundred years one of the most urbanized of the rich Western democracies. Just over a hundred years after the first fleet's arrival in 1788 Adna Weber's comparative study of international urban growth published in 1899 pointed out that in Australia nearly one-third of the entire population was settled in and about the capital cities, 'a most remarkable concentration'.[1] Contemporary Australia must, by any standard of comparison, rank as one of the most highly urbanized countries in the world, with 85 per cent of its population living in towns with more than a thousand people according to the 1971 census. And this urbanization has been concentrated in the state capitals, as the population table on page 8 indicates.

Yet historians, political scientists and sociologists have traditionally looked to the outback, the bush ethos, for an explanation of Australian development and for the ideas and beliefs that make up the Australian heritage, and have asked very few questions about the process and politics of urban growth, and the nature and quality of the urban life that most Australians have experienced. One of the few scholars to

Year	Adelaide	Percentage of S.A.	Melbourne	Percentage of Vic.	Sydney	Percentage of N.S.W.
1891	133 000	42	491 000	43	383 000	34
1901	162 000	45	496 000	41	482 000	36
1911	192 000	46	612 000	46	630 000	38
1921	255 000	52	801 000	57	899 000	43
1931	324 000	55	996 000	55	1 201 000	47
1941	350 000	58	1 115 000	57	1 337 000	48
1951	443 000	61	1 331 000	58	1 795 000	55
1961	588 000	61	1 985 000	65	2 183 000	56
1971	809 000	69	2 503 000	68	2 725 000	59

Source: State Year Books

break with this tradition is the economic historian N. G. Butlin, who wrote of the period from 1860 to 1900 that

> the outstanding characteristic of Australian economic history was ... the exceptional rate of urbanisation of the local population and the extraordinarily early orientation of economic activity towards commercial-industrial specialisation and the tertiary services of urban society. By 1891, two-thirds of the Australian population lived in cities and towns, a fraction matched by the United States only by 1920 and by Canada not until 1950. Most of Australian capital equipment went into growing towns, most of the expanding workforce was employed in urban occupations and the greater part of gross product came from urban activity ... The process of urbanisation is the central feature of Australian history, over-shadowing rural economic development and creating a fundamental contrast with the economic development of other 'new' countries.[2]

Colonization from Britain was the starting point in the history of Australian cities, which were peopled, financed and equipped from outside. Australia was a distant part of the British, European and western-world economic system. Trade was initially limited by the lack of exports, until wool filled the need for a staple in the 1830s and gold was discovered in the 1850s. The role of the early cities as entrepôts for the maritime trades, the wool trade and then mining is familiar. Without the demand of commerce for bases and fishing grounds, and of English industry for wool and metals, the cities would hardly have grown as they did—ports before they were cities —or where they did.

By mid-nineteenth century, transportation of convicts had ended, free migrants were taking their place, British investors were placing some of their money in Australia, and self-government was on the way. The discovery that Australia could produce the wool that Britain needed was the trigger of this transformation. The people who migrated were affected by the class structure of the home country in obvious ways: convicts who were mostly convicted of offences against private property; entrepreneurs with modest capital in search of a fortune; workingmen in search of independence, their own patch of land and better wages; peasants in search of urban comfort and income. But it is equally significant that the class structure of England produced a concentration of surplus funds in the hands of private owners in search of dividends. The public transport systems of the Australian colonies, and a good many other public works, were financed in the late nineteenth century by the inflow of this private British capital, a situation more aptly described therefore as 'agency capitalism' than as 'colonial socialism'.[3]

Wool growing, with its low labour requirements, reinforced the dominance of Sydney over its hinterland. The gold discoveries confirmed this urban domination, precipitating Melbourne almost overnight from small town to metropolitan centre. Australia was launched in the 1850s on a long period of prosperity which continued until the early 1890s. The roots of this prosperity lay in Australia's place in the expanding British world economy. 'Australia received British migrants and plentiful British capital, found a buoyant British market for its exports, and flourished under the Pax Britannica as the resources of a new continent were brought into production. Modern Australia began to take shape, a shape that persevered until World War II'.[4] This was the first great period of city building. Between 1860 and 1890 the building industry absorbed about one-third of total Australian investment, reaching a peak in the metropolitan building booms of the 1880s, the over-supply of houses, and the collapse of the market in the early 1890s. In each city the building boom went far beyond the housing market and became an urban land boom, with suburban subdivisions and land speculation extending well ahead of building, and housing development racing ahead of the provision of other urban facilities, with the result that 'Australian towns and cities grew primarily as a sprawl of detached cottages with only primitive commercial, industrial and social equipment'.[5] Sydney grew from 54 000 in 1851 to 400 000 in 1891, 35 per cent of the New South Wales population. Melbourne, a mere 29 000 in 1851, had grown to 473 000 by 1891, 40 per cent of Victoria's population.[6]

From the beginning Australian cities straggled across plentiful land, using the English country cottage as its model dwelling, creating suburbs well before most other urban industrial societies. From walking-distance cities up to the 1880s the capitals developed as public-transport cities with the large investment in that sector at the end of the century. By 1891 New South Wales had built over 2194 miles of railway, Victoria 2764 miles and South Australia 1665 miles.[7] Most city growth in Australia took place after the nineteenth-century revolution in transport which suburbanized even old-world cities, and Australian cities remained public-transport cities until economic and technological changes ushered in the motor-car age in the 1950s. With labour shortages and high wages, home ownership was much more of a possibility for most people than it had been in the old country. The 1911 census, the first to provide this information, showed that half of all housing was owner-occupied, a proportion barely reached in the United Kingdom by 1971. The proportion had probably been much higher in 1891 following the building boom.

While a small patch of urban land was accessible to a majority of city workers, this was not true of rural land, despite the intentions of the land acts passed in the southeastern states in the sixties and seventies. In the twenties the Crown gave away land or sold it for a small sum, but in 1831 it ceased to grant free land to new settlers. No Crown land was to be sold for less than 5s an acre, and in 1842 the minimum price was raised to 20s. Sheep owners who grazed flocks on Crown land were not hurt by the rising price of land. By the sixties, when their pastoral lands began to be resumed for auction under the new land acts (whose intention was to 'unlock the land' for small farmers), it was the pastoralists (or squatters) who could most afford and most readily obtain bank loans to purchase the freehold. Thus the more the democrats legislated against squatters the more they strengthened the squatting monopoly. Sheep runs paid better than small farms and banks were more willing to lend money to the pastoralist to purchase his lease than to lend to penniless selectors. Under the land acts, intending settlers were allowed to select and occupy a farm area of 40–320 acres. They had to pay a quarter of the price of the land and reside on it for three years. Then, if they paid the balance, the land was theirs. While the government was spending as revenue the millions of pounds flowing in from the sale of the public estate, it saw no urgent need to arrest a process by which 96 men acquired the freehold of 8 million acres in New South Wales and 100 men in Victoria secured the freehold of 1.5 million acres. The small class thereby created of large rural property owners, who gained for themselves majorities in the state upper houses, elected on a restricted franchise, were to be a major hindrance to the urban reformers of the twentieth century.

The initial prosperity and growth of the cities dried up in the depression of the 1890s. With the withdrawal of overseas capital and the collapse of speculative companies, profits fell, wages were forced down, and severe unemployment continued for the next ten years. For the next twenty years Australia lived in the shadow of the 1890s depression. Gone were the golden days of easy expansion, for the British world economy was constricted by competitors who had overtaken it technologically and carved out rival empires. Between the 1890s and 1914 Australia gained its reputation as a country of advanced social legislation. In this period the powers of the new federal and old state governments were used to guide and direct the economy and during this time of recovery and self-examination the town planning movement first emerged, closely allied with other movements for social reform.

Australian cities were built by a partnership of public and private enterprise in which the public authorities provided the essential services and private business did the rest. The state governments, which owned the land, employed large amounts of labour, borrowed large amounts of capital, and were responsible for peopling and developing the new country, naturally needed to intervene in the economy to some extent. But this state intervention was not, as it has usually been called, 'colonial socialism'. Its purpose was to create the conditions in which private enterprise could flourish. In the period of industrialization from 1920 to 1970 (interrupted by depression and war in the thirties and forties) the inflow of private capital was again heavy and played a major part in the expansion of several industries that had a large influence on the cities—cars, electrical goods, electronics.

Thus the particular pattern of physical development of Australian cities depended on class relationships outside them, specifically the exploitative relationships which concentrated large amounts of investable money in the hands of British and American businessmen. But the situation was not one of total dependency, for the very inflow of capital was dependent on local events, notably the ascendancy in the two long booms of Liberal Party politicians who actively sought overseas investment.

British Influence on Town Planning Ideology

It was not only our political and social institutions (parliaments, constitution, private property, the nuclear family) and the process of capital formation and investment that were derived from overseas. So too, logically, was Australian thinking, especially thinking about our cities and their problems. This chapter looks at the derivative nature of the town planning movement which emerged around the turn of the century and was consolidated by the end of World War I. It will first look at some of the key concepts of British thinking of the time, tracing their influence in the personalities and ideas of members of the Australian planning movement, and examine the political, economic and social assumptions behind and implications of these ideas. The extent of British influence is evident in the importance of immigrants in the early planning movement, in the exodus to Britain between 1912 and 1915 of public servants from each state to study and report on British developments, and in the frequency with which British examples were cited in Australian discussions and reports.

The development of town planning as a reform movement in Britain originated in the concern of some intellectuals and politicians about the social and economic consequences of the industrial revolution. Since the beginning of the nineteenth century, while Britain grew wealthy from her industrial cities, many poets, novelists and essayists—Wordsworth, Ruskin, Morris, Engels, Kingsley, Cobbett—pictured this development as a deterioration from the pre-industrial golden age. Two lines of thought developed from these origins. Writers and philosophers condemned the life of industrial cities, but more practical-minded men sought to improve the cities materially by sanitary reform and by creating model industrial villages.

The movement for sanitary reform was the result of an awareness of some of the alarming qualities of the new congested districts. 'Even if he were not his brother's keeper, every man of property was affected by the multiplication of thieves; everyone who valued his life felt it desirable not to have a mass of carriers of virulent diseases too close at hand.'[8] There were signs that such dangers did exist and to look into their extent and nature were the tasks of the famous investigations, public and private, of the thirties and forties. Their titles indicate the problems: *The Moral and Physical Conditions of the Working Classes of Manchester* by J. P. Kay, *The Health of Towns* by a House of Commons Select Committee (1840), *The Sanitary Condition of the Labouring Population of Great Britain* by poor law commissioner Edwin Chadwick (1842), and *The State of Large Towns and Populous Districts* (1844–5) by a royal commission. It was immorality, criminality and disease that were causing concern. Overcrowding, poverty, crime, ill-health and high mortality were conditions found together, and a causal relationship was assumed.

The reform proposals of the select committee report on the health of towns involved a radical departure from existing practice. But the grounds on which their framers sought to justify them are indicative of the terms in which urban problems were seen. There were two principal arguments. Firstly the unhealthy conditions created an economic loss, in reduced labour productivity, which affected the whole community. Secondly towns fostered unrest and defiance of the law, which threatened the social structure. Remedial efforts were therefore desirable on grounds of both humanity and expediency. The select committee of 1840 declared that 'some such measures are urgently called for, as claims of humanity and justice to great multitudes of our fellow men, and as necessary not less for the welfare of the poor than the safety of property and the security of the rich'.[9] Property was a dominant theme and major consideration of all reformers. The need to keep it inviolate was not only an argument for social reform but more importantly imposed drastic limitations on the reform that might be attempted.

Precious little urban reform was attempted in the nineteenth century. The whole subject of sanitary improvement no doubt seemed of minor importance when set beside the achievements of industry and commerce. By the end of the century there were two main approaches to urban problems. The first, derived from the writers and philosophers, advocated the abandonment of both technology and the profit system and a return to pre-industrial values. The second, less radical and derived from the sanitary reformers and utopian town planners, wanted to 'quarantine' the technology (by separating it from residential areas) but to leave untouched the economic structure and means of production. There was doubt about achieving much more along the old lines of public health and housing policy and some sought a more comprehensive approach which they called town planning. Their models were the new towns and villages and garden suburbs of the late nineteenth and early twentieth century. Their theorist was Ebenezer Howard, clerk, farmer, court reporter and inventor, and author in 1902 of *Garden Cities of Tomorrow*.

Howard, in his own words, 'swallowed whole' Bellamy's vision in *Looking Backward* (1888) of the communistic Boston of A.D.2000.[10] Howard and the Garden City Movement fostered basically anti-city planning. They emphasized environmental health, housing and sanitation, to make living conditions healthier and less visibly grim. Howard's concept of town-country was intended to foster the advantages and discard the disadvantages of both town and country life. His fundamental idea was to create independent new communities of limited size, with land in community ownership. This was to be the key to the economic problems of the community. Profits accruing to the community from public ownership of the land were to be used to eliminate poverty and care for the disadvantaged. Howard never discussed or apparently considered how, in a society where power rested with vested interests in property, the transition to public ownership of land might come about. Like most planners before and since, he was innocent of questions of political and economic power and social control, and failed to see that his planning proposals provided yet another means of social control which could be used by those in power to prevent conflict and preserve the status quo.

Howard wanted to recreate the social mix of the country town but to change its economic structure. But the radical economic aspects of his proposals were not taken up by later disciples. That was not surprising given the class background of those who joined for example the Garden Cities and Town Planning Association, a group that purported to speak in the name of the urban poor but drew its membership from the middle and upper classes and directed its appeal to 'influential people'. Letchworth and Welwyn garden city were the natural offspring of such a movement. Their layouts provided a dramatic contrast to the rigid grid-iron layout with small backyards which had been the almost universal rule for the homes of all but the very rich. But this was made possible only by the adoption of comparatively low densities, which acted as an automatic means of social segregation in commercially based suburban development, where the price of the land was beyond reach of the poor.

Low density became the overriding principle of planning, enshrined in the Housing and Town Planning Acts of 1909 and 1919. Low density was not seen as inconsistent with two other key aspects of planning ideology, the concepts of community and social integration. The origins of these concepts can be traced back to a reaction against the loss of the church's concern for the whole spiritual life of man as a result of changes taking place in the nineteenth century. The idea of community arose as compensation for some of the changes involved in the transition from a feudal, land-based society to an industrial society. The idea of social integration arose in opposition to the social and physical manifestations of inequalities in the distribution of capital. Both concepts however looked backwards to the social structure of a rural society with its supposed organic solidarity (neglecting the inequalities in the distribution of land and power that characterized those societies) rather than forward to a less class-stratified society where power and opportunities would be shared more equally.

The values behind these concepts were affirmed as early as Howard and as late as the National Council of Social Service's report in 1943 on the size and social structure of a town. Among their recommendations were that housing development should be based on the 'neighbourhood unit', regarded as a community with a maximum of 2000 dwellings and furnished with the facilities necessary for the full development of the life of the neighbourhood; and that in the interest of social variety each neighbourhood unit should be socially balanced', containing houses of different types and sizes and inhabited by families of different incomes. This report was a milestone in the documentation of the ideology of physical planning. It contained proposals that foreshadowed most of the early post-war reports, acts and planning practice. But up to World War II, town planning was limited in function, if not in intention, and regarded mainly as a means of controlling new development to enhance architectural and amenity standards.

By 1900 a number of strands of earlier reform movements had been put together in a series of arguments for town planning as the best means of co-ordinating the reform and future growth of urban areas—utopian urban design, promotion of public health, improved working-class housing, better service provision, and reform of urban government. The Housing and Town Planning Acts of 1909 and 1919, in which health, housing and planning were linked for the first time in national legislation, were the climax of the first phase of town planning. But that legislative approach was remedial and palliative. It did not attack the cause—the economic system and the problem of poverty—of the ills the planning movement sought to improve. This was not surprising given the class background of the reformers. They sought to ameliorate harsh social conditions and to avoid divisive conflict. Planning was seen as a means of maintaining social harmony and was therefore presented as an issue that transcended class and party divisions, benefiting all sections of the community, from workers and middle-class citizens to landowners (by maintaining the value of developed land by zoning to preserve the 'character' of particular areas) and capitalists (by cultivating a healthy workforce).

The ideas of community and of social integration, presented as beneficial to all classes, were always assumed to be achievable by physical arrangements. This assumption that physical arrangements, rather than economic and political change, could bring about the social reform that planners desired is a weakness in the social theory of city planning that persists to this day. The first indication of a change of direction in Australian thinking was revealed in Hugh Stretton's *Ideas for Australian Cities*, written in 1970 by an academic rather than a planner. He predicted that

> metropolitan planning must one day be integrated as the land use and communications branch of central economic planning . . . The 'chief planner' will have to be the Premier. The chief 'planning document' will have to be his budget. His chief executants will probably include massive development corporations directed by economists and dealing in as much as a third of all new urban land.[11]

He added that these notions 'are still no more than radical theorists' dreams of the twenty-first century.' No member of the early planning movement in Australia, with the exception of the radical Sydney University economics professor R. F. Irvine, perceived that, in order to achieve most of their social aims, physical or town planning must be closely allied with economic planning. One of the great weaknesses of the planning movement in Australia, as elsewhere, is that this has not been done.

Social, Aesthetic and Administrative Concerns

By the turn of the century Australian cities had become the subject of wider public discussion. The expatriate English architect John Sulman (1849–1928), who later became first president of the Town Planning Association of New South Wales and lecturer in town planning at Sydney University, gave several addresses after his arrival in

Australia in 1885. One of these, 'The layout of towns', delivered to the Australian Association for the Advancement of Science at Melbourne University in 1890, contained the earliest use of the term 'town planning'. Sulman's British origins were evident in his preoccupation with disease, unsanitary conditions and public health. When misuse of land and the privilege of private ownership 'takes so glaring a form as originating conditions that must inevitably tend to produce disease it is the absolute duty of the state to interfere', he argued.[12] He did not mean however that the state should interfere with the system of private ownership, the cause of the evils that disturbed him. Rather he advocated regulatory powers: fixing a minimum size for building lots, limiting the area of suburbs to a maximum of one square mile with open space between suburbs of at least one-eighth of a mile, and refusing subdivision approval unless satisfactory water supply and drainage schemes were provided for.

But Sulman was ahead of his time even in these concerns, for most discussion about cities around the turn of the century focused on municipal problems. Australia had not kept pace with overseas developments during the depression of the 1890s, and Sydney, by 1900 the largest Australian city with a population approaching half a million, had not kept pace with advances in city government that were occurring in centres like London and Birmingham. Looking back in 1917 Charles Reade (1880–1932), a New Zealand journalist who worked for the Garden Cities and Town Planning Association of Great Britain and organized their Australasian Town Planning Tour in 1914, claimed that 'the stress of local evils pressed more heavily upon the New South Wales capital' thereby producing 'some of the early developments of the movement which has set Australian cities definitely in search of city planning reforms'.[13] Sidney and Beatrice Webb, during their short visit of 1898, compared the local government of Sydney to that of London 'prior to 1885' and advocated the establishment of a Sydney county council to supersede the functions of the forty municipal councils. These views were similar to those of J. D. Fitzgerald (1862–1924), who since 1890 had been active in movements for town planning, civic improvement, better housing for workers and municipal reforms. He was one of the first Labor members elected to the New South Wales Legislative Assembly, minister of local government and public health in the national government from 1916 to 1919 and chairman of the Housing Board which planned and built the model Daceyville garden suburb. Fitzgerald had met John Burns (principal author of the British Housing and Town Planning Act of 1909) on a visit to England, and on his return in 1898 he addressed the Sydney Toynbee Society on 'Municipal Statesmanship in Europe', attacking the lack of interest in municipal affairs in Australian cities. Two Greater Sydney conferences in 1900 in which he was involved foundered on the failure to reach agreement about unification or federation, a conflict that repeatedly foiled attempts to create one central government for Greater Sydney. City aldermen favoured unification but suburban aldermen favoured federation. Each group was anxious to protect or increase its own powers.

There were other reasons besides the issue of municipal reform, though, for an increasing interest in the problems and development of Sydney. Slum reform in particular was a very important component of the town planning movement that emerged formally in 1913. The slum issue was first raised in 1896 when Archdeacon Boyce (1844–1931) predicted catastrophe in health or crime or both if something were not done about Sydney's slums. In March 1900 bubonic plague broke out in the Darling Harbour Wharves area, almost paralysing the activities of the city and forcing the government to act. This crisis crystallized a number of issues concerning redevelopment. Perhaps the most important result was the establishment of a statutory authority, the Sydney Harbour Trust, which signified the entrance of the state into an area previously a private preserve.

This body of appointed rather than elected commissioners was criticized by Fitzgerald for being 'entirely independent of municipal control'. Similar complaints had been made in 1902 at the annual conference of the Political Labour League when it was resolved that members of the Water and Sewerage Board and other boards and commissions should be elected by adult suffrage. These demands indicated recognition by Labor supporters that councils and boards had powers that affected them and should therefore be subject to democratic control. They recognized, at least implicitly, that decisions concerning city development and redevelopment were not only technical but political, that they involved distributional and access questions. But others less politically committed to the interests of a particular social class resented the intrusion of 'politics' into questions of improvements, arguing that the chief criteria should be financial viability and technical expertise. Sulman was an exponent of this view. In his *Improvement of the City of Sydney*, written in 1907, he argued that 'one competent expert will produce a better scheme in less time and at less cost than any board or combination of representatives'—the classic British paternalist, elitist view of the planning process.

The differences of approach of Sulman and Fitzgerald were evident in their attitudes to the Wexford Street redevelopment scheme in inner Sydney. Sulman thought the scheme 'undoubtedly good insofar as it gets rid of a congested area of low-class property'. But Fitzgerald criticized the proposals for their lack of provision for 'rehousing of people'.[14] In 1906 Fitzgerald published *Greater Sydney* and *Greater Newcastle*, arguing for united city government and for a

Housing of the Working Class Act. He wanted a body that could deal with Sydney 'on one harmonious and artistic plan' and that would have the power 'to improve the city area by resuming and demolishing slum quarters and rebuilding on a better plan ... and to erect or provide model lodging houses for the poor, as the great British municipalities do'. Sulman had not yet become interested in workers' housing but he and Fitzgerald eventually worked together on the planning of the Daceyville garden suburb in 1912–13 and united two strands of the emerging planning movement, the social and the aesthetic concerns.

The growing interest in the 'improvement' of Sydney culminated in 1908 in the appointment of a royal commission on the 'Improvement of the City of Sydney and Suburbs', which sat for twelve months. Its final recommendations included proposals for wholesale demolitions, creation of new streets, subways, tunnels and arterial thoroughfares a hundred feet wide from city to suburbs, street widening, construction of an underground railway, the promotion of a building act, powers to municipalities to resume and remodel unsanitary areas, provide workmen's cottages, playgrounds and so on, and finally to enable councils to make and execute town planning schemes on the lines of the British Act of 1909. D. Winston lamented in *Sydney's Great Experiment* (1957) that, apart from the Daceyville housing scheme, little was done to implement the recommendations of the royal commission. But the odd amalgam of values and conflicting approaches to city improvement evident in the list of recommendations made any concerted action unlikely. The emphasis on the 'monumental' or aesthetic approach (the preoccupation with majestic thoroughfares and civic grandeur) suggested an effort to imitate Baron von Hausmann's achievements in Paris under the autocratic rule of Napoleon III with no clear realization of the economic or social consequences. No doubt the fact that ten of the principal witnesses to the commission were engineers and three were architects contributed to the dominance of this approach. It was probably only the participation of Fitzgerald in the inquiry that ensured the inclusion of the social welfare goals of workers' housing and slum clearance.

The McGowan Labor government, elected in 1910, was concerned about slum areas and rising rents as a factor in reducing real wages and established a Housing Board in 1912. Fitzgerald became chairman of this body, the creation of which may have been encouraged by the passing of the Workers Dwellings Act in Queensland in 1909. But it differed from the Queensland act in a way that illustrated the influence of town planning ideas. For rather than supply advances for the erection of random dwellings the Housing Board proposed the building of a garden suburb. Work on it began in 1912 and Sulman, as supervising architect, came into contact with Fitzgerald. Sulman's interest in planning at this time was also stimulated by his friendship with the newly appointed economics professor at Sydney University, R. F. Irvine, who was appointed by W. A. Holman in 1912 to investigate the provision of workingmen's housing in Europe and America. The report produced by Irvine in 1913 was published as a government white paper and not long after its release the Town Planning Association was formed at a meeting in the Sydney Town Hall on 17 October 1913.

Class Origins of Town Planning Associations

The years 1913–15 were a period of intense activity for the emerging town planning movement. The various strands of the reform movement coalesced in the formation of town planning associations in each state; three state governments sent civil servants overseas to study and report on planning and housing; and in 1914 Charles Reade, accompanied by W. Davidge, began the Australasian Town Planning Tour on behalf of the British Garden Cities and Town Planning Association, receiving official recognition and financial support from all state governments as well as from municipal and other bodies.

The formation of Australia's first town planning association in New South Wales in 1913 brought together men with widely differing political views and approaches to planning. The main aim of the association was 'to advocate proper planning of Australian cities and towns'[15] but its many sub-aims revealed the diverse interests of its membership, which included the figures who dominated the Sydney movement from 1900 to 1930—architects Sulman, Walter Burley Griffin (designer of Canberra) and W. L. Vernon, municipal politicians like Sir Allen Taylor (a prominent businessman) and J. Garlick (later a city commissioner), engineers like J. J. C. Bradfield, real estate developer and company director R. Stanton, George and Florence Taylor, editors of the *Building and Real Estate Magazine*, and housing and social reformers like Irvine and Fitzgerald. The concerns of the association ranged from housing and the report of 'nuisances' such as smoke, to parks and reserves, water supply and lighting, disfigurement of the city by hoarding advertisements, road widths, and public health. The association also supported a modern building act and the establishment of a chair of architecture and town planning at Sydney University, but saw its most important task as that of reporting and publicizing the town planning cause.

George Taylor's views were representative of the 'right wing' of the planning movement. His book *Town Planning for Australia* (1914) was preoccupied with civic beauty, vistas, spectacle and visual drama. He supported zoning as a means of 'distributing population into districts of varying character . . . [because] human nature will never be levelled'. His conservative view of human nature extended to the belief that people got the kind of city they deserved.

> The Jerry Builder has long been a scape-goat for bad suburban construction, but he is only a product of the people. Those for whom he builds get what they ask for. Let them request decent homes and be prepared to pay for them and they will get them . . . It is useless to expect a decent city unless we have a decent people.[16]

This was not typical of most members of the planning movement, who believed that a physically improved city would improve the morals, health and welfare of its poor people. But Taylor opposed 'fool legislation' like the Fair Rents Act and 'state socialism' building people's homes.[17]

Such was the conservative strand of the movement. At its most radical extreme was Irvine, whose interest in town planning was part of an overall socialist critique. In 1914 he put forward the theory that unequal income distribution was a major source of economic crisis, concluding that at almost every stage of industrial evolution had existed a fund that might have been redistributed more equitably without in any way impairing the efficiency of production. Trained in economics and history Irvine believed in applying these skills on behalf of radical social change. He appeared on behalf of workers at major investigations into wages and conditions in 1913, 1920, 1921 and 1930. In his evidence in 1920 to the Piddington royal commission on the basic wage he showed that Australia's percentage of rent to total wages was the highest in the world despite inferior housing standards, and suggested a Henry George type of land tax, municipal ownership of outlying land and a public brickworks to keep down housing costs. In his book *The Roots of Our Discontent* he attacked the idea that capitalism could be regarded as a permanent economic system and analysed the vested interests opposed to social change. He showed the social ills resulting from allowing the laws of supply and demand to determine economic life, attacked property as the real source of poverty and industrial unrest and criticized the concentration of credit power in private hands. To protect the standard of living of the workers he sought a series of solutions—social legislation, co-operation to raise productivity, experiments in industrial democracy, and co-operative ownership. He also advocated rent control, building licence control, town planning and control over land and speculation. Irvine's 1913 report to the New South Wales government on workingmen's housing was one of three comprehensive reports prepared for state governments in this period. He was 'obsessed with town planning and wrote prolifically on this question' during the war.[18]

In Perth the inspiration behind the town planning movement was W. E. Bold, Perth City Council's town clerk. Bold reported to the council in 1910 on the importance of planning the growth of the metropolitan area, quoting experience in Britain, Belgium, France, Sweden and America. He related land values to transport access, noted the importance of betterment and directed attention to the importance of public ownership of land on the outskirts of cities in order to control future development. He recommended zoning, control of building density and room densities, and the undergrounding of telephone, telegraph and electricity cables. In 1913 the Perth City Council sent Bold on a world tour to study municipal conditions and to attend the Imperial Health and Town Planning Conference, at which Howard, Raymond Unwin and Seebohm Rowntree were speaking. Bold's subsequent report stressed the need for a city plan as the key to successful municipal effort. The Western Australian Town Planning Association was formed in 1916, 'partly as a consequence of Bold's report . . . partly as a public reaction to a remarkable series of public addresses in 1915 by Charles Reade on town planning and partly as a means of securing legislation'.[19]

Meanwhile in Victoria in 1915 J. C. Morrell's *Report on Town Planning* was submitted to the minister of public works. Morrell was an architect in that department. His report stressed overseas innovations and lamented that Australia was falling behind in important areas of social progress. He was particularly concerned about housing and referred to Letchworth garden city as the desirable model. He argued too that planning should be anticipatory, rather than just mending past mistakes, and he attacked those who confined their thinking to the City Beautiful. Like Irvine, Morrell was impressed by the British Housing and Town Planning Act of 1909 and the power it gave to local authorities to control the future growth of a town, in particular the powers for zoning, for insisting on the adequate provision of services in all subdivisions, and for preventing overcrowding by limiting the number of houses to the acre and thus avoiding slums. Like most of the social reformers of the time, Morrell worked from an assumption of physical determinism and an awareness of the cost to society of a bad environment.

Who can say of the vast array of the unemployed how large a portion of the industrially inefficient are so because of lowered physical vitality caused by disadvantageous living conditions? To what extent is the forbidding atmosphere of so many homes an element in the problem of inebriety? Of the burdens which the State is called on to bear in the support of alms-houses for the dependent, hospitals for the sick, asylums for the insane, prisons and reformatories for the criminal, what portion can fairly be attributed to early adverse environment?[20]

Like the professional middle-class members of the British planning movement, Morrell adhered to the concepts of community and social balance. While not believing it desirable to 'mix the dwellings of all classes together indiscriminately', he did believe it desirable and possible 'that all classes of a community may and should live together in close relationship; that a wide variety of classes and types of people produces a healthy, interesting and openminded society.'[21]

This concept of social mix has been criticized by radical social scientists as a device for oppressive social control, for the idea of social mix explicitly accepts the divisiveness of class and tries to mitigate some of its worst results. This divisiveness was particularly apparent in the nineteenth century,[22] the formative period for planning ideology. The development of an industrial, capitalist economy produced not only a very large and very poor urban proletariat but also a severe estrangement between the middle and working class which was seen as a threat to the fabric of society. This estrangement was basically associated with relationships between the owners of capital and the sellers of labour, but it manifested itself in a growing spatial segregation in cities and in the development of a distinctly working-class culture. Notwithstanding the contributory effect of spatial segregation, it was in the market-place rather than the neighbourhood that the estrangement was most severe. Middle-class planners sought gently to soften the divisive realities of class in the market-place through the face-to-face meeting of the classes in the neighbourhood. Whatever may be said of these intentions in theory, they were plainly innocent of the economic and political realities of the 'market city', in which the poor simply cannot afford to buy land and housing in middle-class areas.

Morrell's report, so typical of planning ideology in its espousal of zoning, social balance and the like, influenced the thinking of the Victorian Town Planning Association which had been formed in 1914. In South Australia the visit of Reade and Davidge the same year led to the emergence of the South Australian Town Planning Association. In New South Wales the association had started strongly, partly because its members were well placed to influence government policy—Fitzgerald in state housing, Bradfield in transport, Garlick in local government, and at the university Sulman and Irvine. With influential individuals in each state the planning movement was ready to make the transition from the propagandist to the administrative and legislative phase.

From Ideas to Legislation: Failure and Reassessment

Charles Reade claimed in 1917 that the lecture tour he and Davidge made in 1914 had had permanent results in educating public opinion and paving the way for the introduction of legislation. With bills for the reform of urban administration before the New South Wales and Victorian parliaments in 1915 and a town planning and housing bill (drafted by Reade) before the South Australian parliament in 1916 the success of the town planning movement seemed assured. But the euphoria did not endure. Both the Greater Sydney and Greater Melbourne bills were defeated by hostile upper houses on the issue of broadening the franchise and the South Australian bill met a similar fate because those in power saw it as a threat to their property rights.

After the failure of these legislative efforts to secure status and power for town planning there followed a period of sober reassessment, evident in the themes that emerged from the two Australasian town planning conferences held in Adelaide in 1917 and Brisbane in 1918. With 300 delegates in Adelaide and 600 in Brisbane the views expressed at these conferences can be taken as representative of planning thought at that time. Sulman's paper 'The cities of Australia and their development' was typical of most delegates' statements, which went beyond the desire for economic and orderly development, aiming for social improvements of various kinds. He argued that new suburbs should be separated from each other by boundaries of open space, that employment opportunities should be provided in new areas, and that a sense of identity could be achieved by community centres. He argued that the most urgent question before the conference was the limitation of city growth, by which he meant 'the prevention of continuous building and confining all new centres of population within a limit of about 30,000 inhabitants divided from the next centre by at least a quarter of a mile of open country.' This was essential because 'Sydney is already subdivided to ten to fifteen miles out and will soon all be built over unless steps are taken to prohibit it.'[23] Sulman's thinking was clearly derivative of Howard's garden city theory but it omitted the most radical element of that theory, municipal ownership. It may be that Sulman thought public ownership far too radical for the contemporary climate of opinion. It is more likely that it was too radical for Sulman's own brand of reformism.

Sulman was not only concerned with the planning of new areas. But in his thoughts about improving existing cities he revealed the reformers' dilemma. Utopian solutions were all very well for new areas, but the existing cities were far more complex problems and more urgent in terms of immediate need. Sulman's town planning lectures, published as a book in 1921, worried about 'congestion during the hours of work and congestion in the dwelling, the chief evils to be combated.' He argued that those dispossessed in slum reclamation should be rehoused in garden suburbs and provided with cheap land and transport. Sulman now saw town planning as 'covering almost everything that makes for the commercial and industrial expansion of cities and the convenience and health of their dwellers',[24] but in common with others in the movement he felt the need to show that planning was a paying proposition.

Fitzgerald, in his presidential address to the second conference, said of the first that

> it is an unchallengeable fact that our movement will change the destiny of urban populations and that our propaganda will make our civil conditions better . . . our citizens healthier . . . that our town planners' devices will save millions . . . The hardest task of the first conference was to convince a doubting public that we were not a mere band of dreamers . . . that we could stand the severest test of a Chamber of Commerce.[25]

This statement suggests that war and the 1915 and 1916 legislative defeats had not dimmed the optimism of the movement. On the contrary, it felt itself to be on the verge of great influence and success. This confidence was based partly on the expectation in most states that planning legislation was imminent. But Fitzgerald's own approach had changed insofar as he expressed a new criterion for the movement, that it 'could stand the severest tests of a Chamber of Commerce'. This stress on financial viability had always been important to some figures in the movement but not, generally speaking, of those politically left of centre. Yet this was now a preoccupation expressed in the papers of most delegates. Councillor Rigby, vice-president of the Victorian Town Planning Association, argued that 'even the businessman, the unidealistic person of utilitarian outlook, should remember that city planning attracts industries, commerce and visitors; it produces better transport facilities, improved hygienic conditions and better and less expensive living quarters and food supplies. *City planning is a business proposition of the first importance*'[26] [my italics]. Similarly W. Scott-Griffiths, later South Australian government town planner, claimed that his principal aim was to supply evidence to those who doubted 'the commercial or business value of town planning'. Even the advocates of garden cities used economic profit as their rationale. T. Price, the mayor of Toowoomba, announced that it was now possible 'to so plan industrial cities that they will turn out a far greater quantity of material wealth at less cost.' W. E. Bold illustrated the social control aspects in his paper 'The distribution of parks, playgrounds and open spaces', which argued that 'provision of parks and playgrounds pays a city—in *increase in land values*, attraction of population, improvement of public health and *reduction of delinquency*' [my italics]. The planners' argument for zoning was given its true economic basis in a paper by H. F. Halloran, a surveyor, real estate agent and auctioneer. He explained that New York property owners welcomed zoning as necessary 'in the interests of public health, safety and general welfare, and for the conservation of property values'.

It may be that the most effective arguments that reformers could advance were those that demonstrated reform to be economically profitable. If Australian reformers used this argument as a stratagem (rather than from genuine conviction that economic profits were the most important issue), this indicates much about the political scene. If their perception of the situation was that change would only be possible if it were in the economic interest of those groups who held economic and political power, the possibilities of radical reform were indeed limited, especially in the area of land reform and property rights. If, on the other hand, economic arguments were used in the conviction that this was an important issue, this suggests much about the reformers' ideology. It indicates that their reformist intentions were limited to palliatives that would strengthen rather than threaten the status quo.

The second preoccupation of these two conferences was with the administrative and political problems of a planning authority. Most delegates recognized the need for some kind of planning legislation, but there was little agreement either about the best way to allocate planning powers or about the scope of those powers. The consensus that finally emerged in 1917 was that 'full town planning powers be conferred on local authorities, with right of control by the State government'. But a more modified and ambiguous resolution emerged out of the continuing debate on this issue in 1918, proclaiming that it was not advisable to set up an arbitrary body of experts, but nor was it wise to give individual councils the absolute right to decide whether they would or would not plan, irrespective of adjoining councils or statutory bodies. This issue has never been satisfactorily resolved in subsequent legislation and persists as an enduring dilemma to this day.

At the end of the 1918 conference Fitzgerald remarked that he had never been in any deliberative body so large and so important in which there had been so little friction. It was true that all the resolutions proposed at the conclusion of the conference were passed unanimously, except for one. But the one that failed raised a vital point and suggested that the consensus approach to planning that had prevailed in the two conferences was only possible because discussion was confined to uncontroversial matters that involved no basic economic or political changes. The resolution that failed was put forward by Alderman Branston of Sydney and asked for 'provision to be made to prevent speculators from monopolising business and residential allotments in towns, that an immediate assessment of the unimproved land values of the State be made and the enactment of legislation reserving all future increments to the State . . .'[27] The resolution was opposed by two speakers. E. H. Cowdrey, from the New South Wales Town Planning Association, argued that the proposals were political and had 'nothing to do with the conference at all'. Councillor Rigby said that the latter section of the resolution 'if it means anything, means the nationalisation of land. I am not in favour of that. (Applause).'[28] What is important, apart from the approving applause for Rigby's opposition to land nationalization, is the suggestion by Cowdrey that if proposals were 'political', they should not be presented to the conference. This was not an uncommon attitude among planning advocates. Sulman for example saw 'no valid reason for political party issues being introduced' and believed that municipal government was 'administrative and not legislative.'[29]

This belief that municipal government is administrative rather than legislative belongs in the same ideological mould as the belief that planning decisions are technical rather than political. This unwillingness to come to grips with politics, which has been a feature of the planning movement for the past seventy years, can best be understood in terms of its historical origins. Consistent with the middle-class backgrounds of most members of the movement was the desire for non-partisan appeal and the aim of ameliorating class differences and promoting social harmony. Significant to this developing ideology was the fact that Irvine, the only radical thinker active in the movement, withdrew after 1917, no doubt because the trend of the movement in favour of this consensus view of politics and social change was not in his view the way to solve the main problems of society, especially the problem of poverty. The waste and inefficiency of cities troubled those reformers who involved themselves in the planning movement and they prided themselves in trying to reduce it. But most regarded utopian thought as a luxury and radical thought as both alien and foolish, especially when many businessmen, politicians and civic leaders saw planners as woolly visionaries. Proposals expressing or implying deep dissatisfaction with the present order would only have provoked further criticism, which they could ill afford. This was evident in the treatment of Irvine by the business community. City banks and insurance companies agitated for the foundation of an economics society to offset Irvine's radical ideas and their influence on students. He was eventually forced to resign from the university, ostensibly over a private matter. But in an exchange in the New South Wales parliament one of Irvine's adversaries, Sir Daniel Levy, argued that 'it is not right that men in public positions should express views on contentious political matters' and a Labor parliamentarian claimed that Irvine had been 'victimised because of his radical views'.[30]

Sulman, unlike Irvine, was an apolitical man (which does not mean that his views had no political implications) who worked cautiously from within the system. He participated on numerous boards and commissions, yet his achievements over a forty-year period were minimal. Herein lies a central dilemma for the planning movement. Although it was initially inspired by a social reformist zeal, it submerged the broader problems of social and political change in its concentration on day-to-day problems and in its efforts to win political respectability. This may have been partly because the rapidity of urban growth, especially in the 1920s, demanded 'practical' plans and immediate decisions, and partly a decision (which all reformers must face) to accept the attainable improvement rather than to struggle, probably unsuccessfully, for more ambitious and probably unattainable ideals.

Conclusions

City planning in Australia developed around 1900 as a reform movement concerned with conditions in Australian cities but heavily derivative of British thinking and values. The movement was organized by middle-class reformers who were disturbed both by what was happening to the cities aesthetically and by the living conditions of the urban working class. But their motives were not simply altruistic. They believed that slums threatened their cities physically by breeding crime, violence and disease, politically by breeding discontent, and economically by lowering industrial productivity.

Partly because of their conservative nature the reformers held what has been called a 'facility-centred theory of social change'.[31] They believed that if the poor were provided with a set of properly designed facilities, ranging from a house and garden, which the poor were expected to pay for, to better work places and parks and playgrounds, they would not only give up their slum abodes but would also give up the pathologies associated with poverty. This theory of social change, based on assumptions of environmental or physical determinism, was the conventional wisdom of the early town planning movement and was supported by many businessmen, property owners and their economic and political associates (banks, councils and the like). These groups were interested in ensuring that the slums did not 'infect' the central business area. They were concerned primarily with buildings and facilities and they made common cause with the early reformers.

What the poor needed most was economic aid, some redistribution of the national product, as well as parks and playgrounds. The reformers could have developed anti-poverty programmes, reorganizing the industrial economy so that unemployment and poorly paid employment would be eliminated. They could also have recommended land nationalization, reservation of development rights for the community, or collection of a betterment tax, as Irvine did. But Branston's radical resolution at the 1918 conference was howled down, and

Sulman, who adopted most aspects of Howard's garden city theory, rejected the most important element, that of municipal ownership of land. Irvine was in fact the only member of the town planning movement to advocate fundamental structural changes. The rest failed to do so because politically they were quite conservative. They had no desire to change the economic system or the social order. Their concerns were health, convenience and amenity; order, efficiency and beauty.

2

Adelaide: Property, Privilege and Power

> Town planning ought to be taken out of the hands of land-
> lords and their agents, who desire mainly to see how many
> houses can be got onto a given space.
>
> J. Gunn 1915[1]
>
> ... the rich were used to cosy but lawful relations between
> business and government.
>
> H. Stretton 1970[2]

Structure of Power

In 1836 South Australia was founded by private colonizers, disciples
of the theories of Wakefield, who banned the importing of convicts
and therefore had to rely on free labour. The only way to attract that
labour was to subsidize emigrants' fares, and that was done by selling
Crown land for 12s and later 20s an acre. Beyond the areas surveyed
for sale, squatters leased land to run sheep and cattle, but they also
accumulated large freeholds by purchase at government auction sales.
For by the 1860s, after twenty years' operation, many of the squatters
whose land was opened to selectors had the resources to spend heavily
at the sales. In this way three-quarters of the land offered was sold to
squatters.[3]

Capitalism is a system of power based on or organized in the form
of property. Property, in the form of land, was the most important
basis of political power in South Australia. Those with capital bought
land. Land generated more capital. Land ownership entitled one to
vote and stand for the Legislative Council. It was common practice
for men who had become wealthy in trade or a profession to acquire
land and run sheep without moving from the city. Country and city
capital were thus connected. Merchants and professional men
invested in mining and grazing while pastoralists found seats on the
boards of banks and insurance companies.[4] This propertied elite, often
called the Adelaide Establishment because it comprised a quite small

number of old, interrelated families, exercised 'a degree of financial influence and control probably unparalleled by any group in any Australian state ... they were economically, socially and politically conservative ... they fought to preserve a nineteenth century constitution, a socially hierarchical order, and a *laissez faire* economic system'.[5] And they had the necessary political power to achieve these ends. Lacking any popular base but possessing money, property and influence, their natural habitats were the Legislative Council (elected on a restricted franchise which gave votes only to those owning or renting property valued at £25 or more), the property-dominated Adelaide City Council, the Liberal Party organization, and a political structure that sheltered them. 'Their political influence derived not solely from ability and social prestige, but also from the role the old families played in staffing and financing the party organisation'.[6] Their natural allies, to become formal allies in the Country Party merger with the Liberals in 1932, were the 'Yeoman proprietary', core of the Country Party, cautious guardians of the small-farm economy (more successful in South Australia than the eastern states because the soil of the plains and highlands near Adelaide made it more profitable) and dedicated preservers of rural interests and values. Neither of these two groups were potential supporters of city planning, with its connotations of state intervention and constraints on individual economic freedom, and above all its likely constraints on land, the basis of their wealth. Farmers in fact gained considerably from government intervention, with railways, cheap rates, Roseworthy Agricultural College, land laws. So they didn't mind state intervention if it favoured them, but this was not a distinction they made out loud. Their hold on political power was tight and unassailable, as indicated by their almost unbroken reign in state parliament from 1917 to 1965. (In these years Labor held office only twice, 1924–7 and 1930–3). A ratio of 2 country seats to 1 metropolitan was enacted in 1901 with the provision that country electorates should have half as many electors as city districts. Thenceforth farmers were the largest single social group in the House of Assembly. The Country Party was given a guarantee when it merged with the Liberals that this ratio would be maintained. Consequently, under the 1936 and 1955 redistributions, the extra-metropolitan region had 26, the metropolis 13 seats.

The powers and composition of the Legislative Council were modelled on the mid-nineteenth-century House of Lords. It could reject or amend any bill, including money bills. Franchise provisions were restrictive, based on the head of the household. Therefore as late as 1965 only 38 per cent of assembly electors were on the council roll. Boundary arrangements accentuated the inequality in the distribution of voting power. Three of the five four-member

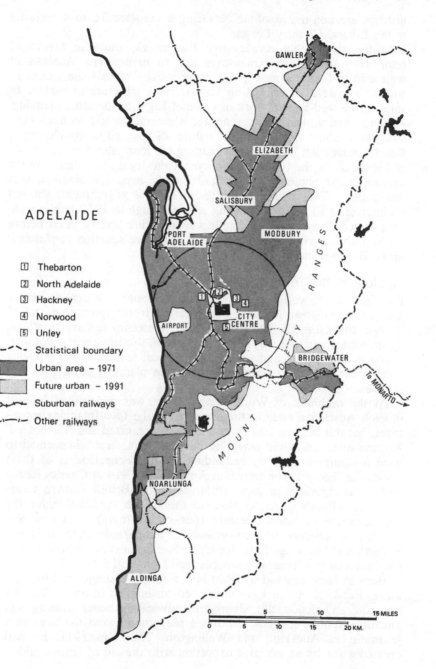

ADELAIDE

1 Thebarton
2 North Adelaide
3 Hackney
4 Norwood
5 Unley
- - - Statistical boundary
▓▓▓ Urban area – 1971
░░░ Future urban – 1991
o—•—• Suburban railways
-•-•- Other railways

GAWLER

ELIZABETH

SALISBURY

MODBURY

PORT ADELAIDE

RANGES

CITY CENTRE

AIRPORT

BRIDGEWATER

To MONARTO

MOUNT LOFTY

NOARLUNGA

ALDINGA

0   5   10   15 MILES
0   5   10   15   20 KM.

districts are non-metropolitan, ensuring a constant 16 to 4 majority to the Liberal Country League.

Within this highly conservative framework, those in favour of reformist town planning measures had to manoeuvre. Analysis of their efforts to implement planning proposals reveals the extent to which they were victims of an impenetrable structure of power. In spite of the well-known work of Colonel Light in its initial planning, Adelaide had to wait eighty years for a second theorist to think constructively about the desirable nature of the city's development. Charles Reade left in 1920 after battling for four years for acceptance of his ideas. In the following nine years the legal and administrative apparatus for planning, which had largely been his creation, was dismantled. From then on, successive Liberal governments showed no interest at all in town planning and, although in 1950 public pressure forced them to reconsider, it was a further sixteen years before a new Labor government finally gave legislative sanction to planning ideas. But to begin at the beginning . . .

Ideology of the Town Planning Movement

By 1914, in a world-wide context, a reasonably articulate set of thoughts about town planning had emerged from separate streams of thought formed in the latter half of the nineteenth century: aesthetic aspirations about the City Beautiful; social thoughts about housing, overcrowding, health and slums; and political and economic thoughts about metropolitan administration and the planning of utilities and services.

At the outbreak of World War I there was widespread interest in each Australian state in the concepts of the town planning movement, but this interest was by and large unorganized and fragmented. No one involved in the emerging movement in Australia seemed to have a comprehensive understanding of the connectedness of these streams of thought. The arrival in Australia in 1914 of Charles Reade and W. R. Davidge as representatives of the British Garden Cities and Town Planning Association (in the British Association for the Advancement of Science lecture tour of Australia), overcame this problem of direction and co-ordination, temporarily at least. Reade in particular left a significant legacy in South Australia, where he was employed as government town planner from 1916 to 1920.

Born in New Zealand in 1880 into a family distinguished in literature, Reade seems to have developed an interest in and a flair for exposing and denouncing slums and advocating better housing and amenities (public gardens, children's playgrounds and the like) as a journalist in Auckland and Wellington. There, in 1911, he had created a stir by an effective exposure, with the aid of lantern slides, of unsanitary housing in those cities. In New Zealand he had written articles on housing projects in Australia, Britain and Germany, which in 1912 led him to Britain, the heart of the new town planning movement. There he was assistant, then acting secretary of the Garden Cities and Town Planning Association, which had been responsible for the creation of Letchworth garden city and other projects and had been influential in initiating the 1909 *Housing and Town Planning Act*. His interest in Australia was heightened in November 1912 by Davidge's lecture 'Planning the new Australian capital' and in 1913 he accompanied Davidge on the Australian lecture tour to 'promote up-to-date planning legislation'. It was in this interlude in Britain that Reade accumulated the body of knowledge concerning planning legislation and experiments in Britain, Europe and America that he was to expound so energetically in his six years in Australia, and later in the Malay States, Rhodesia and South Africa before his suicide in 1933. No personal impressions of Reade the man seem to have survived apart from a few obituary comments which appeared in the *Town Planning Institute Journal* describing him as 'a man of delightful personality, with a strong sense of humour and a rich fund of anecdotes. He did great work in unsettled districts, under trying conditions and often against a distinct hostility towards town planning in local official quarters'.[7]

Reade certainly met with considerable hostility, criticism and opposition from various public bodies in Adelaide, from the city council and from some politicians and technical bodies, particularly from the Surveyors Institute and the Licensed Landbrokers and Real Estate Agents Institutes, and not a little of this must have been provoked by his outspokenness. For example he alienated the Adelaide City Council within twenty-four hours of his arrival in 1914 by remarks about the 'smugness and complacency in Adelaide' and by challenging the city council in a lecture entitled 'Garden Cities versus Adelaide slums and suburbs'. From then on he had an enemy in both the acting mayor of the day, Lewis Cohen, and the city council, which was later to prove a major obstacle when planning proposals largely drafted by Reade came before Parliament in 1916 and 1920. But his energy and enthusiasm attracted and converted many to the cause, including the Liberal attorney-general of 1917–20 and minister in charge of town planning, H. N. Barwell (premier 1920–4), many local councils, and at least two local left-wing newspapers, the *Critic* and the *Daily Herald*.

Since Reade provided not only the inspiration but most of the intellectual sustenance of the movement for town planning in South Australia, his ideas deserve some attention. In general terms his proposals for Adelaide are revealed in a pamphlet *Recommendations in regard to Planning*, written with Davidge in 1915 after their Australasian tour. He advocated a town planning act to deal with both undeveloped areas adjoining the city and with the improvement of areas already built up. The essential provisions of such an act should include power to lay down street and building lines, vary the width of roads, prescribe the maximum height and character and limit the number of buildings to the acre, prescribe special districts for factories and other purposes, acquire lands for open spaces, park belts, street and city improvements, acquire unsanitary areas for the building of garden suburbs at the government valuation prior to the initiation of the town planning scheme, and secure for the public a proper proportion of the betterment arising from any public improvement under town planning. He believed that all main or arterial roads should be subsidized or maintained by the state; that cheap and rapid transport provided by the state should be an integral part of town planning schemes; that tenement houses should be strongly discouraged and the principle of one family, one house firmly maintained; that scenery and natural features and objects of historic or scientific interest should be preserved and belts of open country permanently reserved on the outskirts of cities and new suburbs and that the principles of the garden city movement should be applied or adapted to every scheme of town planning and to every new town created in the state.[8] He approved of the low-density spread of Australian cities but wanted their layouts improved, slums abolished, good homes built for workers, and public parks, open spaces and children's playgrounds provided. His plan for Colonel Light Gardens, the garden suburb created after an act of 1919, embodied his views of enlightened town planning—no through traffic along residential streets, zoning of areas according to their best use, residential and commercial areas designated, building line requirements laid down, and the number of houses to the acre specified. Sites were provided for open spaces and public buildings and provision made for wide tree-lined streets.

At a meeting of the Municipal Association of South Australia in September 1919 Reade spoke on the economic as well as social difference between 'planning' and 'subdividing' land, emphasizing that new areas should be planned *as a whole*, not subdivided piecemeal. To do this, councils needed town planning powers. The mere control of subdivisions, or any legislation attempting to solve existing difficulties under this head, he argued, was doomed to failure. Councils must be able to plan areas *in anticipation of development* and to determine the uses to which land should be put, to regulate the number of houses to the acre, and generally to encourage the orderly development of new districts.

It was no use telling a man he should not waste his money; he was a victim of his environment, and while that was permitted to be squalid no improvement could be expected. Men in such conditions troubled little about the effect of their actions on other people ... Besides the immediate effect of slums, the harm to future generations had to be considered. People who lived in slums took little care of their children.[9]

Reade then recommended to the Smeltors Company that they build a model garden suburb for their workers, for humane as well as for sound business reasons.

The extent of Reade's influence on the South Australian planning movement is obvious in the reorganized constitution in 1916 of the South Australian Town Planning and Housing Association, a body formed after Reade's initial visit in 1914. The objectives of the association are clearly derived from Reade's 1915 pamphlet of recommendations for town planning in South Australia. They included provision by parliament of an up-to-date town planning and development act and housing act 'under which existing shortage and overcrowding will be replaced by modern garden city and social welfare facilities, including the removal of existing unhygienic conditions which are a menace to the public health and national welfare', supplemented by a modern building act; state loans at low interest rates for financing town planning and housing schemes; substitution of modern schemes of town planning and garden city development in place of haphazard growth with the general objective of securing 'convenience, health and amenity'; zoning factory, commercial, recreational and residential areas, including limiting the number of houses to the acre, the proportion of land which could be built on, and the height, use and character of building generally; public adoption of garden city methods of housing and estate development; and 'provision of parks and open spaces, including facilities for recreational institutions or clubs and the encouragement of social welfare generally'.[10]

A significant feature of the planning movement in these enthusiastic early years was its emphasis on the social benefits accruing from town planning, especially for children. In 1916, as part of a child welfare exhibition, the Town Planning Association had prepared an exhibit and declared that 'the welfare of the child demands a Town Planning Act without delay'. Reade delivered a lecture on 'Playgrounds and recreation in garden cities' arguing that 'it was now recognised that by providing for the welfare of the child they were providing for the welfare of the future citizen' and gave an account of the playground movement in the United States, United Kingdom and Canada. He was a strong believer, as were most reformers of the day, in environmental or physical determinism, and argued that 'when slums had been replaced by properly planned suburbs equipped with well designed playgrounds there had been a remarkable decrease in infant mortality and in various diseases, convictions for crime had diminished, and drunkenness had decreased'.[11]

The town planning movement in South Australia reached its zenith in 1920 with the passing of the Town Planning and Development Act and with the publication of its official journal, the *Light Journal of Town Planning and Housing*. The first, and last, issue appeared in June at the high point of public debate over the planning legislation then before parliament, and much of it was devoted to supporting 'the Bill, the whole Bill, and nothing but the Bill'. Its editorial announced that the purpose of the new journal was to give detailed publicity to town planning and housing and kindred activities. It ran a feature, 'Subdividing versus town planning', supporting Reade's work in drawing up garden suburbs. It printed a letter from Ebenezer Howard to a 'prominent Adelaide citizen' (probably Reade) which referred to the concentration of half of Australia's population in five cities and argued that the best corrective was decentralization in properly planned rural garden towns. 'I can see no way of correcting the current overpopulation of big cities, interesting people in the productive enterprises of the soil, except by taking to the country all the advantages of the modern town or city', Howard had written. This solitary issue of the journal was funded from donations of members of the Town Planning Association which itself appears to have been short-lived. But in the early days of the town planning movement (1914–20), when Reade had given it direction, inspiration, energy and intellectual substance, what had been achieved? Outside the legislative sphere (in which the reformers had no direct power and only a little indirect influence, but nevertheless where their major goals lay), on a smaller, piecemeal scale, their efforts were not completely fruitless.

Reade, in his position as government town planner, drew up many subdivision plans for private landowners on 'model garden suburb lines', the first of which, for H. Allchurch at Kurralta Park, proved such a success that the owner donated £5 to the Town Planning Association's publicity education fund. Reade's plan had deducted 5 acres from the total area of 120 acres for parks and open spaces, but still provided 1500 feet more in sellable frontages than had been originally proposed. A similar model suburb of 120 acres adjacent to the port road, in which 10 acres were devoted to open spaces and public buildings, also pleased its owners.[12] So in cases where Reade was able to convince private enterprise that there was no conflict between good planning and private profit-making, he made small gains for his methods. Other marks left on the suburban landscape by Reade were parks and recreation ovals at Thebarton and Prospect, South Australia's first 'garden suburb' at Colonel Light Gardens, the West Terrace children's playground, and many plans of subdivision for private owners. Outside the metropolitan area he was responsible for a major community effort in Port Pirie to build a children's playground, for the Victor Harbour foreshore improvement scheme and for civic 'beautifications' (parklands, recreation ovals, playgrounds and the like) in Jamestown, Kadina, Kapunda, Goolwa and Victor Harbor.[13] All better than haphazard development and private enterprise exploitation, these achievements nevertheless were small-scale, piecemeal and remedial and came nowhere near the comprehensive, anticipatory planning that Reade had tirelessly advocated. For *that*, legislative action was necessary, and that legislation was the major ambition of Reade and the Town Planning and Housing Association. But it was in the parliamentary arena that the town planning movement first foundered.

Legislative Efforts 1916–20

For the state's first planning legislation the Town Planning and Housing Bill introduced by the Labor Party in 1916 showed an encouraging directness and lack of modesty in its appreciation of what was wrong and what needed to be done. Perhaps it was an indirect compliment to the impact that Reade had already made that the Labor Party felt confident about introducing such radical proposals, though in restrospect it looks more like a case of political naivety. For within a week the bill had raised some, and within six months most, of the dilemmas that have dogged the progress of planning since then; questions of the relative distribution of power between local councils and a central authority; struggles within and between government departments over responsibility in this new field of government activity; debates over how much 'planning' is compatible with 'democratic rights' and how much power ought to be vested in one man, the planner; rival concepts of 'community welfare', and widely differing judgements as to the extent of state responsibility for underprivileged groups.

The second reading speech of the bill provided an extensive analysis of the role, powers and weakness of local government. Criticism ranged from the inability of local governments to secure adequate street widths, directions and uses, to their inability to prevent overcrowding of small houses in new suburban areas, regulate building, or provide special areas suitable for industry and commerce. But the two most crucial inadequacies in local government powers were seen as their inability to provide low-cost housing and the fact that there existed no means of co-ordinating the various functions of municipal and statutory authorities in the development of extensions to city and suburbs.[14] To remedy this the bill proposed a town planning commission of three experts (a town planner, an engineer or architect and a financial man), with executive control to be exercised through the treasurer, whose functions would be to control all town planning works throughout the state, to prepare town planning schemes in co-operation with local councils within the metropolitan area and to prepare model town planning by-laws for application outside the metropolitan area. There were also enlightened provisions for co-operation with the State Bank to finance workers' homes, and the New South Wales government's garden suburb Daceyville was seen as exemplary. The commissioners were, if necessary, to override existing by-laws and local government objections in order to execute town planning schemes. It was understood, again through Reade's reports, that 'a central authority is essential to carry out a town planning scheme'.[15]

The bill was received surprisingly well in the press, the *Advertiser* editorial following the second reading speech seeing its object to

> remove the evil of slums and congested districts, provide open spaces in populous areas, and render the development of cities and towns something other than the haphazard affair it has always been
> ... no time should be lost in providing the machinery whereby the growth and improvement of populous centres will be regulated for the first time on scientific principles ... Mr Vaughan rests the case for the Bill in great part on its hygienic value, as being likely to recommend it to the more utilitarian of its critics ... A town planning scheme on liberal lines might go far to solve more than one social problem and might be the means of introducing a little brightness into the lives of the poorer sections of the community.[16]

But there was no such benign reception by the Adelaide City Council. Reade had already aroused the wrath of city councillors by his references to Adelaide slums, and it was significant that the Adelaide City Council was the only metropolitan council that had not affiliated with the Town Planning and Housing Association by 1919. For this bill, Reade had prepared slides and an exhibition to accompany the second reading speech to prove beyond doubt that slums did exist. The city council was duly outraged. Within a fortnight the mayor, Isaac Isaacs, a land agent and chairman of the Adelaide branch of the Liberal Country League, had called a meeting to draw attention to the 'drastic conditions in the Bill' and to recommend that strong action be taken by the council to oppose this measure 'which would take away many of the privileges and powers now enjoyed'. The mayor also thought it the duty of the council to warn local councils of the dangers and to assist them in protecting their interests.[17] The same meeting attacked Reade's motives. Councillor Forwood thought this seemed 'to be a Bill for the benefit of

Mr Reade' and that 'in [his] opinion the organiser of the town planning movement had been in Adelaide for two years planning to make a job for himself.' The city council's reaction in turn provoked a bitter counter-attack the following day in the *Daily Herald* editorial:

> The City Council is going to fight against the Town Planning and Housing Bill because it is afraid that some of the slum areas and overcrowded residential districts may be brought into more prominence than hitherto . . . It is a well known fact that enormous profits are reaped by slum landlords . . . It is sheer nonsense on the part of the City Council to pretend that "there are no slums in this fair queen city". When the Premier introduced the Bill he quoted instances of overcrowding in city areas . . . These cases . . . are in themselves an indictment of the City Council as a representative public body that has not only failed to do its duty, but is now trying to block urgent and practical reforms . . . The City Council . . . seems to want slum owners left untouched so that the landlords may reap their harvest of gold while the poor of this city reap their harvest of suffering, disease and other ills associated with bad housing.

These sentiments had been voiced in the house by the Labor member for Adelaide J. Gunn who argued that 'town planning ought to be taken out of the hands of the landlords and their agents, who desired mainly to see how many houses can be got on to a given space'. The *Advertiser*, while not going so far as to accuse the city councillors of self-interest, continued to support the measure despite their hostility:

> An attitude of unqualified hostility toward the measure is wholly unjustified. It is far too late in the day to sneer at town planning as though it were a mere sentimental fad . . . Even in Adelaide the reformer is far from being unnecessary . . . There must be, as Mr Reade contends, a central authority, competent to design and coordinate schemes for the whole area in cooperation with the local councils . . . The town planning question, and the measures necessary for its satisfactory solution, emphasise the long acknowledged defects in the present system of city and suburban administration. These afford the ground for the motion submitted by Mr Gunn and carried by the House of Assembly yesterday, declaring that the time has arrived for the establishment of a Greater Adelaide . . . but parochial jealousies, as well as a difference of opinion on the question whether the municipalities should be unified or simply federated, have hitherto prevented any serious action toward the accomplishment of the reform . . .[18]

That the local councils were not at first unduly worried by or opposed to the bill is indicated by a meeting in October 1916 of the Suburban Areas Municipal Association, which had appointed a subcommittee to consider and report on the bill. This committee recommended to the meeting that the association express its approval and endorsement of the general principles of the bill. Their recommendations were adopted, as was a further recommendation in favour of notifying the Legislative Council that the association hoped the bill would be passed without delay. It was not. The Legislative Council held up the bill while the Adelaide City Council set out to undermine it, and by June 1917 they had generated sufficient discontent for the Legislative Council to feel justified in allowing the bill to lapse.

The tactics adopted by the city council were to call a conference of representatives from each metropolitan council to discuss amendments to the bill. The proposed amendments were to eliminate entirely the proposed central town planning commission, sections related to the provision of housing by the state, to make town planning solely a function of *councils* vested with *absolute authority* to plan, and to strike out all clauses relating to powers compelling a council to observe or carry out a scheme authorized by parliament. Clauses relating to compulsory land purchase and compensation (which under the bill were similar to those already possessed by the South Australian Harbours Board and the commonwealth government) were stated to be 'unnecessarily drastic and may possibly work hardship on owners'. In conclusion the conference proposed a reversion to earlier acts and accordingly the Legislative Council allowed the bill to lapse at prorogation.[19]

In February 1917 the Labor Party had split on the conscription issue. When parliament first met for the year in July, Liberal opposition leader A. H. Peake proposed an adjournment motion. It was carried. The Labor premier then resigned and Peake formed a ministry which included three ex-Labor Nationalists. The new Liberal administration did not take up the Town Planning and Housing Bill. Reade's own retrospective comments on his bill are interesting. In 1920, giving evidence to the select committee of the Legislative Council on the Town Planning and Development Bill, he explained that he

> quite realised that we were not going to get that Bill through Parliament. Frankly, it was a propaganda measure, and it had the desired effect. It secured the interest of the local governing bodies and made them think more about town planning. It brought them into contact with ourselves, and it resulted in numerous lectures and discussions, and considerably widened the outlook on the whole question of town planning practice and ideas.

Whether or not this was the intention of the 1916 bill, its effect was certainly more ambivalent than Reade cared to acknowledge. It may, as he argued, have stimulated discussion and understanding, but it also brought his enemies out into the open, particularly those in the

Adelaide City Council and their allies in the upper house, and started an active campaign *against* his proposals. As a political strategist, then, Reade may have been an amateur out of his depth. The reactions to and tremors after this bill set the tone and defined the limits for the much more cautious Town Planning and Development Bill introduced in 1919.

In the meantime a Control of Subdivision of Land Act passed in 1917 gave the surveyor-general wider discretionary powers to refuse approval of unsatisfactory subdivisions, particularly with regard to the width of roads, the suitability of the site and the orientation of any buildings to be erected on the land, a tacit admission of the validity of some of Reade's criticisms. But Reade himself commented on the passage of this act,

> It is one of those temporary expedients which, while removing some of the glaring anomalies of the Surveyor-General's position, cannot provide for the proper planning of town extensions (including arterial roads, open spaces, factory areas, limiting the number of houses to the acre, etc.) merely by increasing the powers of an executive officer to refuse his sanction to plans for the subdivision of a particular block of land ... The new law is merely the continuation of an obsolete method of regulating town development which has been tried and failed in other countries. The remedy is town planning.[20]

Reade was here making a clear distinction between the limits of mere regulatory planning and the possibilities of what is today known as 'development planning'. He was correct in his belief that most of his 'reformist' ambitions—(for example better-designed, low-cost worker housing and more equality of access to the good things of life) could only be achieved through development planning. The difference is evident today between an authority like the National Capital Development Commission, which actually develops virgin land, and most of the work of the state planning authorities, which have only regulatory powers of zoning and subdivision control.

More to his liking therefore was the Garden Suburb Act of 1919 which provided for 300 acres of state-owned land to be developed as a garden suburb and for 600 homes to be provided by the State Bank. M. F. McNamara (acting inspector-general of the State Bank and treasurer of the Town Planning and Housing Association and of the South Australian executive of the Australasian town planning conferences in Adelaide in 1917 and Brisbane in 1918), was appointed garden suburbs commissioner and Reade subsequently prepared plans for what was to become Colonel Light Gardens. But even this was only a minuscule portion of the city and Reade's real aspiration was for comprehensive planning legislation embracing the whole metropolis. The Town Planning and Development Act which was finally passed late in 1920 went some small way toward meeting this aspiration.

How intractable were the problems facing town planning as seen in 1916 and 1917? Did the intervening four years change the nature of the problems, or of attitudes toward them, or neither?

According to the attorney-general (H. N. Barwell), introducing the Town Planning and Development Bill into parliament in September 1919, everything had changed for the better. He believed that the three Australasian town planning conferences of 1917, 1918 and 1919 had led to a widespread appreciation of the benefits of town planning and that many who had formerly opposed the idea had been won over. But he was a convert to the cause of town planning and this may well have clouded his political judgement of the real strength of the opposition to it. For in retrospect the events of 1916–17 appear as a mere dress rehearsal for the real drama that took place following the introduction of the 1919 bill. Yet that bill was far more cautious and circumspect than its predecessor.

Two lessons had been derived by the new government from the experience of the 1916 bill: no town planning measure could survive if it threatened either the limited autonomy of local government or the independence of the Adelaide City Council. Accordingly Barwell's introduction of the bill explained that a new bill had been drafted, based on the conclusions of the second Australasian town planning conference, which had unanimously decided that 'Councils, public bodies and central Government Departments should act in cooperation, the council to be responsible for initiating and carrying out proposals in its own area'. He emphasized that the autonomy of local governments had been adequately protected from 'autocratic extremism' by the central department. (In practical terms this meant that, compared with the 1916 proposals, the central authority no longer had the power to initiate and control town planning schemes. Local governments could initiate planning if they chose to but it was not mandatory, and they could not be overridden by the central authority.) And he explained that the City of Adelaide would be excluded from the provisions of the bill until a resolution of *both* houses of parliament directed that it should apply to the council.[21] Other departures from the earlier bill included the omission of housing sections, the creation of a minister for the Department of Town Planning to be the central administrative and technical authority, the provision for proper planning of all new towns or extensions laid out by the state, and the consolidation of all existing laws relating to subdivision. Unlike the Labor government, which had emphasized the radical reforming possibilities of planning, the Liberal government adopted a low-key, cautious approach and stressed that everything would be gradual and mild, that inquiries and conferences between public authorities and private owners would precede action, and that precipitate action would be most unlikely. Yet despite reduced aims, tactics of appeasement, and cautious language there was public outcry from various groups within a week, and the course of the bill through the upper house was long and arduous.

First to move against the bill was the Licensed Landbrokers Institute, which requested that the attorney-general appoint a parliamentary committee to take evidence from experts and then amend the bill in view of the costs it would impose on landowners wanting to subdivide their land. They were supported by the Surveyors Institute, which objected to the delay in business that would be caused by the new regulations. Their actions drew strong words from the Town Planning and Housing Association.

> This move to refer the Bill to a Select Committee will mean a delay of another 12 months. It is made evidently in the interests of those who primarily are responsible for the subdivisional methods which . . . have resulted in houses and gardens being crowded onto small allotments in new areas and numerous other evils . . . Public interest and welfare demand that any further delay in making the proposed town planning powers operative be not entertained by Parliament (and that the Bill be passed) without recourse to amendments proposed by those either opposed to town planning or responsible for the exploitation and spoliation of our cities.[22]

The following week the *Advertiser* ran an editorial claiming that the Town Planning Association's protest against the action of the Surveyors Institute, the Licensed Landbrokers and the Real Estate Agents Institutes had been reinforced by vigorous support from local councils in both town and country.

> The West Torrens district council in particular points out that a further subdivision of their district has been made without the Council being consulted or a plan submitted to the Surveyor-General. They state that land was being offered for sale through a leading firm, one of whose principals was simultaneously active in publicly denouncing the proposed legislation.[23]

Labor members of the house were outraged at the exclusion of the Adelaide City Council from the bill. Accordingly when the bill reached the committee stage, A. A. Edwards (Labor member for Adelaide) made revelations about Adelaide's slums which were so grave that the attorney-general decided that the clause dealing with the omission of the City of Adelaide should be struck out.

In response to the protests of opposition groups the Legislative Council set up a select committee which heard evidence from the town planner, architects, surveyors, landbrokers, local councillors, the head of the Municipal Tramways Trust, and the City Council.[24] Reade found himself bitterly opposed by the professional institutes (surveyors, architects, engineers) who protested against the wide powers he was to be given as head of the proposed Town Planning Department and argued that the Town Planning Act should not be administered by one man but by a board of professional men. Added to this was a personal attack on Reade by the secretary of the Surveyors Institute (A. J. Blakeway). These protests were attacked by the Town Planning and Housing Association in an urgent memorial sent to members of the Legislative Council. They argued that the petition by the landbrokers, surveyors and architects was an unjustifiable attempt to secure a central controlling board representative of their own professions, professions which, being dependent for their living on commissions from private clients, were likely to interpret planning powers in less ambitious ways. The effect of such a move, the Town Planning Association argued, would be to render the government town planner subservient to the board and to destroy all individual initiative and responsibility. 'It might be very difficult for the government in the circumstances to secure the services of an experienced and competent town planner to administer the Act under such conditions', they warned. Their memorial continued as follows:

> The petition presented to the Legislative Council in favour of the proposed Board is signed by numerous persons dealing in land and building operations, who, in recent years, have been the principal agency for the wholesale subdivision and cutting up of suburban areas . . . as well as precipitating overbuilding and other conditions, which town planning now seeks to remedy. Whilst the repetition of old errors in new areas have been in course of perpetration by these petitioners they have been the chief factor in opposing and delaying the Town Planning Bill, notwithstanding repeated protests from councils, public societies and others interested in maintaining the highest welfare and efficiency of our towns and cities.[25]

Reade took a similar view of their self-interested motives in a letter to the minister in charge of town planning: 'It is to be hoped that Mr Blakeway is not incensed by the fact that this Department refused to agree to a plan of subdivision surveyed by him in the district of West Torrens, which sought to evade the Control of Subdivision of Land Act 1917'.[26]

The principal issue that emerged from the select committee inquiry was disagreement about which department and who would ultimately hold the power, and the extent of these powers. The surveyors argued that there was no need for a Town Planning Department at all. Planning duties could be carried out quite adequately by the surveyor-general. Exponents of this view showed no understanding that town planning meant anything beyond control of subdivision. Only one witness supported strong powers for the town planner—the president of the federal council of the Australian Institutes of Architects and of the South Australian Institute of Architects. He criticized the bill for being neither comprehensive nor powerful enough and thought its great imperfection was that

> there is no comprehensive scheme for dealing with town planning as a whole. It is absolutely fundamental that a scheme should be prepared for zoning and districting the whole of the municipalities. Provisions should be made for the appointment of a Commission to set out the future development of the metropolitan area . . . The Town Planning Department is not given power to do what I am suggesting. The little municipal councils are given power to do it in their own districts, but it is absolutely fatal to town planning that they should do what the Bill contemplates—i.e. that each of them should set out a town planning scheme for its own little district.

He went on to criticize the omission of the City of Adelaide from the bill's provisions, 'The most important parts of town planning would be the regulation of traffic and transportation and those are the very things which would affect the City of Adelaide more than any other district,' and to argue for a Greater Adelaide scheme.[27] The outcome of the committee's report was verbal support for 'the need of town planning legislation' and the recommendation that an advisory board be created to administer the act rather than the town planner.

Opposition to Reade and to the bill was not confined to South Australia. George Taylor, secretary of the Town Planning Association of New South Wales wrote in his paper *Building* that the South Australian government should strongly reconsider the bill in the light of reviews from several Australian planners and architects. He argued that the bill was 'too autocratic in giving to one person too much power' and emphasized that the new department would be able to deal with 'the demolition, erection, construction, alteration, etc. of buildings'. Thus there would be 'a great possibility of its interference with legitimate private enterprise in architecture and building, thus superseding architects and builders in private practice as well as seriously interfering with existing government departments.'[28] Taylor was probably behind a mysterious eleventh-hour effort to sabotage the bill late in November 1920. On 24 November, when the bill was in 'a critical period before the Legislative Council owing to severe destructive criticism and opposition by vested interests and others,'[29] the *Register* published a telegraphic message, ostensibly supplied by J. J. C. Bradfield, the New South Wales planning advocate, condemning the bill outright. After a letter from Reade expressing his disappointment in an old colleague, Bradfield wired denying any knowledge and disclaiming authorization of publication of such an article. In a personal letter to Reade, Bradfield explained that he could not discover who had deliberately misrepresented him (by quoting out of context from a speech he had given to the Town Planning Association) but hinted that he suspected it was Taylor, since he was the only person to have a copy of the speech.[30]

In a personal letter to Bradfield on 3 December 1920, Reade reveals his feelings about the long ordeal of bringing legislation to fruition:

> Our Bill was passed in the closing hours of the session last week, thanks to very strenuous effort and fighting, and despite the determined efforts of certain interests both in Adelaide and Sydney to kill it.
>
> We did not get the whole measure but all the provisions of immediate importance were approved, including the permanent establishment of the Government town planner and his department, independent of the Board which will be advisory on certain matters only instead of administrative . . . The mischief and misrepresentation that time and again have come from Sydney apparently are very deep seated . . . and without any justification whatever. That decent people cannot attempt to do decent work for the good of Australia without personal malice and misrepresentation to hinder them is a disgrace to the democracy of this country . . .

This goes some way towards explaining why, within a month of the passing of the Town Planning and Development Act, Reade had left Australia to become town planner for the Federated Malay States, never to return. Although his services had been in demand in a good many places, he was being paid only £700 a year by the South Australian government. The Malay States offered £2000. But if money had been of major interest to him it is unlikely that he would have accepted the position in South Australia in the first place. Rather it seems that he regarded Adelaide, with its heritage of Colonel Light's layout, as the most fertile opportunity to achieve modern town planning legislation but in the process of the struggle was disillusioned and finally turned away by the grip which he came to realize 'certain vested interests' had over the city.

Nevertheless his legacy of planning legislation was remarkable for its time. The Town Planning and Development Act of 1920 created a Town Planning Department with the government town planner as its permanent head. His main duties were to prepare plans and reports for new towns and extensions to existing towns, including garden cities and suburbs and industrial areas; to replan or improve existing towns including land subdivisions; to plan public open spaces, reserves and so on. Expenses were to be met out of moneys provided by parliament for the purpose. A central advisory board was created, comprising the government planner, the surveyor-general, a civil engineer, an architect, and two people nominated by the Municipal Association and the Local Government Association. Its duty was to advise and assist the government planner according to the minister's directions. There were also provisions for local councils to form town planning committees, comprising the mayor and as many other members as were necessary, to which the council could, if it chose, add two people with professional qualifications. The town planner was given complete control over subdivision approvals (but control of resubdivisions remained with the local council) and subdivision procedures were specified. Applications had to be approved by the registrar-general of deeds, the surveyor-general, the council, any public body whose powers or functions were involved, and by the town planner. In addition, approval was conditional on the decision of the commissioner of sewers as to whether allotments could be economically and advantageously sewered, a useful provision which was deleted in the superseding act of 1929 and not reinstated until 1955.

That this moderate act was not to survive beyond the end of the decade Reade himself could probably have predicted. The next section explores this demise of town planning in South Australia in the 1920s.

Decline and Fall 1920–9

Given the extent of Reade's influence in 1914–20, it may seem logical to conclude that his departure was the major cause of the decline and fall of town planning in the 1920s. But the individual is rarely the sole mainspring of history, and to focus on the individual is to ignore the social forces at work around him. The quality of Reade's successors was reasonable, as can be seen from the annual reports they produced in 1921–9. But some of their statements indicate some of the wider forces at work which were to thoroughly undermine town planning by 1929.

The 1921 report by Reade's first successor emphasized the need that 'a unified plan be prepared immediately providing a scheme for the future extension of the metropolitan area and anticipation of future growth', and in his conclusion he drew attention to the principal weakness of the 1920 act,

> [the] lack of any method of making the principal features of any plan binding upon the land included within it. The main purpose of a unified metropolitan plan for Adelaide is to correlate the public works undertaken within the city and suburbs so that, without duplication or waste, each of them may form part of a scheme

adapted to the fulfilment of the needs of the next 30 to 50 years. Useful as a plan without binding force is, it inevitably fails in many particulars unless the observance of it is made obligatory.[31]

Those were large, clear thoughts to be written in 1921, and more followed, all of which were to be repeated in the late 1950s. W. Scott-Griffiths's town planner's report for 1922–3 reinforced his predecessor's plea for a unified plan of metropolitan Adelaide.[32] The chief emphasis of his 1924 report was the need for parliament to pass the amendment to the Town Planning Act before it, 'as it is difficult for me to check, under existing conditions, the practice of defeating the main effects and intentions of the Act, which is entirely due to the divided control in regard to resubdivision.'[33] This remark points to the main practical problem of the planners in the early 1920s, that of controlling the subdivision and speculative boom taking place in these prosperous years following the initial recession that had set in immediately after the war. It also indicates where the most determined sources of opposition to planning were likely to arise. No surveyor, land agent or landowner making quick profits from this subdivision boom would look kindly on the detailed subdivision application procedures laid down in the 1920 act.

The 1925 report was the last which contained intelligent discussion of major planning issues and problems and significantly it coincided with the parliamentary 'beginning of the end' for planning. Reports for the last three years of the Town Planning Department's existence (1926–9) were reduced to a bare three pages dealing only with statistics of subdivision applications, indicating the precariousness with which Scott-Griffiths now regarded his position. His perception of the hostile opposition to planning is more fully revealed in a private letter dated January 1925, though its optimism about the future was in retrospect misplaced.

My two years administration of this Department has convinced me that it could be much improved ... but one has to be exceedingly discreet and exercise much care and 'hasten slowly' ... just prior to my entering upon my position here there was a very strong agitation by several bodies to annihilate this Department and it has only been with the greatest care and discretion that all opposition has been caused to vanish and I am pleased to state this Department is now working smoothly with all classes and my relations with the surveyors and land agents etc. are most pleasant. Enclosed is a copy of my amending Bill which has only been trimmed and a few additional powers inserted as I don't desire to raise another rumpus, because after all, we are still in the educative stage and any shattering of this, the only Department administering town planning in Australia, would seriously affect the chances of similar legislation contemplated in the other states ...[34]

Who were these bodies agitating to annihilate the Town Planning Department? Scott-Griffiths here identified the surveyors and land land agents, but felt that the major difficulties were now easing. He was wrong. This period was only the calm before the storm, temporary shelter being provided by a sympathetic Labor government from April 1924 to April 1927. Soon after its defeat by an alliance of the Liberal and Country Parties the ship of town planning was wrecked on the rocks of the Adelaide power structure, in which land agents and landowners played a major part.

In July 1922 the Surveyors Institute wrote to the government suggesting that no town planner be appointed in charge of a separate department after the present planner's term expired. They advised that the Town Planning Department be abolished and that the administration of the Town Planning Act be vested in the surveyor-general. 'The Surveyors Institute regards the Surveyor-General as the head of the surveying profession—and town planning as only a part of the surveying profession—consequently a part which should be controlled by the Surveyor-General.' The reasoning advanced for this drastic move was that it would mean one less department for the general public and for the surveyors to deal with, hence 'facilitating business'. This was both a professionally and materially motivated challenge to town planning. But it was more than a standard inter-professional power struggle. It was conflict between professions whose living and status depended on private property owners and on government respectively. The Town Planning Association answered the professional threat in a letter by its president (H. W. Uffindell) asserting that 'indeed surveying is but a branch of town planning' and accusing the Surveyors Institute of wanting to get for their profession a monopoly of town planning.[35] The material challenge was countered by a plea from some of the victims of the profit-oriented subdividers. During 1922 the Town Planning Department received letters from the district councils of Mitcham, Walkerville, Yatala South, Campbelltown and Woodville (all areas at different points on the periphery of the urban expansion of that time) requesting amendment to the Town Planning and Development Act to provide for the formation and construction of new roadways in subdivisions being made by the owners of the land being subdivided before it could be offered for sale. The request from the town clerk of Yatala South put the issue concisely: 'It is felt by the Council that as most of the subdivisions now being made are for speculative purposes, and that large profits are being made by the vendors, the Councils should not be called upon to make the roads, involving as it does a very large expenditure from the district funds.'[36]

In response then to pressure from some local councils, from the

Town Planning and Housing Association and from the Town Planning Department, the Liberal government introduced into parliament late in 1923 the Town Planning Act Amendment Bill. It contained three main provisions, the most important of which was designed to curb excessive and undesirable subdivisions, 'to remedy the present position whereby plans of resubdivision may or may not be presented to local governing bodies [which means that] where a person wants to avoid resubdivision being turned down by a local governing body he usually goes over their heads to the Lands Titles Office—which can and does pass resubdivision plans without the knowledge of either the Town Planner or the local governing body concerned.'[37] The bill proposed therefore to give all subdivision and resubdivision control to the town planner. Secondly it provided for any council to apply to the government for the issue of a proclamation declaring that council's area, or part of it, to be residential. The third provision aimed to compel subdividers to construct or provide for the construction of roads before blocks were sold.

The bill provoked immediate and hostile reactions from those whose operations it sought to curb but found an unexpected ally in the Surveyors Institute.

> It has been brought under our notice that certain land agents and auctioneers in the city have been instrumental in getting the Landbrokers and Auctioneers Association to use its influence with members of Parliament to secure the defeat of the Town Planning Bill now before Parliament ... The Bill is the outcome of long conferences with the Institute of Surveyors, the town planner, Lands Titles Office and Town Planning Advisory Board, and is supported by the Town Planning Association ... The Landbrokers Association's protest to clause 25 sums up the whole trouble in a nutshell. To give councils the right to call upon owners of land to make the streets when subdividing will undoubtedly check the promiscuous cutting of land into allotments all over the metropolitan area irrespective of need or of likelihood of it being built on ...[38]

The bill had not been passed by the lower house before the elections of 1924 brought the Labor Party into office. The new government then restored the bill to the house, adding to it a further provision for the government to control advertisements relating to new subdivisions to prevent 'misrepresentations and omissions'— that is, dishonest advertising. The bill was heavily amended in the committee stage in the assembly. The clause relating to control of advertising was removed and clauses giving all subdivision and resubdivision control to the town planner were amended to provide that local governing bodies be consulted. After lapsing at prorogation the bill was restored to notice in the council in 1925, where it provoked drastic reactions. The upper house not only sought to amend most of the bill in ways that would render its provisions quite ineffective, but sought also to abolish the post of town planner and to merge the Town Planning Department with that of the registrar-general. When the Labor majority in the assembly refused to agree to these amendments, the bill lapsed. But the forces of reaction had served notice that they meant to put an end to the Town Planning Department when they could, 'for causing confusion, delay, and irritation to people, and hindering the development of the State'.[39] When the Liberal and Country Party alliance won the election of 1927, there was nothing to stop them doing just that.

The Town Planning Act of 1929 was the culmination of thirteen years of mounting opposition from those sections of society interested in profiting from land dealings, to the rising movement in favour of town planning, which among other things sometimes threatened people's 'rights' to profit from their properties. In the debates of 1929, town planning was discussed as though it was synonymous with control of subdivision (for this was the aspect of planning that the new Town Planning Department had been most occupied with) and the 1929 act was little more than a control of subdivision act, enumerating (and diluting, compared with the provisions of 1920) details for the minimum size of allotments and width of roads. 'It is now possible in the light of ten years experience, to state the rules about town planning in much simpler form ... The government has taken the opportunity to simplify town planning legislation and clear up difficulties which arose under the old Act.'[40] 'Simplify' was the understatement of the decade. The principal 'reform' proposed by the bill was the amalgamation of the Town Planning Department with the Lands Titles Office. This had been recommended by the classification and efficiency board, in a report initiated by the debates of 1925, for three main reasons: there had been a reduction in the volume of work connected with town planning due to the subsiding of the subdivision boom, considerable economy would be effected by transferring the town planner to the Lands Titles Office (the expenses of the Town Planning Department had averaged £1000 per year), and it would be much more convenient for the public. One rather obvious reason did not get a mention: it would be much more convenient and profitable for landowners if the teeth were extracted from town planning legislation.

Those who wanted to oust planners and replace them with surveyors were seeking to bring in a profession dependent for its greatest rewards on commissions from big operators in the private sector. Planners were threatening to create a profession not tied in the same way to property and the profit motive. The ruling class naturally preferred engineers and surveyors to planners because the former were accustomed to living mainly from fees from big companies and could be relied on to be 'realistic', while planners were initially threatening because their loyalty was to the public and they lived off salaries rather than consulting fees. Planners only eventually won the acceptance of the power holders when they demonstrated that they were compliant and docile—estate managers of capitalism in the sense that they did only the kinds of things that the powerful appreciated.

An appropriate epitaph to this period was provided by the *News Pictorial:*

> Adelaide was the first city to have a town planning Act but here alas we are content to rest on past laurels. There is so much in this line still to be done, and the surge of enthusiasm that brought the Act into being has gone. Except for control of local subdivisions we are doing nothing to govern, in a broad general way ... the growth of this wonderful city.[41]

Building the Economic Base 1930s

From the gloom of the 1929 Town Planning Act, South Australia plunged into the darkness of world-wide economic depression. Her rulers emerged from it in the early 1930s with one very general observation and one single-minded goal. The observation was that the depression had revealed starkly and tragically the great dependence of the South Australian economy on commodity prices in the world market because of her overdependence on primary industry. The goal therefore was the encouragement of manufacturing. South Australia became the first of the Australian states, with the possible exception of Victoria, consciously to undertake the transformation of its economic structure by shifting its base from primary to secondary industry.

How they proceeded to do this is a story that has been well told elsewhere.[42]

> The state should re-assert the economic sovereignty it appeared to have surrendered to some mixture of misguided federalism and misunderstood individualism. Then (1) government should supply industry with suitable land, docile labour, cheap credit, physical services and various planning and advisory services; and (2) it should use political power to limit local costs of living and therefore costs of production, in order to make its territory an advantageous one from which to export manufactures to the rest of the country.

Some of the means, especially state housing, and some of the effects of this programme reshaped the city, and 'though seldom thought of then or since as a method of metropolitan planning', it was in fact a 'practical and powerful one, adaptable to other places and purposes.'[43]

The establishment in 1936 of the South Australian Housing Trust ('while the rest of the world was founding conscience-stricken Housing Commissions to clear slums and shelter the suffering poor')[44] was an essential part of the industrialization of the state. The rationale behind this is clear in the report of the auditor-general, J. W. Wainright, quoted extensively in the debates on the South Australian Housing Trust Bill.

> With the recovery from the depression rents have been rising, and with rents, wage costs. If, however, the industrial expansion so vital to South Australia is to continue, rents must be prevented from rising ... It is fundamental that any policy of fostering secondary industries in this State must be based on a lower cost of living than Melbourne or Sydney. There is very little the State can do to prevent rises in prices of food, groceries and clothing, without autocratic and arbitrary control ... The item of cost which can be most easily and equitably kept at a reasonable level is rent, and rent forms at present about 25 per cent of the total cost of living of families with low incomes.[45]

Realizing the disadvantages facing manufacturers in South Australia, the government granted concessions to industry in the fields of company taxation, freight rates and port charges, it assisted them in securing factory sites and essential services (water, drainage, electricity), and provided technical advice. To assist local enterprises, the Industries Assistance Corporation was formed in 1937 to advise and provide funds for progressive local enterprise, the growth of which might be impeded if it had to rely on orthodox channels of securing capital.

The rapid industrial development that then took place and was stimulated by World War II brought marked changes in the social and urban fabric. More women joined the workforce and there was an increase in the number of skilled workers. Manufacturing in the immediate post-war years accounted for 29 per cent of the workforce, an increase of 7 per cent from pre-war years, while farming and domestic services declined. The social pattern also changed in another important way. As real investment was undertaken almost without exception in the metropolitan area, job opportunities drew people from country areas. Consequently in 1935–45, for the first intercensal period in South Australian history, country population decreased and the ratio of metropolitan to total population increased from 54 per cent pre-war to 59 per cent in 1945. In the seven years from 1939 to 1946 the metropolitan area gained 70 000 people, half of them 'rural immigrants'. While the housing trust battled to accommodate the influx, it was rapidly changing the nature and degree of urban problems.

The more conventional forms of town planning might have stood still, indeed retrogressed, in 1920–50, but the state's development had not, and by the end of the war the state's encouragement of industrial growth meant that a whole new set of conditions arose. In effect the government's industrialization policy meant that its contribution to and participation in the growth of Adelaide was vastly more significant than in any other city except Canberra. This dramatic expansion was scarcely a triumph of *private enterprise*. The fast-growing wealth of local entrepreneurs was brought about by *state political power* and encouraged an intimacy between business, politics and administration that proved to be a major obstacle to the progress of planning after the war. How it did is part of the story in chapter 6. No matter how Playford, leader of the Liberal Country League and premier from 1937 to 1965, 'might deal with occasional predators, the State power still belonged to the farmers and old oligarchs so it had to be used without general damage to their interests, a condition which did not hinder industrialization on public land, but would presently cripple any town planning of private freeholds.'[46]

3

Melbourne: Bureaucracy Tempered by Anarchy

> It is not to be expected, however, that the proposals of town planners will meet with universal and ready assent. No reform is ever popular at first, and no far-sighted movement is ever widely understood. The inertia of habit and custom is always slow to move, and the opposition of those whose interests or prejudices are affected is always bitter.
>
> Councillor Rigby 1917[1]

> An English visitor recently described the Australian system of government as 'anarchy tempered by bureaucracy', and it is tempting for an epitome of the politics of Victoria simply to reverse the terms.
>
> A. F. Davies 1960[2]

Power

Although Victoria shared with other states the enthusiasm and reforming zeal of the early town planning movement, it has been tardy in giving legislative support to planning ideas. Victoria waited until 1944 for its first planning legislation, until 1954 for its first plan, and until 1968 for this plan to be given statutory force.

Planning has suffered in the past from the political naivety of its more idealistic advocates. The political obstacles confronting attempts to implement planning, particularly planning that emphasizes social equity considerations, are, as I have shown in South Australia, formidable. The structure of political power in both South Australia and Victoria has been such as to protect property owners and pamper rural interests while excluding any serious debate on the structure and goals of our cities or encouraging any far-sighted policy of urban development. This rural and conservative bias—so antipathetic to urban planning—is built into the very political institutions and processes through which efforts have been made to implement planning: lower houses dominated by coalitions of country and city rich, upper houses at the mercy of rural conservatives, city councils whose members have a vested interest in protecting existing property and privilege or in real estate and land speculation, and a Liberal Party organization dependent on the support of the financial 'establishment'. A. F. Davies has written of the Legislative Council (the upper house), 'While discussion of major Bills in the Assembly brings them into public focus few Cabinets in Victoria have been permitted to feel that this was their proposal's main hurdle ... Always in the background like a malicious, mechanical anti-coconut shy has stood the unreformable Legislative Council, pitching back bills and bits of bills ... Until recent years this veto worked by a sort of compulsive shudder of the property instinct from which even the moderate proposals of conservative Cabinets were not always immune.'[3]

Until 1950 rural interests made up half the council's membership, a predominance maintained by the extraordinary weighting to rural areas in the distribution of seats. In 1881 there was a ratio of 100 metropolitan votes to 61 rural, in 1936 it was 100 to 49 and in 1950 still 100 to 55.[4] The ratio of metropolitan to rural voters has made it impossible for the Labor Party to gain a majority of seats. The rural conservatism of the council was evident in the four years of the Hogan Labor ministries (May 1927 to December 1928, December 1929 to May 1932), in the crucial period when the report of the Metropolitan Town Planning Commission was being considered, during which twenty-nine government bills were rejected by the council, one of them a town planning bill. It was evident again in 1947 when the council dramatically dismissed the Cain Labor government from office on the issue of bank nationalization. In specifically town planning matters the council rejected legislation in 1913, 1915, 1930, 1936, 1937 and 1952–3.

The lower house has had a similar record of conservative and rural bias. A significant over-representation of farmers (26–30 per cent in the house, only 8 per cent in the population)[5] has meant that since the formation of the Country Party in the 1920s, that party has always held the balance of power. Electoral distribution has thus allowed the Country Party ('the only political group ... without any ideas at all beyond the make-believe of rural-urban jealousy')[6] to stamp its mould on a whole generation of state politics. Redistribution at the end of the nineteenth century had set the city vote at a firm discount which, through neglect and manipulation over sixty years, has hardened into deprivation of a growing metropolis. In 1926, 100 city votes were worth 47 country, in 1943 it was 100 to 39 and in 1945, 100 to 57. By 1942 the Country Party had doubled its 1920 parliamentary representation with more than a third of Assembly seats. Instability of ministries became endemic from the early 1920s till 1955 and in consequence, 'the sort of men who rose to the top were wire-pullers, horse-traders and wheeler-dealers of the most

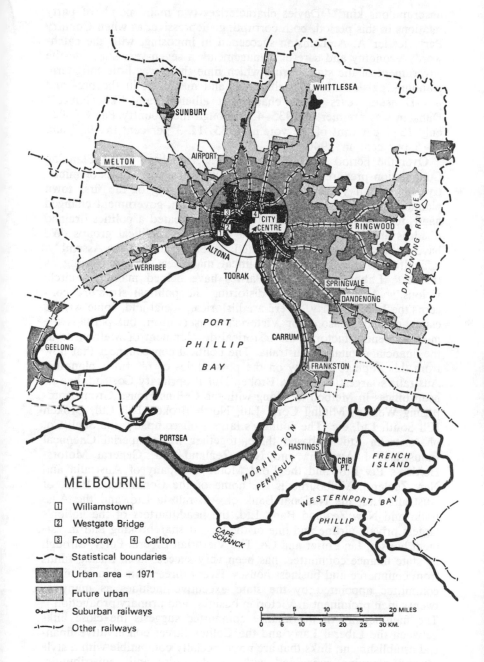

MELBOURNE

1. Williamstown
2. Westgate Bridge
3. Footscray   4. Carlton

-⌒- Statistical boundaries

░ Urban area – 1971

░ Future urban

o⌒o⌒o Suburban railways

-ı-⌒ Other railways

unscrupulous kind'.[7] Davies characterizes two main moods of party relations in this period, both corrupting: depressive, as when Country Party leader A. A. Dunstan succeeded in imposing, with the catchwords 'economy and careful management', a seven-year stasis on the government of the state during which time there was little long-term planning, particularly of Melbourne; and manic, as in the pre- and post-Dunstan years when 'changes of alliance rang like chimes'.[8] Dunstan was premier in 1935–43 although the Country Party polled only 13·7 per cent of the vote in 1935, 11·3 per cent in 1937 and 16·5 per cent in 1940.[9]

Over the period 1922–9, when the Metropolitan Town Planning Commission prepared its report, there were twelve changes of ministry. In the ten years 1945–55, from the passing of the first town planning act to the production of the first plan, government changed hands ten times. 'As a sustained mode this created a politics drained of ideas and left deep scars on the outlook of political groups. We have already noted the mean-spirited, 'shrewdie' tone of the Assembly: difficulties of recruitment to political machines so unrewarding as the state Labor and Liberal Parties have helped make the circle vicious.'[10] A further element distorting the political structure concerns the Liberal Party. There are historical, social and, some writers claim, climatic reasons for Victoria's conservatism, but perhaps the most influential factor is the historical development of Melbourne as the financial capital of Australia. The political consequences that flow from this impinge strongly on the possibilities of reformist planning. Australia's largest company, Broken Hill Proprietary Co. Ltd, has its head offices in Melbourne along with the Collins House Group comprising Western Mining Corp. Ltd, North Broken Hill Ltd, Broken Hill South Ltd, etc. The country's largest oil company, the Shell Co. of Australia Ltd, is based there, together with Imperial Chemical Industries of Australia and New Zealand Ltd, General Motors-Holden's Pty Ltd, and the Ford Motor Company of Australia and New Zealand. Melbourne is the home of the Commercial Bank of Australia Ltd, the National Bank of Australasia Ltd, and the Australia and New Zealand Bank Ltd, the headquarters of the nation's largest private airline and one of the largest sharebroking and investment houses, Ian Potter and Co. The Victorian Liberal Party, through its state finance committee, has been very successful in raising funds from commerce and business houses. Every three years a fund-raising committee appointed by the state executive includes as many as twenty men prominent in Victorian business and primary production.[11] The membership of the finance committee suggests the close links between the Liberal Party and the Collins Street conservative financial establishment, links that are not especially compatible with a style of city planning concerned with social equity and redistribution.

Trustees of the finance committee have included Sir Ian Potter (rated by the *Financial Review* as 'the monarch of Melbourne finance') and Sir Maurice Nathan, former chairman of Paterson's Aust. Ltd and lord mayor of Melbourne. He made an investment-seeking overseas trip with Bolte early in his premiership.[12] It seems reasonable to suggest that these economic forces behind the Liberal Party, with their laissez-faire ideology and profit-oriented interest in politics, must have been especially influential since 1955 (the year after the Melbourne and Metropolitan Board of Works produced its metropolitan plan) when the Liberal Party under Bolte was elected.

Such is the conservative political structure within which those advocating a reformist approach to town planning have had to work. One offshoot of this imbalance, highly significant to the fortunes of town planning, has been the bleak history of the Labor Party in Victoria, particularly in the inter-war period. As D. W. Rawson has shown, the apparent impossibility of attaining office and power, far from promoting a doctrinaire intransigence, bred a characterless and dispiriting respectability.[13] The ALP was not, in this period, an advocate for the social benefits of city planning, and its political weakness may have discouraged those who were interested in town planning from allying themselves with and working through the Labor Party. Between the wars, then, the town planning issue was in the hands of middle-class reformers and professional men. This gap between the politics of the Left and planning advocates, noticeable after World War I, has encouraged the development of a purely 'technical' approach, a class of planners (and civil servants) who espouse an 'apolitical' approach which places maximum emphasis on efficiency considerations. And however independent this 'technical' activity might appear to be, in fact it has made planning conservative. These political constraints have naturally affected the kind of planning that has been done. There has been no attempt to initiate or control urban development. Planning has simply aimed to improve the efficiency of that development.

Moves to Reform Urban Administration, part 1

It was in the 1870s that the 'drift to the cities' first became marked. People left decaying mining towns and hopeless selections and made their way to Melbourne. In 1881, 32 per cent of Victoria's population lived there and in 1891, 43 per cent. In 1871 three-quarters of Melbourne's population was concentrated in the city and inner suburbs of Carlton, Collingwood, Fitzroy, Richmond, Prahran and North and South Melbourne. There was little suburban expansion until railways were built in the late 1870s. The collapse of gold mining in the seventies had closed the main avenue of speculative investment and, to a great extent, suburban land speculation now took its place. Transport was essential if land values were to be inflated to the point where subdivision yielded spectacular returns. Political influence was therefore important. Before, and even after, the passing of the act of 1884 transferring railways from ministerial control to a board of commissioners, lobbying on the construction of suburban railways was notorious.[14]

As subdivision activity spread, original suburban townships were swallowed up. In 1874 local government was given wide borrowing powers, which many used to build pretentious town halls while ignoring other needs of their areas. As subdivision continued, provision for future parklands was almost entirely neglected. Sewerage and responsibility for public health were in the hands of individual councils, with varying results. Local inspectors often tolerated great abuses. But the shortcomings of the water supply and sewerage arrangements were beyond remedy by any single municipality. In 1874 a municipal conference proposed a scheme for the appointment of a board of works to deal with the problems of water, sewerage, gas, trams, river control, noxious trades, parks and hackney carriages within a radius of ten miles of Melbourne. Finally, following the recommendations in 1889 of a royal commission on the sanitary condition of Melbourne, an act was passed in 1890 to provide for better management of the metropolis by the creation of the Melbourne and Metropolitan Board of Works (MMBW), which was given responsibility for water supply and sewerage. Its formation and subsequent gradual accumulation of other responsibilites illustrates the process of extension of powers, ad hoc institutional development and subsequent rationalization, which have been a major source of planning difficulties in the 'naturally' growing cities. Legislation for the board was modelled on that for the short-lived London and Metropolitan Board of Works. A. Briggs claims that the London board failed because its two-stage election process—aldermen to councils, then from councils to the board—was not a sufficiently democratic process.[15] This criticism is still made of the Melbourne board today, and as an issue it has been crucial in determining the fate of various efforts at metropolitan co-ordination.

The formation of the MMBW was the first step in the progress of one aspect of planning thought, that concerned with the more efficient provision and administration of essential services to the metropolitan area by means of central co-ordination of activities. From 1890 to World War I there was lively interest in this 'Greater Melbourne' issue. A 1902 royal commission investigated the question of unification or federation of municipalities but recommended that the time was inopportune to attempt either. One of the problems that prompted legislative efforts for a Greater Melbourne was the existence of several bodies controlling separate tramway systems. The 1911 royal commission on the railway and tramway system of Melbourne and suburbs recommended that metropolitan tramways should be vested in and controlled by a Greater Melbourne council. In 1912 the MMBW proposed an enlargement of its functions to include fire brigades, Yarra River improvements and others. In the same year a conference of municipalities recommended the formation of a metropolitan municipal authority to be known as the Greater Melbourne Council.

If ever a policy seemed to have widespread support, it was this. Accordingly the Liberal premier, W. A. Watt, introduced the Metropolitan Council Bill in 1913 to establish a metropolitan council of thirty to forty members, directly elected by constituencies similar to the existing municipal districts. The bill lapsed, but was reintroduced in 1915 by the Peacock Liberal government. It provided for the 'federal control of Melbourne's general utilities', including transport, gas, electricity, lighting, water, sewerage, drains, fire protection, rivers, creeks, parks and gardens, markets, abattoirs, noxious trades, hackney carriages, and regulation of buildings.[16] Since the government had the numbers, the bill did pass the assembly, but not without opposition. The case argued in an *Argus* editorial was typical of all opposition that foiled the Greater Melbourne issue. The *Argus* attacked 'three fundamental defects' of the bill.

It proposes to depart from the long established and essentially just municipal franchise, which gives property holders one, two or three votes according to the value of the property for which they are assessed, in favour of the system of one ratepayer one vote. It also proposes to abolish the MMBW and to laboriously build up another representative body, merely . . . for the sake of change. Thirdly the Bill proposes to vest in this new body the very difficult and highly specialised work of managing the tramways . . . The Labor opposition will have difficulty dissembling its delight when a measure is presented which will . . . inevitably hand over the municipal control of the metropolis to Labor . . . No necessity exists for the adoption of revolutionary proposals. The Ministry has ready to hand the MMBW [whose powers] can be amended and extended to suit the growing needs of the city . . . It is amazing that they [the government] should attempt to introduce a municipal franchise which would make Melbourne an arena for socialistic experiments carried out at the expense of the defeated property holders.[17]

A meeting of the Victorian Employers Federation condemned the new franchise,[18] as did the Prahran Council, which urged other councils to oppose the bill and 'protect the interests of the people who will be called upon to find the money to finance the Council, and whose property will be mortgaged in consequence.'[19] Clearly there was some agreement on the need for a metropolitan authority, but the issue was submerged by the fear that this

> would mean the handing over of the Metropolis to the Labor Party ... Immediately it gained control the Labor Party would never rest till it made its grip secure. We should have such insistent demands for the broadening of the franchise that Parliament could not long resist altering one ratepayer one vote to the lodger vote, and from that it would be a short step to one adult one vote.[20]

The Labor Party's attitude throughout its opposition to the Greater Melbourne bills was uncompromising. It demanded unification, adult franchise, and payment of members, none of which the Liberals were willing to approve. A different kind of opposition came from the property owners in the Legislative Council. It shelved the bill and there was a waning of interest in the question for the next ten years. A separate Metropolitan Tramways Board was created in 1918 and the same arrangement was made for fire brigades.

Local Government and Planning

From 1900 to 1930 significant changes began to take place in the pattern of urban growth. The old core of the metropolis became less important as a residential area as secondary industry expanded during the war and needed more space close to transport outlets. The displaced residents moved outwards, along the pre-existing railway and tram lines. Railways were electrified by 1923, trams by 1919, in time to cope with the boom period of the 1920s during which Melbourne's population increased from 750 000 (in 1920) to a million (in 1929). Suburban expansion and more road traffic increased the urgency for metropolitan planning. Efforts to centralize and co-ordinate controls over metropolitan growth were unsuccessful, but some control over development through municipal regulation began around 1900.

The Local Government Acts of 1903 and 1914 introduced building and site regulations, empowering councils to prescribe minimum areas, depths, widths of frontages, and spaces around dwellings; to regulate their height, ventilation and lighting; to reclaim insanitary, low-lying or overcrowded areas; and to regulate subdivision proposals according to specified standards. In the metropolitan area, plans of subdivision *could* be refused if the area could not be economically and advantageously sewered, but the power was discretionary and hence easily avoided. According to the final report of the 1914–18 royal commission on housing these few regulatory powers that did exist were used reluctantly and sparingly, if at all.[21] The same was true of the earliest land-use controls granted to local councils by the Local Government Act of 1921. This enabled councils to make by-laws 'prescribing areas within their districts as residential areas' and prohibiting from these areas any other uses that the by-laws specified.[22]

It has been said of American cities that 'most graft in American local government today arises from the administration of zoning controls'. Zoning has traditionally been the responsibility of local governments but R. Mathews argues that

> although they may be safely left with the responsibility for administering detailed zoning ordinances in accordance with a metropolitan-wide plan, it is dangerous to entrust them with the task of planning land use. This is because they are likely to be more concerned with maintaining or enhancing private property values, which are the basis of the bulk of their revenues, than with promoting community welfare in a wider sense . . . Zoning needs to have regard to such matters as aesthetic considerations, the need for recreational areas and the planning of housing and other development in such a way as to make effective use of public service facilities. A metropolitan authority is more likely to give due weight to such matters than local councils elected by private property owners. When this is permitted to be undertaken for private gain without regard to public interest, it may result in disorderly development and throw unnecessary burdens on public authorities responsible for providing roads, sewerage, water supply and other urban services.[23]

Hindsight has shown that zoning, one of the 'conventional wisdoms' of the early planning movement, is not the wholesale remedy for urban problems it was once thought to be. Zoning could be used in a conservative way by middle- and upper-class areas to protect themselves from 'undesirable land uses', which could cover anything from industrial encroachment to working-class housing. Until empirical research has been done on the matter, we can only guess at the extent to which zoning has been used as a conservative tool by local governments in Australian cities. One local historian records that local councils were tardy in exercising the few powers they did possess. Weston Bate argues, in the case of Brighton, that in the period of rapid growth and material advance of the 1920s local councils were ill-prepared and no one clearly saw what was at stake. Planning was associated with provision of playgrounds and reserves, and the 'knowledge upon which a constructive overall plan might have been based was rare in Melbourne.'[24] Bate's study suggests that planning at local council level was not a going concern before World War II, but until more case studies are completed we can only speculate about the probable conservative impact of local zoning powers, as Robin Boyd does in *Australia's Home*: 'In the early 1920s many municipal councils in Sydney and Melbourne began to ordain Brick Areas, insurance companies noting with satisfaction that no timber houses were approved in such areas ... Weatherboards never appeared in rich streets, bricks seldom in poor streets. The brick areas were created for snobbish reasons.'[25]

Discretionary local zoning powers were a far cry from the prescriptive land-use control of the whole metropolis that those active in the planning movement advocated. These shortcomings were explained and condemned by the authors of the 1929 *Metropolitan Town Planning Commission Report*, itself the culmination of the early enthusiasm for planning that Victoria shared with other states during World War I.

Town Planning 1914–18: Housing and Social Reform

The 1914 lecture tour by Reade and Davidge triggered the formation of the Town Planning Association in Victoria, as it did in other states. The concerns of the Victorian body, which incorporated the pre-existing Anti-slum Committee and the National Parks Association, were with housing, designing new cities, and preserving parks, open spaces and native wildlife.[26] Their first president and leading member for twenty years, James Barrett, a Toorak doctor, lieutenant-colonel during the war, and later vice-chancellor of Melbourne University, was a member of the Liberal Party and the Melbourne Club.

In 1913 a joint select committee appointed by the Watt Liberal government had investigated slums and reported that the housing of the people in some parts of the city was a disgrace, a menace to those concerned and to the health of the community at large. This led to the establishment of a royal commission in 1914 to inquire into working-class housing conditions. The commissioners, two Labor men and five Liberals, presented two progress reports before completing the final report in 1918. The first dealt with the failure of local councils to make by-laws to enable them to control subdivision. It also criticized the 'meanly avaricious spirit displayed by certain owners of large estates or their agents ... in thwarting, in the absence of local enactment of legal obligations and in the presence of moral obligations to the community, attempts made at the beginning of settlement to establish reasonably necessary conditions of subdivision.'[27] The second report emphasized the need for 'State purchase of lands and State provision of dwellings and traffic facilities, as complementary to private enterprise in reducing the shortage of proper housing accommodation and so encouraging exodus from overcrowded areas.'[28] The minutes of evidence (which ran to 510 pages before printing was abandoned as too costly) reveal the breadth and depth of the inquiry and the influence of the planning movement. Among those consulted were twenty-two policemen, twenty-eight social workers (that is, ministers and church workers), seven representatives of health authorities, fourteen men interested in housing (among them Sir Allen Taylor, member of the Legislative Council, New South Wales, and T. H. Thomas, secretary of the Workers Homes Board, Western Australia) and nine 'town planning' representatives—Reade, Davidge, Fitzgerald, Sulman, Irvine, George Taylor, Morrell, Stanton and the lawyer and Sydney city councillor E. Milner Stephen—who were all asked to prepare statements on the housing of the people.

Sulman recommended that urban growth should be on garden city lines, the essential feature being the limitation of the number of houses or people per acre. He favoured *private* control of garden suburb development rather than government or municipal control, but within stictly limited conditions as to layout, upkeep, speculation in land values, and the devotion of profits beyond 5 per cent to the benefit of the estate.[29] His model obviously was Letchworth garden city. The wide-ranging and radical concerns of the commission are evident in the kinds of questions it posed to witnesses. Sulman for example was asked by the chairman, Labor parliamentarian J. H. Solly, 'What are the principal advantages to the community of Town Planning?' 'In connection with any reform movement, who do you think are the proper persons to take control . . . individual municipalities . . . or a Greater Melbourne Scheme adopted to absorb the municipalities . . . and with power over all public utilities?' 'Are you likely to get a Town Planning system such as we advocate under private enterprise?' Solly suggested to Sulman that the slums of Sydney were indicative of the failure of private enterprise, and when Sulman rose to the defence of the work of private enterprise in the suburbs the commissioner replied that 'the better class dwelling in a suburb is the result of a demand by a certain class in the community who have the means to pay for it', to which Sulman could only agree.[30]

Irvine, who was asked for his views 'with regard to the man who really cannot help himself—the man who is forced into the slum area through being only able to obtain casual employment at very poor wages', said that the problem could not be solved unless rents were brought within the limits of the wages paid to that class of man, and added that from this point of view he considered Daceyville garden suburb a failure. 'The ordinary worker cannot afford rent up to 17/6d. a week . . . Daceyville is really a suburb for the moderately well-to-do.' Charles Reade's fifty-page contribution discussed housing and speculation in Europe, the garden city movement in Britain, the 1909 Housing and Town Planning Act, slums and replanning of overcrowded areas, constructive aspects of continental town planning for Australia, cheap transit in Belgium, problems of Australian cities, and tentative recommendations for a town planning act and its administration.

In 1918 the royal commission delivered its final report. It was highly critical of municipalities for not using powers given them in the Workers Dwellings Act (1914) to acquire land and borrow for construction of low-rent workers' homes.

> In searching for an adequate explanation of the councils' aloofness ... it is evident that a constant hindrance to initiative on their part is the influence of persistent demands by ratepayers to cut down expenditure, to say nothing of the probable opposition of vested interests in small house properties. But ... such explanations cannot be regarded as justifications.[31]

The commission therefore recommended the introduction of measures 'to enable either the Government, or associations under Government control, to take up the work of reform, instead of leaving such work to be developed by the uncertain operation of an adoptive section of local government powers'. It urged *government intervention to enforce* control of subdivision, uniform building regulations and health regulations, and to proceed with slum clearance and low-rent housing. Nothing ever came of this four-year undertaking. For although the reports were signed by all commissioners, the influence of the Labor chairman was conspicuous. But Labor was not in office when the final report was tabled, nor in the years immediately following. For the Liberals, the four-year inquiry had obviously been a convenient way of defusing the issue.

Business and Town Planning 1920s

During World War I there was a remarkable interchange of ideas between states, especially through the two Australasian town planning conferences and the Victorian Royal Commission on Housing. Neither the nation-wide exchange of ideas nor the reformist emphasis of the movement survived long after the end of the war. After 1918 each state became preoccupied with its own problems and, since the twenties were a boom period, attention was directed at facilitation of growth rather than concern for its social consequences. Between 1920 and 1930 Melbourne's population increased by 195 000, and 70 000 houses were built in the metropolitan area.

> Land speculators were operating again, more concerned with attaining a maximum frontage to sell than with providing open space and other amenities, or with coordinating one subdivision to another. The areas subdivided were far beyond the needs of the day. With a population near the one million mark, Melbourne had begun to sprawl, although for some time various organisations had been advocating legislation to prevent this.[32]

Eventually this advocacy (by the Town Planning Association and, through its president in 1919, Councillor Frank Stapley, the Melbourne City Council), resulted in the Metropolitan Town Planning Commission Act of 1922. This act established a nine-member town planning commission (four local councillors, one Melbourne city councillor and four 'technical experts') to 'inquire into and report on the present conditions and tendencies of urban development in the metropolitan area' and to set out 'general plans and recommendations with respect to the better guidance and control of such development, and estimates of the cost involved in the construction, maintenance and administration of the recommendations.[33] The commission had to consult with all municipalities and every public authority on any of its inquiries that affected the powers of these bodies.

The final report was presented to the minister for public works (J. P. Jones, Labor member of the Legislative Council) in March 1928. He agreed that a town planning bill be prepared. The commissioners then conferred with the parliamentary draughtsman and the resulting bill was to make it mandatory for every municipality with populations over 2000 to prepare or adopt town planning schemes. The minister was to be empowered to order a municipality to prepare and enforce a scheme, though no penal provisions were included. A central authority of 'town planning experts' would administer the act. Municipalities were to have the power to resume land, prevent development contrary to the scheme, compensate those injuriously affected, and collect betterment from those who benefited from schemes.[34]

In July 1928 a first draft of the bill was submitted to the commission for comment. The revised bill was not submitted to parliament for, in the meantime, a National ministry had taken over from the Labor ministry. The new government prepared a new town planning bill, did not forward it to the commission for comment, and did not submit it to parliament before dissolution in November 1929. The authors of the 1954 planning scheme attributed this to the depression. 'The thoughts of politicians turned to what they considered more realistic things than town planning.'[35] But the report had actually been delivered to the government in January 1928, at least eighteen months before the depression was felt, which suggests two further explanations of this failure. In April 1930 the chairman of the commission remarked that since it had been established there had been twelve changes of ministry, with consequent changes in the portfolio for public works.[36] The unstable three-party situation that existed through the 1920s was characterized by the inactivity of successive ministries. The Labor Party held power from December 1929 to May 1932, but only with Country Party support. During this time the original town planning bill was submitted to parliament, but failed because of the opposition of country representatives.[37] For the next eleven years the Country Party governed and, with the hostility of country interests to any money being spent on the city, planning became a dead issue.

So much for the politics of the Town Planning Commission. What of its policies? Were they so radical as to justify conservatives' fears? The commission's report, published in 1929, was the first general stock-taking of the urban system in the ninety years since its foundation. It concentrated on three areas: the introduction of a metropolitan-wide system of land-use zoning, the planning of a metropolitan main road network, and a programme to increase the amount of open space. Traffic surveys had shown an increase in city traffic of 31 per cent between 1924 and 1926 and an eight-fold increase in car registration, from 21 152 in 1917 to 158 468 in 1928. Consequently the report agonized for 120 of its 300 pages on 'traffic congestion' and how to overcome it by building more roads.

Little was said of social reform: much on the financial benefits and scund business principles of planning.

> A city must be planned with two objects in view—that of conducting its business in the most efficient manner, and that of conferring the greatest benefits on the greater number. City planning aims to bring about order in urban physical development . . . and to provide for the requirements of commerce and industries.[38]

Zoning, recreation, open space and housing proposals were justified in economic terms. The commission commended the Local Government Act of 1921 (which had empowered municipalities to zone areas residential and prohibit non-residential uses) because it 'has had the effect of stabilising values' and preventing undesirable conditions in residential areas. It thus proposed a metropolitan zoning system which 'would have a very beneficial effect by stabilising the value of property.' The recommended zoning proposals would have made any form of new housing other than detached units of one or two storeys virtually impossible to build. Indeed the proposed zoning and building regulations were further justified in terms of their ability to 'ensure that the principal housing districts of the metropolis would be of character consistent with the Australian ideals of housing.' It thus appears that the pattern of suburban development and home ownership that had emerged in the 1870s and 1880s had come to be regarded as characteristically Australian and unquestionably desirable. The final reason advanced to justify zoning the metropolis was that it would reduce service costs. It was proposed that 123 713 acres be zoned as residential, an area which it was estimated could accommodate 3·7 million. Yet elsewhere the report lamented the fact that 'there are few, if any, cities of a population of one million which occupy such a large area as does Melbourne to its suburbs. The relatively low average density of population . . . has presented many problems to those charged with the responsibility of supplying the various public services.'[39]

The commission's findings on housing were less substantial and less welfare-oriented than those of the earlier royal commission. The report noted that no local council had bothered to use the powers granted them by the Housing and Reclamation Act of 1920 but was not curious as to why this was so, made no suggestions for housing low-income earners and clearly had no intention of suggesting inter-ference with the private enterprise system. The commissioners' values are implicit in the title of one section—'Encouragement of Home Ownership'. Unlike the 1918 royal commission, the 1929 report gave no attention to sociological variables such as income distribution. Nor apparently were they concerned about the locational inequalities of the developing metropolis. New working-class areas were develop-ing mainly in the outer western suburbs despite poor transport facilities and inferior provision of services in those areas. While no mention was made of this important social fact, much was made of the 'material aspect' of open space provision, in that it 'invariably increases land and property values in the vicinity' and access to open air invigorates workers and increases their 'productive capacity.'[40]

The commission recognized the need for some form of centralized control in a metropolitan construction authority and suggested three ways of constituting such a body, but did not indicate its own prefer-ence, obviously preferring to avoid political controversy. Their report did attempt to formulate planning proposals on a metropolitan scale, but it was hardly a radical document. It reads far more like a Chamber of Commerce proposal than a revolutionary manifesto. Yet nothing ever came of it. And the city's growth continued under the system of laissez-faire which had prevailed in the nineteenth century.

Housing and Town Planning 1930s

That more humane strain of thinking which had characterized the early planning movement and given priority to issues like housing of low-income workers and slum abolition, revived in the 1930s. While the record of action in these years is bleak, Victorians seem to have at least had a talent for producing intelligent reports on the ever-worsening situation. After two further decades of neglect since the 1918 royal commission report on housing, yet another probing inves-tigation was forthcoming. Its authors were the Housing Investigation and Slum Abolition Board, a group appointed by the Dunstan Country Party government in 1936 in response to persistent agitation through-out the decade on the slum problem. The deputy chairman of the board, F. Oswald Barnett, had led this public campaign.

Barnett was a former school-teacher who presented a thesis entitled

'The Economics of the Slums' to the Faculty of Commerce at Melbourne University in 1932 and published it as a book, *The Unsuspected Slums*, in 1933. His findings on the occupations, habits and values of slum dwellers provided the framework for the social survey conducted by the 1935 Board of Inquiry. That survey asked questions about the income, occupation, drinking habits, criminal record, and parental background of husbands in slum households, and whether the wives loved and cared for their children, drank and appeared slovenly. It compiled statistics on the conditions of homes, incomes and occupations of slum occupiers and details relating to children in the houses inspected. It was found that 64·7 per cent of male occupiers were unskilled workers, that 43·5 per cent of the inhabitants of all houses inspected were children and that 21·8 per cent of those over fourteen years were unemployed. The passage of twenty-five years since the 1913 select committee report on housing had 'aggravated almost beyond description the appalling conditions of the same slum areas and of the inhabitants'. Land had been used 'so avariciously in some instances that two or three houses have been erected on an area which was originally intended to be a backyard'. Rents were so extortionate 'that many families . . . have been reduced to a state of semi-starvation'. Industrial encroachment had accentuated overcrowding. Displaced occupants of demolished inner-city homes 'crowded in on the already over-crowded houses in the same neighbourhoods'. Thousands of men, women and children were living in what could only be described as 'miserable hovels'. The report concluded that 'the housing of the poor in the metropolitan area is a standing reproach to this State'.[41]

The board had set out to formulate both a short-term policy of rehousing for those areas needing immediate treatment, and a longer-term policy embracing considerations of town planning and co-ordination of transport and other services. Their *first progress report* argued that a direct cause-and-effect relationship existed between bad housing and a variety of social problems. Statistics on infant mortality, ill-health, delinquency, crime and the disproportionate use of social security and welfare services in slum areas were used to infer this relationship. The authors were aware too of the revolutionary potential of such impoverished surroundings, which could 'engender a hatred of and revolt against a social system which permits such housing conditions to exist'.[42] These arguments provided the political impetus for the establishment of a public housing programme for they appealed to Christian humanism, to economic reason and to political prudence.

More recently sociologists and social workers have discounted many of these earlier propositions. There is certainly still a coincidence between, on the one hand, some kinds of social pathology, and on the other, bad housing and certain poorer residential areas, but the causal link is difficult to sustain. In fact a deeper understanding of different ways of life and the importance of social relationships has led to an acknowledgement of real strengths in some areas of poor housing. In many respects the pendulum has swung to another extreme. Some conservationists, sociologists, social and community workers who are impressed with the network of relationships and the richer and more varied community life in areas of poor housing give the impression that everything should be preserved as it is now, in perpetuity, regardless of the physical standard of the accommodation or the merits of rival land use.

However, it makes little difference to its victims whether bad housing is a result or a cause of poverty. It is an integral part of being poor. And this economic reality was squarely faced by the 1937 inquiry.

> The problem of the slums is essentially the problem of poverty . . . the problem of the tenant who, by reason of his low wage-earning or the number of his dependants, is unable to pay the full economic rent of a dwelling of reasonable standards . . . Economically, the slum problem is the wage problem and a solution must be found by either increasing the earnings of the persons concerned and/or by providing lower rental dwellings . . . The slum dwelling has been and still is being used as an instrument for the shameful exploitation of the poor.[43]

The report's recommendations were strong medicine to an essentially laissez-faire society, for they argued that the free market had failed and the urgency of the situation demanded a state social service, which could not be expected to be self-supporting. It was 'futile to attempt to deal with the problem as a cold commercial proposition'. The board argued for an authority that would take over municipal powers relating to health, building and subdivision regulations, proclaim and treat reclamation areas, condemn and demolish insanitary buildings, acquire lands compulsorily to replan and rebuild areas, and act as landlord and let houses of the authority to tenants. It recommended legislation to deal with overcrowding in houses and on sites, with zoning and planning, and to create the power for the proposed authority to introduce differential rental scales for tenants of state housing, to control the activities of public utilities and private trusts for building, to make and enter into 'treaties' with constituents of the building industry, and to make building by-laws. This extensive investigation into the plight of low income earners' living standards, and its findings, was different in only one significant respect from its predecessor of 1914–18. Something did come of it. The Housing Commission of Victoria was established in 1938 as the outcome of the 1936–7 Board of Inquiry.

The premier and Country Party leader, A. A. Dunstan, explained in his second reading speech that a housing commission would be established to 'improve existing housing conditions and provide adequate and suitable housing accommodation for persons of limited means, that is, persons with an income up to £260 p.a. or £5 per week.'[44] £500 000 was allocated to the commission for its first year's operations and provision was made for future allocations from consolidated revenue.

The important consensus that emerged from the debates on the housing bill was the acceptance of the principle that the state must intervene, even at financial loss, in the provision of housing. Significantly absent from the debate was any discussion of planning issues or of the connection between planning and housing that the Housing Investigation and Slum Abolition Board had insisted on. This board had set out to formulate a short-term policy of rehousing and slum reclamation for the immediate future, and a long-term policy covering a much wider area and involving considerations of town planning, co-ordination of transport and other services. It had recommended legislation to deal with zoning and planning and to control the activities of public utilities and private trusts for building. None of these suggestions or concerns were dealt with in the housing act.

Victoria's public housing began as an attempt to abolish slums and rescue slum dwellers, unlike council housing in the United Kingdom which began as an attempt to build houses—good and cheap—for ordinary working-class families (the more 'respectable' the better), and unlike the South Australian Housing Trust, which began as an attempt to promote economic growth and keep rents down for workers in growing manufacturing industries. This difference in origins helps explain the different results in standard and quality of buildings, their density and location (inner-city or suburban), and the attitudes of housing managers to tenants.

Why, though, did a Country Party government pass an act providing for *state intervention* in the free market to supply houses mainly for the *urban poor*. Was it economic reason or political prudence that prevailed? or Christian humanism? Dunstan argued in his presentation of the bill that 'even though we do lose some money as a result of the passage of legislation of this kind, indirect benefits of a substantial nature that cannot be measured in terms of pounds, shillings and pence will be achieved'. By 'indirect benefits' he may have meant political and social harmony and goodwill among men. But the Country Party only governed with Labor Party support and presumably felt the need to pass at least one piece of legislation urged by Labor. Perhaps too Dunstan expected that at least some of the Victorian Housing Commission funds could be channelled into housing for the rural poor.

Moves to Reform Urban Administration, part 2

The Melbourne Metropolitan Council Bill of 1936, presented by H. S. Bailey (chief secretary in the Dunstan Country Party government) as an attempt to implement the recommendations of the 1929 Town Planning Commission report, met a similar fate, for similar reasons, to its precursors of 1913 and 1915. It made provision for control of water supply, sewerage, tramways, buses, bridges, highways, fire brigades, for the taking over of local councils' powers under the Health Act and of housing, reclamation and regulation of buildings, as well as the creation of new powers to zone the whole metropolis and to purchase land for the provision of parks and gardens. The proposed council was to have thirty members directly elected on a population basis, and was to be financed by property rating powers.[45]

Some of the complexity of the politics involved in creating a metropolitan authority with co-ordinating powers emerges from the lengthy debates on this bill. There was immediate opposition from the United Australia Party (UAP) on the grounds that it would create 'a much too powerful new authority which would eventually rival Parliament' and would be 'another taxing body ... placing increasing demands on the Government for heavier rating and extended borrowing powers'.[46] Both inner and outer municipalities opposed the bill, the former afraid that their rates would be used to finance development in the outer areas, and the latter afraid that their interests would be swamped on such a council because their lesser population would give them less representation. While the bill was being debated in parliament a conference of municipalities decided to oppose it. The conference concluded that, although a metropolitan-wide authority was necessary, the MMBW was the appropriate body to handle the proposed new functions. Local councils found it impossible to agree on these issues but were unanimous in their fear that any new central authority would eventually supersede them. Faced with such many-sided opposition, the government introduced amendments excising from the bill control of tramways, cemeteries, fire brigades, metropolitan gas undertakings, transfer of local powers under the Health Act and their power to make building by-laws, and the transfer of municipal abattoirs, thus emasculating the original conception. Yet the same objections were again raised.[47]

The constitution of any metropolitan authority was a seminal issue. Should it be elected or nominated? Should members be paid? The Labor Party supported an elected body returned on the basis of one ratepayer one vote, and one member from each municipality. This convinced the UAP that the bill was 'undoubtedly in conformity with the socialistic policy of the Labor Party, which wants a municipal franchise based on the principle of one adult one vote'. Local councils sent letters of protest 'against such an unnecessary and revolutionary change in the municipal government of Melbourne, and in support of increased local council powers 'rather than relegate these councils to the subservience of a coterie of central administrators'.[48] Given that there was so little agreement on the need for a bill of this kind, let alone for its mechanisms, why did the Country Party introduce it? The accusations of the UAP member for St Kilda were accurate:

> The government has obviously brought down the Bill at the dictation of the Ministerial corner party. The action of the Government would appear to have justified the boast of Mr Kennelly, organising secretary of the Labor Party, when he said—We are not keeping this Country Party Government in power for nothing. We are getting while the getting is good.[49]

With Labor Party support the amended bill did pass in the assembly but was shelved by the Legislative Council, members of which saw themselves as defenders both of local councils and of property owners. 'It is necessary that we should protect our ratepayers and help in every way we can the owners of property.'[50] The only consensus to emerge was that the MMBW was doing a good job and should not be dissolved in favour of any new metropolitan authority. Not surprisingly therefore a bill for the reconstitution of the MMBW was introduced by the same government in 1937. From the beginning, UAP members accused it of being the 1936 bill in disguise. The 1937 bill proposed to expand the powers of the MMBW to include town planning, roads and bridges, parks and gardens, foreshores, and housing and reclamation. To finance its new responsibilities there was to be an increase in its rating power of 2d in the pound and, most significantly for the final fate of the bill, the election and representation system for the MMBW was to be changed. Each municipality was to be represented on a population basis, one member for areas with a population between 20 000 and 52 000, two members for areas from 52 000 to 85 000 and three members for areas from 85 00 to 117 000. The franchise was confined to ratepayers, but plural voting was to be abolished.[51] Opposition to the bill was similar to that voiced against the Melbourne Metropolitan Council Bill of 1936. Sir Stanley Argyle, a Toorak doctor and former premier (1932–5), delineated the four 'objectionable features' of the bill; one ratepayer one vote, ratepayer franchise, payment of members and the financial effect on the metropolitan ratepayers. He argued that the proposal was 'the thin edge of the wedge for the accomplishment of the clearly avowed policy of the Labor Party, to obtain by constitutional means complete control of the government not only of this state, but also of this great city.'[52]

Clearly the issue was no longer whether there was a need for reform in metropolitan administration—the original intention of the bill—but centred around the political implications of any such reform Both the UAP and the Country Party feared the consequences if, having created a centralized body with wide-ranging powers over the growth and development of the metropolis, Labor were to capture control of it. The bill reached the committee stage, then lapsed. The real issue, concerning the need for an authority with co-ordinating powers over the metropolitan area, had been obscured by 'sovereignty' fears, from members of parliament to local councils, property owners, and existing statutory bodies, that their traditional power bases were to be undermined. The only real support for the bill, introduced by the Country Party, came from Labor. That the bill was introduced as a political manoeuvre by the Country Party to appease Labor, without whose support it could not remain in office, is evident by the lack of enthusiasm with which the Country Party defended the measure. The press was quick to pick up the observation of T. T. Hollway (UAP, Ballarat) that not one Country Party member had spoken in support of the bill.[53] And their lack of commitment was painfully obvious in the speed with which they dropped it as soon as it proved controversial.

Within parliament little enthusiasm for the measure could be heard, but public attention was being focused on the matter through the backing it received in the *Age*. In its reporting of the debates, the *Age* used pejorative adjectives to describe the speeches of the opposition—feeble, floundering, footling, petulant, parochial, petty plaintive, irrelevant, lamentable, soured, vague, uncertain, unconvincing, rambling—while referring to those speeches in favour of the bill as reasoned, progressive, prompt, more effective, improved, and vigorous.[54]

The support of the *Age* for this issue is analogous to the support of the *Sydney Morning Herald* in the same period for 'town planning'. Both issues were popular when discussed at the level of general principle but met rigorous opposition once decisions had to be made about means and methods and powers.

Conclusions

Melbourne had suffered a slight decline in population from 1929 to 1932 and only exceeded the 1929 level again in 1935. By 1939 the population was only 41 000 above the level of the previous decade. In the depressed thirties the issues of traffic congestion, industrial encroachment and the need to plan for expansion, all of which had loomed large in the twenties, seemed less pressing.

Thinking about planning from the turn of the century until World War II followed a cyclical pattern that was primarily a reflection of prevailing economic conditions. In the period of growth of the 1920s, planning thought focused on providing the facilities to enhance and encourage expansion, 'to bring about order in urban physical development', as the 1929 Town Planning Commission's report said, particularly through improved transport and communication services. 'Growth' was not only believed to be a good thing but was regarded as essential to the nation's survival. There was never any suggestion that it should be restrained in any way. At most it should be rationally supervised. In such a period the social reforming aspects of the planning movement were submerged. Social welfare concerns came to the fore in times of hardship: at the turn of the century following the effects of the 1890s depression; during World War I, when significant numbers of men were classified unfit for service and startling revelations were being made about housing conditions; and in the 1930s following the trauma of the depression and the cumulative worsening and shortage of facilities like housing for the poor, resulting from decades of neglect.

Action on planning issues was more dependent on the state of politics and suffered accordingly, both from the short-term instability of Victorian politics and from the more enduring inbuilt rural and conservative bias of its political institutions. By World War II some progress had been made in the direction of social reform through housing, but the planning advocates' insistence on the vital interconnection between planning and housing had been ignored. No progress had been made with the other major concern of the planning movement, reform of urban administration through the creation of a metropolitan organization with planning and co-ordinating powers. The issues on and method by which this legislation was defeated in 1936 and 1937 are illustrative of all the minor and major squabbles that have beleaguered efforts to introduce rational planning in Victoria. Rivalry between local government and the state government, between the MMBW and the state government, jealousies between inner and outer municipalities, all presented organizational problems when it came to establishing any planning authority. The tripartite parliamentary situation caused by the electoral gerrymander, the dominance of the Country Party, and the conservative complexion of the Legislative Council presented ideological problems when it came to passing *any* planning legislation.

Paradoxically planning, if it means control of private development (as it mainly did in this period) can only operate during periods of urban growth, when the horse to be steered by the reins of planning controls is going somewhere. It languishes when there is no forward movement. But it was during periods of boom that people said they had no time for planning. Interest revived when the economy flagged. But efforts at planning in those periods were inevitably less effective.

4

Sydney: National Hobby of Land Speculation

Ironically it was in the 1920s that the trend of investment moved clearly in favour of the cities. At the very time when governments gave renewed emphasis to rural areas, Australia was taking off as a manufacturing power—without anyone noticing.

D. Horne 1972[1]

The sanctity of the Australian home as the Australian's castle was the original unquestioned plank in the platforms of all political parties.

R. Boyd 1952[2]

Power in the City

The structure of political power in a city is basic to any explanation of the allocation of resources between different parts of the urban community, and between urban and rural sectors. In Australian cities the matter is complicated by divided sets of responsibilities for resource allocation between local, state and federal governments, but analysis of the power structure at state level gives some indication of the constraints operating against a redistributive approach to city government and planning.

The two previous chapters have outlined some of these constraints in Adelaide and Melbourne—lower houses dominated by coalitions of country and city rich, upper houses at the mercy of rural conservatives, city councils whose members have a vested interest in protecting existing property and privilege or in real estate and land speculation, and Liberal Party organizations dependent on the support of the financial 'establishment'. The broad contours of power and influence in Sydney fall into the same pattern in the period between the two world wars. The Legislative Council has been described as

conservative in purpose, and generally in political complexion and action . . . With life tenure, unpaid membership and a convention

77

... against wholesale swamping, half a century of nominations by middle class governments produced a House that could be trusted to insist on two or more bites at measures to extend the franchise, steepen income tax, break up pastoral holdings for closer settlement, or promote government enterprises and social services.[3]

Country Party influence, as in Victoria, began to play a major role in the Legislative Assembly by the mid-1920s. In 1928, under the non-Labor government, the state was divided for the first time into three zones—Sydney, Newcastle and Country. Seats in the Sydney zone had a larger average number of electors than those in the Newcastle zone, while the numbers for the country seats were smaller still with only two thirds' the electoral population of an average Sydney seat. And the Country Party minister for local government from 1927–30 and deputy premier in the United Australia Party (UAP)-Country Party coalition government from 1932–41, grazier and former army colonel, M. F. Bruxner, 'revelled in the opportunity to use his powers ... in the interests of country people'.[4] (However, aborigines, poor whites and miners, didn't benefit from Country Party generosity.) As minister for transport in 1932 Bruxner virtually stopped railway construction in the city and diverted funds to country roads. In the first full year of the UAP-Country Party government the expenditure of the new Department of Main Roads on country roads increased four-fold to £645 000 and when Bruxner left office in 1941, the department was spending £2 million a year on country roads alone. 'As the years went on the Department took over more functions and more responsibilities ... More roads were classified as state highways, including one which ran past Bruxner's property ... This empire building proceeded with Bruxner's full support and encouragement.'[5] By the late 1930s Premier Stevens could not escape the charge that his government was dominated by the Country Party. The main achievements of his administration were in the country and had been the work of Country Party ministers. 'Capital works in Sydney itself ... had not been noticeable.'[6] This dominance, as Florence Taylor (first woman architect and structural engineer in Australia, life member of the New South Wales Town Planning Association, and editor of *Building* with her husband George Taylor) observed, thwarted implementation of urban planning measures in this period.

> If anything costs money in Sydney it doesn't get done, no matter how vital or urgent it may be. If it did, the Country Party would have something to say about it, and that might lose votes for our administrators when elections come round. Everything, it seems, must be spent in the country, and nothing in the city.[7]

The UAP received the bulk of its funds through a body of trustees outside the party organization who, on the evidence of Sydney's

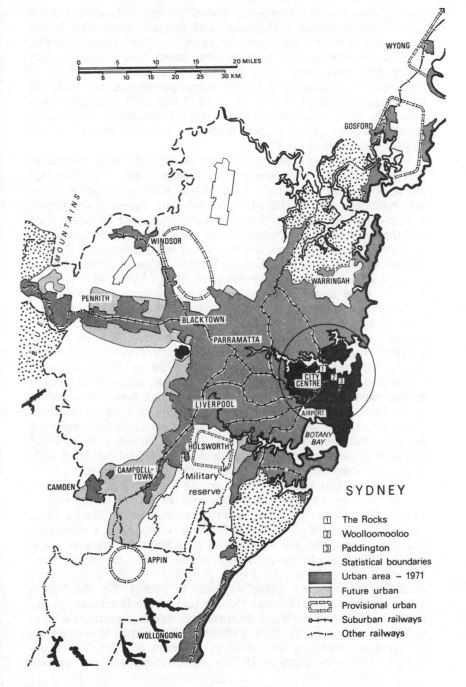

SYDNEY

1 The Rocks
2 Woolloomooloo
3 Paddington
--- Statistical boundaries
■ Urban area – 1971
■ Future urban
▱ Provisional urban
o—o—o Suburban railways
-·-·- Other railways

leading conservative newspaper, 'controlled and influenced a great part of the industrial, commercial and financial companies in the state—that is to say, the largest of them . . . They were, naturally, in close touch with party leaders, with whom they discussed party policy. Not unnaturally, party leaders paid a good deal of heed to their views.'[8] Legislation to reform urban government was defeated by this coalition of interests in 1913, 1915 and 1931. Legislation was passed in 1934 (the Sydney Corporation Amendment Act) which strengthened the power of non-residential property owners on the Sydney City Council (SCC).

Under the Sydney Corporation Act of 1902 the SCC comprised twenty-six aldermen, two from each of thirteen wards which included the working-class residential and industrial suburbs of Darlinghurst, Woolloomooloo, Surry Hills, Chippendale and Pyrmont; the upper-middle-class harbour-side suburbs of Potts Point and Elizabeth Bay; and the central business district, which included as voters both non-residential property owners and working-class lodgers who lived in cheap rooming-houses near Central Station. Property owners with a freehold interest in property worth more than £5 were able to enrol in every ward in which they owned such property, thereby giving property owners a multiple vote. Despite this, Labor aldermen won a majority in 1921, lost it to the Civic Reform Group in 1922, but regained control for three years in 1924. The Civic Reform Group, which alternated with the Labor Party in controlling the SCC in the 1920s, held uninterrupted power from 1930 to 1948. Although claiming to be non-political, above party politics, interested in efficient management, the Civic Reform Group has in fact been the equivalent of the state conservative parties on the council. None of its aldermen have ever lived in the area they have been responsible for, preferring the more salubrious north shore and eastern harbour-side suburbs,[9] but most of them have had property or business interests in the city centre and have used their office to protect those interests.

The issues most keenly debated during Labor's terms in office in the 1920s were the proposed extensions to Moore Street and to Martin Place in the city. The main opponents of the Martin Place extension were the two large banking companies, Commercial Banking Corporation and the Bank of New South Wales, whose land and buildings would have been resumed if the extensions were approved. The will of the banks prevailed, to the detriment of extending the only real 'place' or plaza in Sydney. But the biggest SCC project of the 1920s was the erection of the Bunnerong power station at Botany Bay. While construction was in progress, the non-Labor opposition in the state parliament began questioning certain transactions concerning the letting of the main contract. The opposition's election platform in 1927 promised temporarily to replace the SCC by city commissioners to set the affairs of the city straight and they did just that when they won the election in October 1927. Like the Civic Reform Group's lord mayors of the early 1920s the city commissioners subsequently appointed by the non-Labor state government all lived outside the working-class areas over which they had authority. The Labor Party leader of the opposition, Jack Lang, argued in state parliament that the charges of corruption were not the real reason for the dismissal of the council. 'The real reason for this measure is that a city council election is pending and the results of the last state election, within the boundaries of the City of Sydney [show] ... that the Labor Party would be returned.'[10] The Labor Party has always been vulnerable to clumsy and obvious bribery misbehaviour. Their aldermen have less access to the more 'legitimate' sources of wealth like shares and property than do the Civic Reform Group aldermen. But Labor has usually been able to raise a popular majority. Therefore the conservatives have always had to resort to corruption charges to keep Labor out of office and, when that failed, to (legally) alter the rules of the game to try and exclude Labor, as they did in 1934 by amending the Sydney Corporation Act to exclude the lodger vote.

Unlike the Adelaide and Melbourne City Council, though, the SCC has not been the exclusive preserve of the non-Labor forces. Labor had a majority for part of the twenties, then from 1948 to 1967 when the state Labor government changed the rules, by expanding the area of the council into working-class suburbs, to suit their purposes. To some extent, then, the SCC has been manipulated for the convenience of whatever party is in power at state level. Yet the influence and power of property owners on the council has been an enduring theme for the past fifty years. This is evident in a superficial way in the residential location of Civic Reform Group aldermen and in their occupations. For example the lord mayor in 1935 was an export merchant and company director who lived at Elizabeth Bay. The mayor of 1936–7 was a senior partner in a building and contracting firm and chairman of directors of the Port Jackson and Manly Steamship Company, and the mayor for the last two years of the thirties, N. L. Nock, was managing director of his family company and a director of David Jones Ltd, the largest retailer in the city with three large premises by the late 1930s.[11] But simply to cite their socio-economic status does not prove that the Civic Reform Group governed in the interests of the property and business lobby in the city. To illustrate their effect on the city's development it is necessary to look at what they did and at what they failed to do. Unlike the Labor SCC of the mid-1920s the council under the Civic Reform Group made no moves at all to provide low-cost rental housing for city workers. Nor did it spend money on social services for the poor residential areas. Also, despite warnings for example about traffic congestion by members of the Town Planning Association during the building boom of the 1920s, the council made no effort either to restrict the density and height of buildings in the city or to prepare a planning scheme to give some order and unity to the rapid development. Alderman Walder's activities on the council in the late thirties illustrate the use of office to protect property interests. Walder was knighted in 1933 after serving as lord mayor the previous year. He had developed his father's canvas manufacturing business into that of a general merchant and by 1941 was director of numerous insurance and related companies (and was also a member of the Millions Club). In April 1937 Walder advocated 'a comprehensive city replanning scheme'.[12] But when in 1939 Darlinghurst, East Sydney and Surry Hills were to be declared residential districts, Walder, 'who said that he owned two factories in Surry Hills, asked that a decision on the area be deferred . . . he contended that property values would decline [if zoning went ahead].'[13]

In general, then, property rights and values and profits were protected by the structure of power in Sydney between the wars, and expenditure on the city was neglected in favour of the country because of the power of the Country Party. But these brakes on the possibilities of public sector redistributive spending on the city did not affect the private sector, and in the flourishing economic conditions of the twenties a building and speculative boom occurred, parallelling that of the 1880s, that was virtually allowed free rein. This boom drew the attention of those involved in the town planning movement away from earlier social reformist concerns and towards a preoccupation with equipping the city to cope with its rapid expansion.

Suburban Building and Speculative Boom 1920–9

The Local Government Act of 1919 was perhaps the most concrete achievement of the early town planning movement and was therefore appropriately guided through the Legislative Council by one of the 'fathers' of the movement, J. D. Fitzgerald, ex-Labor politician and social reformer. His speech on the bill was designed to appeal to the 'protection of property' instincts of the conservative councillors, but it also indicates that town planning could be used as a quite conservative tool. Fitzgerald described the improvements that the act would bring,

> the control of new roads, subdivisions and building—and with that improvement the power to control the number of houses per acre that may be erected in a residential area . . . the building provisions . . . will enable us to have town planning on scientific lines . . . if a council declares a district a residential district no one will be able to intrude into that district.[14]

He went on to warn of the perils of industrial location in five residential areas, citing the North Sydney Gas Company's works and the Burwood brickworks as examples. He claimed that the brickworks, 'put right down in the centre of a beautiful district . . . destroy land values and the amenities of the residents of Burwood . . . if we had a system of planning they would have been placed in a suitable locality.' The 'suitable locality', though he neglected to be specific, was usually one of the inner-city working-class suburbs or the Botany-Mascot working-class area. The possibility of protecting the residential amenity of upper-middle-class suburbs appealed to legislative councillors and the bill was passed just before the upsurge in building activity that dominated the twenties.

By 1921, 43 per cent of the New South Wales population was living in the metropolis, 816 000 of them in the suburbs and 110 000 in the City of Sydney. Since the turn of the century the suburbs had expanded steadily while the population of the inner city slowly declined. The following table indicates the extent of 'suburbanizat' '15

Year	City of Sydney	Suburbs
1901	118 211	369 721
1911	119 774	516 614
1921	110 430	816 170
1924	109 180	902 890
1927	109 640	991 550
1930	109 500	1 144 060

The decades 1911–21 and 1921–31 each added 300 000 people to suburban population. These people needed houses, and suspension of building activity and material shortages during and immediately after the war created a demand that inspired the suburban building boom of the 1920s. This boom took many forms: the filling in of older residential suburbs, the beginnings of new ones, the beginning of a subdivision investment market, the expansion of retail and office building in the city centre, and hence pressure on the government for

Year	Index of building	Year	Index of building
1919	68	1927	106
1920	83	1928	108
1921	72	1929	100
1922	71	1930	60
1923	99	1931	16
1924	104	1932	6
1925	96	1933	11
1926	103		

public utilities to keep pace with these developments. The suburban housing boom took place predominantly within a 6–13-mile radius of the city, near public transport routes.[16] The extent of the boom is apparent in the index of all new building activity in Sydney between 1919 and 1933 (page 83), with 1929 as base year, at 100.[17]

The onset of the boom was predicted in the press in 1920.

> Now that the weather is warming up a resumption of subdivision sales is imminent. Agents are already arranging for what many believe will be a record season ... The demand is here already. Whatever may be said of the improvidence of the Australian, he nevertheless has sufficient common sense to acquire his own home or at least strive hard for it.[18]

That more workers than ever were striving for their own home and garden may explain the decrease in population of the inner suburbs, which averaged 10 per cent over the decade. Some moved willingly from crowded inner areas to outer suburbs where land was relatively cheap in the prosperous climate of the twenties. Others no doubt were forced out by the expansion of factories in inner areas. Suburban councils did selectively use the powers given them under the 1919 Local Government Act to regulate the nature of the growth taking place in their areas, mostly to the disadvantage of the poor and migrant groups. Middle-class Willoughby Council applied the residential zoning powers to protect Walter Burley Griffin's 'picturesque waterside suburb' of Castlecrag as a 'first-class, safeguarded, homogeneous, residential waterside suburb.'[19] The 1919 act strengthened councils' powers not only in regulating building and subdivision activities but also in resuming land. Resumption powers were used in the twenties to aid council beautification schemes and to provide more parks. In 1925 the wealthy Woollahra Council resumed 35 acres from Chinese market gardeners to create a new park.[20] No doubt the removal of the Chinese heightened the residential respectability of the area and enhanced local property values.

But not all councils concerned themselves with beautifying their municipalities. Two letters to the *Sydney Morning Herald* on 1 March 1924 in support of the article 'Sydney's lost beauty' bemoaned the fact that while councils had the power to curb land speculators and 'other vandals', 'they would not use them'. The relative disadvantage of the inner working-class suburbs when compared with the wealthier municipalities in terms of access to open space and residential amenity is apparent in the following figures which show the number of acres of parks and reserves in different municipalities in 1931.

Only one group appears to have objected to the 'planning' powers created by the 1919 act and, although they could be dismissed as having a vested interest in laissez-faire conditions, their complaint

Inner working-class suburbs		Eastern and north-shore suburbs	
Alexandria	27	Mosman	272
Annandale	11	Vaucluse	116
Waterloo	13	Manly	605
Newtown	1	Lane Cove	88
Redfern	11	Willoughby	267
Paddington	14	Woollahra	122

Source: *New South Wales Statistical Register*, 1930–1.

in fact raises an issue central to thinking about planning and public welfare. The Master Builders Association objected as follows:

> Sydney cries aloud for homes and more homes for its workers of every class ... building, health and other regulations make it impossible to erect a home at a figure that has any possible relation to the average worker's resources ... It was possible to put up a dozen brick terrace homes on the minimum frontage required for half a dozen detached cottages. Right away, the biggest individual item—the land—was cut in half.[21]

The objection here is similar to that raised by developers in the 1960s and 1970s. By zoning land for specific purposes, and limiting the area available for development, planning authorities or local councils create an artificial shortage of supply that inevitably raises land prices. It is clear that in the market city, with the scarce resource, land, in private ownership, more or less homogeneous areas of deprivation develop and greatly impede any rescue operation, even one that includes radical budgetary transfers of income. This seems unavoidable in a market society unless social space is allocated independently of ordinary market forces. But the question then arises, how costly to the community in real terms is planning that is markedly at variance with market forces? The Master Builders Association clearly thought it was far too costly. Building regulations were in effect depriving workers of their own homes. But land speculation is also very costly to the community, and the private enterprise housing boom of the twenties was paralleled by a speculative subdivision boom that was enhanced by the provision of public utilities but made the provision of those services costly, inefficient and inequitable.

The *County of Cumberland Planning Scheme Report* of 1948, reflecting on the situation in the twenties, made this quite clear.

> Electrification of suburban railways in 1926 and the growth of motor transport meant a far wider choice of residential areas. On the pleasant slopes and in the rural valleys—anywhere within walking distance of fast transport—land speculation was rife. In remote areas too, where there was any chance of profit, lots changed hands. Some of the land was bought by genuine home-builders:

much of it was bought as an 'investment'. Those who acquired lots believed that the value would automatically increase as their neighbours improved the locality for them. Land subdivision was little more than a gamble, in which profit, not housing needs, was the first consideration. This speculation did not result solely from action by land owners. *Very often investment value of the land was enhanced by the provision of railways, tramways, water, sewerage and electricity without there being any coordinated relation with real needs* [my italics].[22]

Critics of the boom in speculative subdivision were few and far between. Most observers were exhilarated at what they regarded as tangible evidence of progress. At the height of the boom a *Sydney Morning Herald* editorial mirrored the general euphoria.

The city proper is invading areas which not long ago were residential or industrial. Greater Sydney abundantly justifies its name by steadily becoming greater still. Bricks and mortar spring up miraculously and cover regions which but yesterday were virgin bush land. Ever since 1923 the annual total of new buildings has been over the 10,000 mark.'[23]

In this atmosphere it was not surprising that the attention of the planning movement turned from social welfare concerns like housing the poor to a preoccupation with equipping the city to cope with its rapid expansion. For this purpose they advocated town planning and particularly transport legislation to give some co-ordination to the direction and servicing of city growth and promoted 'beautification' to make this growth aesthetically palatable, and stress on an apolitical approach to planning and a belief in technical expertise was prominent.[24]

Technological advances in transport and building added a dramatic dimension to the process of urban development in the 1920s, confronting planners with a whole new set of problems which preoccupied thought to the exclusion of just about everything else. The rapid increase in car registrations from 14 000 in 1916 to 28 665 in 1921, 104 675 in 1926 and 171 492 in 1930 provoked planners' increasing worries about congestion and the inadequacy of the road system. And the problem of cars was linked with that other threatening phenomenon of the 1920s, the skyscraper. The capacity of buildings was not adjusted to the load limits of the streets. The problem was recognized by some, like Sulman, but architects and laymen, businessmen and land speculators were all exhilarated by visions of great structures thrusting heavenward. The city-in-the-making was for most people a breath-taking prospect—as editorials in the *Sydney Morning Herald* throughout the twenties revealed—and too often the concomitant problems were overlooked. Growing upward at the centre and outward at the circumference, the urban complex of Sydney was headed in all directions at once. The greatest impetus for suburbanization initially came less from the private car, though, than from the railways and buses. Electrification of the suburban rail system from 1926 and the opening of the Harbour Bridge in 1932 helped the process. And suburban residence was actively promoted by workmen's weekly tickets—concession railway fares. Thus the problems of making a large city function and of servicing a spreading metropolis were given more thought than comprehensive planning or the social problems connected with urban growth. The further into the decade, the more concern is expressed with traffic problems at the expense of issues like housing low-income groups, planning garden cities, eliminating slums, and other social improvements.

Over the decade two attitudes to Sydney's growth emerged. The first, already mentioned, was exhilaration. This attitude, pervading *Sydney Morning Herald* editorials and typical of the business community, held that town planning might make the city more efficient but certainly should not be allowed to interfere with the basic process of growth or with property values. The other attitude was more sobering, but not critical of the basic belief that growth was good. As the records of the Town Planning Association of New South Wales for the 1920s show, some planning advocates, critical of the boom, questioned not 'progress' as represented by the boom, but only its unsightly excesses.

Slums and Questions about Growth 1930s

What was most unsightly in the 1930s however was the social and economic casualties of the growth process, the unemployed and the slums they lived in. The world-wide depression triggered by the Wall Street crash of 1929 began to be severely felt in Sydney late in 1930. Unemployment went from 9·7 per cent in March 1929 to 13·8 per cent in December and 26·3 per cent by December 1930. For the next three years it stayed at that level and only dropped to 17·2 per cent by December 1934. It was December 1936 before the unemployment level receded to its 1928 mark of 9 per cent, which had been the average figure for the twenties. However, unemployment varied considerably between different areas of the metropolis, ranging from the relatively low 16 per cent in upper-middle-class suburbs to well over 40 per cent in most working-class suburbs.[25] There was a seven-fold decrease in building activity in Sydney, the most visible of all urban activities. In no other capital did building close down to the extent that it did in Sydney and it was 1938 before Sydney reached relative parity with Melbourne's post-depression levels.[26]

With the onset of the depression, debate focused on unemployment and on the radical reform policies of Labor premier Jack Lang. The

Greater Sydney issue also revived in 1931 with the minister for local government W. McKell's introduction of the Greater Sydney Bill. Similar bills had failed in 1913 and 1915 in the Legislative Council on the issue of widening the franchise, and the 1931 bill suffered the same fate. Civic Reform Group lord mayor, Alderman Jackson, attacked the bill on predictable lines.

> The Bill will take away the management of the city from the financial, commercial and ratepaying interests. The right to select the government of the city will be handed over to what are largely nomadic *residential voters, who, as a general rule, do not appreciate how the city affects them* ... If the suffrage is to be universal, as I understand, on top of the existing suffrage, the representation of the commercial and ratepaying interests will be practically negligible, probably on ten per cent. [my italics][27]

This same issue was again raised in 1934 in the Sydney Corporation Amendment Bill which proposed unequal voting rights in favour of property owners by abolishing the lodger vote. McKell argued, in opposition to the bill, that

> many lodgers have a greater interest in civic government and civic affairs than a large number of owners. What is the respective position of each? A man owns a property in the city. He may not be a resident of the city but may live on the North Shore line or somewhere else. His only interest in the city may be the property he owns there. On the other hand, lodgers are residents of the city.[28]

The Civic Reform Group lord mayor at this time lived on the 'North Shore line', at Waitara, one station beyond Wahroonga. McKell was using the ancient democratic argument that the wearer best knows where the shoe pinches. The *Sydney Morning Herald* disagreed. 'Instead of allowing those who paid the city rates to elect the council controlling the expenditure of them, "the lodger vote" was introduced, which gave every irresponsible bird of passage a voice in the administration of the municipal funds which other people had to provide.'[29] The passage of this bill reinforced the Civic Reform Group's hold on the city council and hence the power of property owners to determine the fate of the city.

By the mid-thirties the most important issue being debated in various arenas from parliament to press to Parks and Playgrounds Association was the slum problem and how to adequately house low-income earners. A *Sydney Morning Herald* leader in February 1934 was typical of the rising level of concern and illustrates the similarities between the New South Wales and Victorian anti-slum campaigns.

The growth of congested, ill-planned suburbs, of which our cities contain samples, brings a sure burden of ill-health, stunted development, inefficiency and criminal and revolutionary activity much more costly than the direct cost of resumption. It is urged that whereas such evils can only be met by careful planning, housing and zoning, and by providing ample space for recreation, the opportunities for these measures are being lost. This is the case urged by the unselfish efforts of the Town Planning Association, the Parks and Playgrounds movement . . . and similar bodies, and it is in our opinion a strong one.[30]

The *Sydney Morning Herald* had accepted the physical planning principles advanced by the Town Planning Association and the Parks and Playgrounds movement, which had been founded in 1930 by members of the planning movement. It shared the same assumptions about the connections between physical environment and social harmony as its parent association. C. E. W. Bean, a founder of the movement, lawyer and official war historian, had been a leading advocate of planning ideas since the twenties and, through his articles in the *Sydney Morning Herald*, was one of the most articulate laymen to campaign for slum abolition in the thirties. In 1935 he declared that 'a slum is a city area in which . . . citizens whose only crime is poverty have to bring up their families as best they can in surroundings of the underworld. To contend that we have no such areas in Sydney and Melbourne would be simple ignorance.'[31] This was reinforced by two articles on 'Slums. The Shame of Sydney' by N. H. Dick, who advocated a commission with adequate powers and freedom from political interference to deal with the question of slum clearance. Alfred Brown, a New Zealand-born architect and assistant town planner at Welwyn garden city in the 1920s who came to Sydney in 1931 and established the Town and Country Planning Institute, also contributed his knowledge to this press campaign.

The outcome of this public agitation was the decision by the UAP-Country Party government to form a committee to investigate slum clearance and housing reform. The Housing Conditions Investigation Committee was set up in January 1936 with the UAP minister for social services, H. M. Hawkins, as chairman, and representatives from the Master Builders Association, the Architects, Surveyors, and Real Estate Agents Institutes, the Town Planning Association, Sydney City Council, Alfred Brown, and the secretary of the Legion of Christian Youth representing the churches' concern with the problem. They persuaded the premier to introduce a housing bill in December of the same year. This bill was to provide, according to the premier, 'a permanent plan for housing improvement and slum clearance'. But the scheme outlined was to apply only to co-operative societies and a housing improvement board was to further investigate the problem and suggest legislation. The board comprised five members and was to report in six months. But the most significant feature of the housing bill was that the government, unlike its Victorian counterpart, had not accepted responsibility for providing and financing housing for low-income earners. Labor therefore opposed the bill on the grounds that

> the government was shelving its responsibilities, when the only possible way it could deal with slum areas was by itself giving a lead. Some houses would be built, and it would be a fine thing for some of the builders on the Government benches. A housing scheme could be of no use unless workers were paid a decent wage.[32]

At the other end of the political spectrum came opposition from the Country Party, indicating the political difficulties involved in even mild reform efforts. The Country Party member for Barwon opposed the bill because 'it was not the job of the government to introduce a Bill which induced people to come from the country to be housed and "wet nursed" '.[33] Intended to facilitate borrowing for co-operative societies so that they could then lend it to people to buy their own homes, this bill did not tackle the real problem, that poor housing was caused by poverty and inability to pay economic rents. The values behind the bill were made explicit in the premier's stated aim,

> to turn the average Australian working man into a home owner . . . One half of our people already have their own homes. We aim to see that proportion increase . . . The average man aspires to his own home, particularly the man in poor circumstances. For the home is the cradle of our race . . . the basis of family life.[34]

This was no capitalist plot to socialize the workers into the system. Or, if it was, it was thoroughly approved of by the Labor movement. By 1935 the Labor press had taken up the issue of slum clearance. The *Labor Daily* carried the front page headline 'Sydney's Human Warrens and Slums' in June 1935 and the *Australian Worker* followed suit in denunciations of the slums. In parliament McKell, who lived in the slum suburb of Redfern, supported the demolition and rebuilding of his own area and gave radio broadcasts on Labor station 2KY on the evils of slum areas.

But the housing bill in no way helped the poor with their housing problems. The *Sydney Morning Herald* supported the idea of slum clearance because 'such areas are potential danger spots in sickness and disease . . . Socially they are likely to create discontent, and no better way of ensuring a stable community, immune to all types of violent doctrine, can be found than to build up a community of workers [who] . . . own their own homes.'[35] But it also supported the government's housing bill on the grounds that the provision of housing through co-operative societies was to be preferred to any 'expensive socialism'. There was some inconsistency here between desiring the ends yet not being prepared to support the necessary means.

The Housing Improvement Board, which reported in April 1938, exposed this inconsistent thinking. Its report concluded that

> private enterprise is so constituted that it is incapable of viewing the growth of a city from a public or amenity point of view . . . The individual investor, so far as property is concerned, is interested only in the number of buildings he can erect on the smallest space . . . It is only when the public have, through Legislation or concerted action demanded amenities, that private enterprise has seen fit to grant them. Under existing social circumstances it would seem that only by the displacement of materialism, coupled with a rational view of public welfare and aesthetic values, can a well-ordered system of city expansion and housing be evolved.[36]

The board estimated that the cost of rehabilitating substandard areas of the metropolitan area alone would be £30 million and that slum clearance and housing of lower-paid workers must inevitably be carried out at a loss. Their specific recommendations included a special tax of 1d in the pound on income to finance a housing programme, large-scale operations by a central housing authority, the organization of the building industry and its supplies, the planned use of housing funds so that the housing authority would be most active in times of depression, and the overall need for rational planning of cities. The board argued that town planning powers could only be effectively administered by an independent central authority such as a Greater Sydney Council.

These were strong words. Too strong for the government which had established the board. The minister of social services immediately dissociated himself from the report, arguing that it 'embodied the views of the Board and it did not follow that they were the views of the Cabinet . . . The Government had deliberately made the Board an entirely independent body, and even he, as Minister, was not a member.'[37] The government duly ignored the board's recommendations for the remainder of its term of office. Laissez-faire, for the time being, prevailed. But in 1941 Labor defeated the coalition and immediately established the New South Wales Housing Commission.

Car registrations dropped sharply during the depression, but cinemas continued to be built, radios to be bought (101 000 licences in 1929, 177 000 in 1933 and 431 000 in 1939), hotels were extended, and sports were followed avidly. Life in the city did not grind to a halt. There was a boom in flat building at the end of the thirties (flats comprised 41 per cent of all residential building over the decade) and growth in manufacturing industry was substantial, with 184 000 workers in 1938–9 compared with 146 000 in 1928–9. Unbridled urban growth only began to be questioned publicly in the late thirties. To celebrate Sydney's 150th anniversary in 1937 the *Sydney Morning Herald* ran a series of articles on Sydney's growth in an effort to 'arouse interest in the subject of a planned city and to suggest the lines on which it should grow'. In the first article Alfred Brown argued that Sydney was suffering from 'functional derangement of a serious nature' and must be subjected to restriction in order to expand, that a limit must be set to the built-up area and that this should take the form of a green belt of open land preserved in perpetuity from building operations. He thought that satellite towns, built as garden cities outside the green belt, were the solution to Sydney's growth problems, but emphasized that if people were moved out, their work must be too.

A second article by Bean focused on the absence of any means, or machinery, for controlling or supervising growth. He argued that much of the worst development in Sydney's history took place in the twenties

> when immense quantities of land, especially in the southern and western suburbs, were subdivided and sold without any provision of recreation space ... This was due mainly to the fact that no authority existed with the duty of seeing that ground should be reserved; there was no plan, no policy, no recognition even of the fact that there ought to be one. It was, and still is officially, nobody's business to review the needs, look into the future, and make timely provision ... It is, and always has been, the machinery not the money, that we lack.[38]

There was some truth in this observation. No government had been prepared to establish town planning machinery before World War II. But machinery was not much use, say, for land acquisition, unless money was provided to purchase the land, and that became one of the more important post-war problems.

The Town and Country Planning Institute also had published an article written by its 1937 president H. M. Sherrard (an engineer who later became commissioner for main roads from 1953 to 1962 and co-authored, with Brown, Australia's first town planning text *Town and Country Planning* in 1951) on 'The Growth of Sydney— A City without a Plan. Wasted Opportunities'. It criticized the lack of co-ordination between public authorities, the piecemeal method of dealing with problems without regard to the broader aspects of planning, the existence of suburbs where factories jostled with houses, the unnecessarily high infant mortality in such areas, flats with no surrounding open spaces and the lack of recreation areas and playgrounds in many districts. Finally it stressed the importance of a town planning act as the only solution to these problems. As the retiring president in 1939, Sherrard emphasized in another article in the *Sydney Morning Herald* the sociological benefits to be derived from planning legislation. These included

> improved housing, which would tend to check crime, vice and delinquency, lead to better national health and a wider cultural life, and reduce infant mortality; a lessening of distinction between the surroundings of rich and poor houses, which would assist in securing national stability and contentment; and improved layout of roads, which would tend to reduce traffic accidents.[39]

This was a classic statement of the optimistic social reformist school of planning thought which believed town planning could cure everything from health and traffic problems to cultural deprivation, social segregation and political instability. Sherrard argued elsewhere that advocates of planning had for too long been obsessed with things aesthetic, like central city improvements, to the exclusion of everything else, and that they should place stronger emphasis on the 'social gains' that planning could provide. 'The benefits obtained are economic, sociological and aesthetic, and are closely related to national efficiency.'[40]

The reference to 'national efficiency' is interesting. A concern with efficiency had been a pervasive theme of the planning movement since its early days. 'The ideology of national efficiency', as it has been called by one British historian, was a set of ideas which emerged in Britain around the turn of the century concerned with eliminating all elements of waste from social organization. Many of the reformers in the Australian planning movement adopted the rationale of the British conservative Lord Milner in arguing for the reform of slums and the introduction of planning legislation: 'the attempt to raise the well-being and efficiency of the more backward of our people . . . is not philanthropy, it is business'.[41] The cult of the expert, a disparaging attitude towards party politics (because the real choice was not between ideologies but between competence and folly) and eugenics, were the natural offspring of the 'efficiency movement'. Sulman subscribed to all of these views, as did others involved in slum reform in the 1930s.

But reformers have often had to use efficiency arguments to persuade the more hard-headed members of the community to behave more humanely. Most of the town planning and slum reformers were professional people from the social and economic milieu of Sydney's favoured class, and lived on the north-shore or eastern harbour-side suburbs. Basically conservative, they argued for the role of the expert and attempted to keep planning above or outside party politics. Their appeal to business-like values in their efforts to introduce planning legislation indicates their desire to avoid social conflict and to respect property rights. Unlike the more radical Labor politicians and radical intellectuals like Irvine, they did not demand justice for a particular class and certainly did not see the situation in terms of 'class struggle'.

But they were moved by a broad humanitarian impulse, as Sherrard's retrospective comments indicate. 'I was influenced mainly by my own local observations of unnecessary suffering, of inconvenience and of lack of amenity, emphasised by the economic depression of the thirties . . . While some views expressed at the time may appear to be conservative we had to be careful to avoid any charge of socialism, and thus being discredited.'[42]

Part II

Planning since World War II

5

Limits of Reform:
Federal Labor and Post-war Reconstruction

> ... private enterprise will never again mean the comparative
> absence of planning and control that existed before this war.
> If I read right the attitudes of most plain Australians, private
> enterprise in future means, for us, a planned and controlled
> alternative to a more complete socialism on our own model.
>
> C. E. W. Bean 1943[1]

> There would be more room for private enterprise and busi-
> ness initiative after the war than ever before in Australian
> history.
>
> H. V. Evatt 1943[2]

Market City and Reformist Government

People in the liberal democracies have voted pretty consistently for
a market society rather than a socialist society. Australia has been no
exception. There has rarely been mass political support for reformers'
views, let alone those of revolutionary groups like the Communist
Party. Characteristic of the market society is the market city, by
which I mean something both more and less than the P. and P. Goodman's description of 'the metropolis as a department store'.[3] They
had in mind that the main concern of cities in the western democracies—that is, the market societies—was with efficient production
and consumption. Using New York as their model, they outlined the
main characteristics of these cities: populations of several millions,
with production and market concentrated to minimize distribution
services, and work and life centring around the market and infused
by a morality of imitation, emulation and competition. We may not
want to go as far as they do in attributing the demise of all that is
best in man (truth, passion, virtue, sociability) to the organization
of the market city, but it is possible to be more specific about the
effects of this sort of city on people's lives, opportunities, environments, friends and politics.

Left to itself the market city has a changing but characteristic structure, central to which is property ownership of land and its rising capital values and of industrial investment and its location and the jobs it entails. The political power which owners secure tends to reinforce this structure. The distribution of people across the market city takes predictable patterns, determined by income and class, age and household structure, and other determinants of status among which mobility, migrant status and 'deviancy' of various kinds are dominant. These patterns are inequitable in access to jobs, shops, professional and social services,[4] in the quality of the environment (access to beaches, harbour, mountains) and in the density and layout of urban neighbourhoods. But government and public sector services *can* provide opportunities for changing this by providing open spaces and other public facilities and by the very location of public services like hospitals, clinics, schools and transport. The Curtin and Chifley Labor governments of 1942–9 were the first federal governments to take an interest in the fate of Australian cities. In 1942 the Curtin government set up a Department of Post-war Reconstruction to produce a blueprint for a better world when the fighting ended.

The plans for the post-war period involved the continuation of war-time controls and regulations. But once the war ended, so too did the truce between business and industrial interests and the Labor government. As the general manager of the Bank of New South Wales explained, 'We realise that [in war] there have to be sacrifices, and that the sacrifices have to be spread. Hence we submit to a control which should not be tolerated in time of peace.'[5] So with peace came a resumption of the attack by conservatives on state intervention in the economy. This was a seminal period in Australian history, particularly for the future of the cities, for Labor was full of the best intentions for city planning in place of haphazard growth and for decentralization by regional development. None of their ambitious plans, except those for housing, eventuated before the government was defeated in the 1949 elections and the plans were then forgotten for twenty-one years. Partly because the federal Labor government elected in December 1972 has resurrected the issue of the cities, it is important to understand the nature of Labor's plans of the 1940s, the nature of the opposition to them, and above all why they failed and why Labor was defeated, for the dilemmas of a reformist party, revealed by those years in power in the forties, exist today in much the same form. Indeed they are endemic to all parties of the left whose strategy, in a capitalist economy, is to attempt reform from within the system. To succeed they must win overwhelming popular support for their reformist programme and they must be able to find means of implementing those programmes in the face of vested interests and existing power structures. W. K. Hancock has suggested that 'it is a weakness of democracies that, having willed the ends, they try to shuffle out of willing the means.'[6] Was Labor's failure in the forties due to a capitalist conspiracy (as many of its members alleged), to its own failure to invent means of implementing programmes, or to the tyranny of the majority of the population who simply wanted an end put to fuel rationing, strikes and shortages of consumer goods? And how radical were Labor's plans?

The Reformers' Plans

In November 1942 the federal conference of the Australian Labor Party urged that post-war reconstruction be regarded as part of the war effort and sought the appointment of a minister 'whose sole duty it should be to proceed immediately with the preparation of a comprehensive scheme of post-war reconstruction'.[7] In December J. B. Chifley, a former train driver and union politician, was appointed minister for post-war reconstruction, and H. C. Coombs, schoolteacher, wharf labourer and then economist, was made permanent head of the department. They envisaged, in their first major statement in December 1943, full employment policies and continuance of wartime collaboration of government and private enterprise in carrying them out.[8]

What is remarkable about the literature of post-war reconstruction is the unity of themes and recommendations, shared alike by Labor politicians, academics and popular writers.[9] All were concerned with the need for a planned economy and full employment, city planning, population planning, decentralization, regional and participatory planning, and planning to ensure adequate housing for everyone, with special emphasis on the urgency of slum clearance. Within the 'ideology of post-war reconstruction', city planning for the first time was conceived as a national problem that demanded a national strategy. It was seen less in terms of visual appearance, health and amenity and more in terms of social and economic function, and the problem of allocation of land among various uses was perceived as part of the general social policy problem of the allocation of resources. Housing and city planning were among the more dramatic issues and promises of the social reconstruction programme because they raised all the general ideological issues of planning versus a free market. The recommendations of the Commonwealth Housing Commission in 1944, in particular, proposed a revolution in public approach to social policy, announcing that the housing programme would depend on the ability of the state to dominate the market—to control the supply of materials, to fix prices and to purchase directly on its own account.

The period produced an abundance of intelligent research and ideas on social, economic and urban problems: H. V. Evatt's 1942 report on the need for greater federal powers, the Housing Commission report of 1944, the department of post-war reconstruction's report on regional planning in 1949, and the full employment white paper in 1945, and the Australian Institute of Political Science conferences on post-war reconstruction (1944) and decentralization (1948). Chifley was preoccupied with the economic aspects of reconstruction, particularly with the problem of full employment, but Coombs and Lloyd Ross, the director of public relations in the ministry, were more articulate about the social content of the ideology.

> The choice before us is to go back or to go on, to attempt to rebuild the so-called 'free' economy based on individual choice, freedom of enterprise, unemployment and the alternation of booms and slumps; or to go on, by the use of the knowledge and experience we have built up during the war, to an economy *still predominantly one of private ownership and enterprise*, but with an increasing responsibility on the government for the allocation of resources, the prime purpose of which will be the achievement of social objectives of a high and stable level of employment, of rising standards of living for all people, of the development of our national resources and security and opportunity for the individual ... If we are clear upon the objectives we seek ... we have an opportunity to move consciously and intelligently towards a new social and economic system. [my italics][10]

Ross was more explicit about potential conflict and more detailed in his description of the 'new social order'.

> There is real division to be found between those who would move forward to full employment and higher standards of living although these may mean some interference with private ownership of industry, and those who would make their test of judgment the preservation of pre-war property rights and the sacredness of their freedom for their enterprise ... there cannot be any new social order if we return to the nineteenth century conception of either economics or freedom ... Freedom in slums is a farce; but building houses at the end of the war means either we perpetuate inequality or we continue controls; to build houses which will widen the freedom for thousands, *we need to limit the rights of those with money, with land and with building material*; to redesign our cities so that they will recapture the ancient sense of beauty and majesty, a harmony of life that the modern city has largely lost, we need to control the expansion of cities, introduce zoning, alter street routes, and fit design into a general pattern. There could have been no Canberra garden city without a plan and a control [my italics].[11]

But it is evident from their statements that neither of these key public servants believed it was necessary to go beyond a *better-regulated capitalist economy* to achieve the new social order. In this they were reflecting the views of their political masters. John Curtin for instance promised that in the post-war period 'no question of socialisation or any other fundamental alteration in the economic system arises'.[12]

Popular writers who took up these themes emphasized their moral content. For C. E. W. Bean, belonging to the Christian socialist tradition of the slum reformers like F. O. Barnett and W. O. Burt of the 1930s, decentralization was the key to the moral salvation of the nation:

> a people evenly distributed in small or medium sized towns tends to be stronger, morally and mentally as well as physically, than one concentrated in a few big cities. The development of the country towns can easily be fostered ... if the nation determines to decentralise the manufacturing industries ... this would reduce by more than half the Australian problem of town planning and housing.[13]

Bean also shared with Barnett and Burt and with another middle-class housing reformer, Walter Bunning, what could be called a middle-class paternalism towards those low socio-economic groups they were trying morally as well as economically to 'save'.

> We want for our city folk housing conditions in which the 'family system', that our bishops rightly estimate as the sound basis for our moral health, can rear its healthy youth; we want *total* clearance of slums and of the attendant moral and physical degradation ... we want ... community centres for both recreation and culture and .... self-help, to replace the hotel bars as the farmers' and workers' clubs and serve as a kind of people's university.[14]

The simple cause-effect relationship between environment and morals was universally espoused by these Christian social reformers. Barnett and Burt's book *Housing the Australian Nation* (1942), itself derived from the official Victorian inquiry into slums (1937) on which both authors served, had expressed this belief and claimed as evidence for its validity that 'at least ninety-eight per cent of the families removed from slum and substandard houses to the new houses of the Victorian Housing Commission have satisfactorily responded to their new environment'. This book seems to have been one of the most widely read and influential works of the decade. Its findings and recommendations were quoted at great length in Evatt's case for greater constitutional powers for the commonwealth, in the Commonwealth Housing Commission Report (1944), and cited as gospel by all of the 'amateur' reformers (Bean, Penton, Bunning, Luscombe, and Marshall). It clearly influenced the particular prescriptions for housing reform in the forties. Barnett and Burt had concluded that 'private enterprise had not and would never adequately house the poor'. They therefore advocated commonwealth responsibility for and intervention in housing provision, favoured planned decentralization and recommended legislation for a commonwealth post-war housing scheme, quoting Keynes's advice that 'no humbug of Finance should be allowed to stand in the way of our plans for reconstruction'.[15]

In October 1942 the Curtin government made the first public move toward their post-war objectives. Evatt introduced a bill for a referendum seeking approval for a far-reaching enlargement of the ordinary peace-time powers of the commonwealth. The nature of the reconstruction plans and the means by which they could be put into operation would both depend on the commonwealth's constitutional position. A convention of commonwealth and state leaders met in November 1942 in an attempt to persuade the states to refer agreed powers to the commonwealth rather than distract the country by a war-time referendum. Curtin obtained agreement that powers should be granted to the commonwealth for demobilization and post-war reconstruction. But the Liberal states failed to pass the necessary reference of powers agreed upon and Curtin had no alternative but to pursue the matter to referendum.

The 1944 referendum was rejected, but only narrowly, by a majority of voters in a majority of states. The 'No' case had the financial and influential weight of the Liberal-Country Party opposition and their newspaper allies behind it. Curtin then called a conference of commonwealth and state ministers at which he sought a co-operative approach to regional planning within the existing constitutional framework. L. F. Crisp sees this as a major defeat for Labor's post-war reconstruction programme.

> To Chifley's great regret the White Paper [*Full Employment in Australia*] and all his planning commissions and committees had to fall back on slow, clumsy and uncertain 'cooperative federalism' ... Imaginative plans had to be substantially scrapped. In public housing, land settlement, migration, coal development, unification of railway gauges, determination of national works priorities ... resort had to be had to 'government by agreement' ... with all the delays, frictions, compromise and half-measures inherent in that system.[16]

Nevertheless from this beginning came the final proposals for comprehensive regional planning and development involving the commonwealth, the states, and local governments, which are set out in *The History of Progress and Review of Regional Planning Activities through the Commonwealth*, issued by the Department of Post-war Reconstruction in 1949. This was a blueprint for the careful assessment of resources, physical and human, to provide for regional development, decentralization, and the fullest participation of citizens at every level of representative government. In the same way policy was developed for housing as a result of the Housing Commission appointed by Curtin in 1943 to inquire into 'the present housing position in Australia and the housing requirements during the post-war period'.

The Housing Commission produced a plan of immense importance and long-term significance, a blueprint for efficient regulation and supply of housing and implementation of urban planning. It found that housing standards in Australia were very low, especially for the low-wage earner. It pointed to the shortage of housing and the critical need of complete or partial replanning in cities and towns throughout Australia. It envisioned two alternatives to the compound problem of inner-city slums and outer low-density sprawl (with its social and economic costs): the possibility of decentralization of business and industry in satellite towns, or the possibility of integrating town and suburbs in a comprehensive rebuilding scheme involving the principles of zoning, orientation for sunshine, open areas, etc. 'Without some such large scale attack it will be difficult, if not impossible, to prevent the uncontrolled spread of cities.'[17]

It argued that in any area, new or old, a wide range of community facilities needed to be provided, and suggested periodic national housing surveys to determine the total housing needs of the community and the proper location of housing. The commission said that the government should aim to overcome the housing shortage within ten years. To do this it was not only necessary to ensure a normal annual growth in new housing but also to provide for the repair and replacement of substandard dwellings and for slum clearance. The programme would require the erection of at least 700 000 dwellings by 1955 (including single units, attached units, multi-storey dwellings and hostels), which meant an annual target of 50 000 dwelling units, rising to 80 000 by the end of the third post-war year, to be maintained until the shortage was overcome. To achieve this massive programme, the commission proposed a strategy that, had it been implemented, would have effectively provided an urban planning and development base of unparallelled magnitude and effect and of a kind that most cities in Australia sorely lack. The commission argued that a prime necessity was a co-ordinated national effort in a commonwealth/state/local government/private enterprise grouping. Further it set a minimum housing standard and proposed a fifty-fifty government/private enterprise building programme, with the commonwealth sponsoring the efforts of government agencies in the states. It recommended the establishment of a commonwealth housing authority to plan and advise, with state housing authorities charged with the task of construction and administration. Local governments were to have participated in this process, with powers delegated from the state housing authorities.

There was to be national, regional and town planning. The commonwealth was to set up a commonwealth planning authority. State planning was to be co-ordinated through state planning authorities. Regional and town planning legislation was to be enacted in all states. 'We consider that planning is of such importance that the Commonwealth Government should not make available financial assistance for housing unless the State concerned satisfied the Commonwealth that it has taken or is taking definite steps to enact and implement regional and town planning legislation.'[18] And pending the drawing up of full town plans, the control of land use was to be through zoning, the declaration of housing development areas, and the control of land subdivisions.

> National and regional planning may be described as a conscious effort to guide the development of the resources of the nation and their use in productive enterprise so as to provide a rising national income and therefore a rising standard of human welfare, including . . . better housing. In the past, national development has been in the hands of private enterprise and has thus been governed by the possibilities of profit-making rather than by the needs of the community. We consider that national regional and town planning is an urgent national need.[19]

The most radical proposals recommended were those concerning public participation in planning and the need for nationalization of land. 'We stress the importance of setting up an administration which will enable the people themselves to initiate proposals and participate in formulating them.'[20] It was difficult to see in practical terms how these noble ideas could be applied. But the commission was cavalier about 'practical difficulties', as can be seen in its proposals for land nationalization. It agreed with the findings of the Uthwatt committee on compensation and betterment in the United Kingdom that nationalization was the only adequate method of preserving for the people as a whole any increase in land values. But the Uthwatt committee had rejected land nationalization as a practical measure. Not so the Commonwealth Housing Commission:

> We are not in agreement with the objections to nationalisation as stated by the Uthwatt Committee . . . we consider that—political controversy and delay are not valid objections to a desirable policy —that the size of financial operations required should not daunt those used to wartime finance—and that the need for complicated administrative machinery should not be a deterrent in view of wartime experience. There would be considerable public opposition to land nationalisation, both from existing landowners and from many who would fear that such may be a prelude to other similar

measures; but it seems to us that nationalisation is the only effective way to eliminate private profit-making from land and to reserve to the community the unearned increment ... Irrespective of whether nationalisation be effected, we recommend that land resumed by the Government for development purposes should be disposed of on perpetual leasehold tenure and not by sale as freehold.[21]

The report recommended that the commonwealth government set up a special committee to investigate land nationalization. This was never done and this crucial issue was never put forward as a policy or legislative proposal. Neither was the issue of regional planning or the question of public participation. But some of the housing recommendations were adopted in the Commonwealth-State Housing Agreement of 1945.

The main points under this agreement, by which commonwealth funds became available for the states' public housing programmes, were that the states were required to ensure that adequate legislation existed to enable it at all times to control, throughout the state, rental housing projects, slum clearance, and town planning. Further, the housing authority in each state was to allow to low-income tenants a rental rebate equal to the difference between economic rent and one-fifth of family income when that income equalled the basic wage (as the income fell below or rose above the basic wage the proportion varied). The commonwealth government was to bear three-fifths of the financial losses incurred by government-financed housing schemes. And dwellings were to be allotted on the basis of need. The terms of the agreement made it difficult for the states to sell dwellings, and also ensured that the available public housing went only to those on the lowest incomes. South Australia objected to these details of the agreement and did not become an effective partner until 1953 when these restraints were removed by the Menzies government.

Although Jones[22] has questioned the effectiveness of state housing commission policies in reaching the most needy and poverty-stricken groups in the community ('skid row' men and other 'deviants' are consistently discriminated against in public housing policy), the statistical achievement in housing since 1945 has been impressive. From 1945 to 1970 about 36 per cent of all new houses and flats completed in Australia were directly financed by governments on terms and conditions that made them much cheaper than they could have been obtained in the private market. By 1970 about 24 per cent of all existing houses and flats had been financed in whole or in part with public funds; 750 000 subsidized dwellings had been built since 1945. The biggest single group, 310 000, has been built by the state housing commissions.

Housing aside, why did this abundance of good ideas and intentions, great plans and preparations, come to so little? The 1949 election provides the clue.

Capitalist Conspiracy or Tyranny of the Majority?

Between 1945 and 1948 the banks, the judgements of the High Court, the oil companies, the medical profession, and state upper houses resisted, with all the financial and institutional powers available to them, Labor's reconstruction programme. Plans for a national health scheme were shelved after heated opposition from the medical profession. The High Court declared legislation to nationalize all civil airlines in 1945 to be beyond the constitutional power of the commonwealth. The 1944 referendum to extend commonwealth powers was defeated and most states refused to pass legislation giving the commonwealth peace-time powers to control rents and prices. So to some extent there was a capitalist conspiracy against the Labor government, as Crisp has argued. 'Once again business interests hostile to regulation had joined with states-rights doctrinaires. They had been able to use state Upper Houses, in particular, to hobble the National Parliament.'[23] The 1948 High Court decision against bank nationalization legislation, in the opinion of one Labor journalist, endowed the existing capitalist system with weighty constitutional authority and placed 'an almost insurmountable hurdle in the way of economic reforms which in most other democratic countries are left to the free decisions of the electorate through the democratic parliamentary process'.[24]

To some extent, too, Hancock's perception of the weakness of democracies fits the situation of the Labor government—having willed the ends, particularly in the field of urban planning, they did appear to 'shuffle out of willing the means'. No legislation was drafted to implement regional planning and no way was invented of incorporating the public in the planning process. And most neglected in practice was the problem of private ownership of land. Nationalization was strongly recommended to the government. Not surprisingly it showed no enthusiasm for acting on that advice. But it made no efforts to come up with an alternative approach, less politically explosive, that might produce similar desired effects, like nationalizing development rights, introducing betterment, or funding state government land acquisition programmes. But such reformist programmes do require some basic changes to existing structures of power. Men like Curtin, Evatt, Chifley, Coombs and Ross were no revolutionaries. They wanted to increase the efficiency and thereby the distributive justice of the capitalist system. But a redistributive approach to city planning required changes in the system of property rights and ownership; regional and participatory planning required redistributions of power as well as of resources. And the government simply could not get the votes for such changes, as the 1949 election shows. Democracies may have methodological weaknesses, and the capitalist class may have an extraordinarily tenacious hold on power, but we must not disregard the effect of the political preferences of the majority of Australians working through the established political system on factors determining the success or failure of urban planning.

While Labor was outlining its egalitarian utopia, a band of idealists of different political persuasion, 'supported by the manufacturers, the traders, and the pastoralists, painted a rosy picture of possibilities should Australia rid itself of the economic planners and the menace of communism'.[25] The Liberal leader, R. G. Menzies alleged in his policy speech in 1949 that if Labor was returned, they would press on regardless to full socialism. They would find ways to nationalize banks, despite the judicial decision of 1948. They would 'pack' the High Court. They would continue petrol rationing. They would open the way via socialism to communism. The Country Party in particular engaged in this extremist propaganda. Their leader A. W. Fadden argued that a vote for Labor 'will truly be your last will and testament, disposing in your own lifetime of your liberties and your property and condemning your children and your children's children to the living death of socialist regimentation'. But Chifley himself claimed of the 1949 election that 'the real issue, as in New Zealand and Great Britain, was a straight-out fight between the two great forces, socialism and capitalism.'[26] If most Australians saw the election in these terms—and it is likely that they did in the context of the cold war and Berlin wall, and because the three major parties presented it that way—then their choice was quite clear. They chose capitalism. After years of scarcity and rationing, people wanted to be able to have the choice of satisfying different economic and social needs. The reformist enthusiasm born in the heat of war cooled in the immediate post-war years. Patience lost some of its pristine virtue. There is no doubt that much of what occurred was the result of capitalist manipulation, like the campaign waged by the banks on its employees,[27] but it would have been impossible for this to occur if the general political climate had been adverse to such happenings, if the majority of Australians had not wanted precisely the sorts of things they thought those capitalists could deliver. Much of what happened and failed to happen in urban planning in the fifties and sixties can only be understood by keeping this in mind.

The Liberal-Country Party coalition which came to office in 1949 made it clear that commonwealth assistance to the cities would not be extended beyond the agreement already made for funding state public housing programmes. The prime minister R. G. Menzies in December 1950 refused to assist the New South Wales government with finance to implement the Cumberland County Plan, on the grounds that to accept any direct responsibility would establish a wide precedent for commonwealth assistance in urban affairs. Succeeding Liberal-Country Party governments maintained an aloof attitude, leaving the states to cope as best they could with their urban problems through the fifties and sixties.

6

Adelaide: Conservatives, Technocrats and Citizens—Who Plans for Whom?

> The crux of the town planning problem in South Australia is not so much technical as political. During the last thirty years successive governments have done practically nothing to put our house in order, and the establishment of a supervisory authority to control city suburban development is one of our most urgent needs ... A primary necessity is the passing of an adequate town planning Act on the lines of measures approved by the Parliament in 1917.
>
> J. H. Vaughan 1950[1]

> The functions of business at the highest level become increasingly political, while the politician and the administrator become increasingly involved in the conduct of industry. Thus it comes about that business lends government its outstanding personalities, industrialists become Ministers, heads of state agencies, members of state Boards, and political leaders, high ranking officers and senior civil servants are recruited to the Boards of great enterprises. The consequential formation of what has been called a 'power elite' must be viewed not as a kind of conspiracy but as a logical consequence of the unification of business with administration and politics.
>
> P. Shore 1969[2]

Neo-capitalism and the Playford Era

In the middle of the nineteenth century Karl Marx brought the subject of power into economic discussion with a vehemence the world has not yet quite ceased to deplore. The notion of a system of competitive firms he dismissed as an exercise in vulgar apologetics. Production, he argued, was dominated by those who controlled and supplied capital. They set prices and wages in their collective interest. They dominated the society, setting its moral tone. They also controlled the state, which became an executive committee serving the will and interest of the capitalist class.

More recent scholars of the Left have coined the term 'neo-capitalism' to describe the close co-operation between business, politics and administration which has been an observed feature of developed Western economies since World War II. John Playford defined neo-capitalism as the massive entry of business into the institutions of state supervision, planning, co-ordination and control, with all the direct power and influence this entails.[3]

Thomas Playford, premier of South Australia from 1938 to 1965, inherited the broad outlines of a development policy generated by the state in response to the economic crisis of the thirties. His role was to be its political executant. The so-called Playford era saw the transformation of South Australia from a mainly rural to a mainly industrial economy, a process set in motion by the state, which supplied cheap housing, serviced land and so on to industries to encourage them to establish in South Australia. This transformation diversified the old 'power elite' that had centred around the 'Adelaide Establishment', the old families whose wealth derived from land, commerce and banking.

J. K. Galbraith (1967) has argued that the increasing role of the state in advanced industrial societies has changed the source of power in those societies. No longer is the ownership of land or of capital the decisive source. Rather, power now rests with what he calls the 'technostructure', the technical experts who increasingly make the decisions in both state bureaucracies and private enterprise. Changes that occurred in the structure of power in South Australia between the first wave of urban planning (1916–29) and the second (from the late 1950s) are reflected in the efforts to introduce city planning after World War II, in the nature of the opposition generated, and in the nature of the planning that emerged in the 1960s. The influence of new industries, especially car manufacturing, and the role of the technical experts employed by state authorities, especially the engineers, have been particularly significant features of the changing structure of power on the city planning process. But neither has eroded the enduring influence of those older sources of power based on property ownership. Their continuing influence remains an important part of the story of post-war planning in South Australia.

My concern at the parliamentary level is that there has been no far-sighted policy of urban development. This was partly the result of Playford's personal style of government and partly an imperative of industrialization. 'The Premier built around him a team of loyal and able civil servants dedicated to industrial development. Readily accessible to business leaders, he supplemented his civil servants with a wide circle of advisers from private enterprise . . . he bypassed formal lines of communication and responsibility in pursuit of his industrialisation objectives'.[4] This approach had grave consequences for parliamentary politics. Playford's cabinet colleagues were virtually excluded from policy formulation, responsibility for which devolved from parliament to outside bodies and individuals. This shift vitally affected city planning policy in the 1960s.

The premier's economic objectives were not compatible with the restrictions on private enterprise that are a necessary part of radical city planning. Playford made his priorities clear in 1954 in the opening address of the Australian Planning Institute Congress in Adelaide. There would be no town planning until his economic objectives had been realized. And he could execute this economic policy because of his power base. The consideration of where electoral support lies is one of the most obvious factors affecting politicians' behaviour and thinking. Playford looked after the day-to-day interests of farmers and a few city rich and that as well as the gerrymandered pattern of electorates secured him in power for nearly thirty years to do what he liked to the urban majorities whose votes he didn't need anyway. Ironically his long-term industrialization programme not only vitally affected this urban majority but eventually changed its character and distribution sufficiently for it to vote the Liberal Country League out of office in 1965.

The ruling Liberal Country League was largely an instrument of the Adelaide Establishment. The interventionist aspects of Playford's economic policies were a source of conflict between him and the Establishment, in whose eyes Playford was guilty of socialist heresies. Unlike the Establishment, Playford recognized the need for minimal concessions to maintain the conservative order. For conservatism does not entail the rejection of all measures of reform, but survives by the endorsement and promulgation of reform at the least possible cost to the existing structure of power and privilege. For all their acceptance of piecemeal reform and their rhetoric of classlessness, conservative parties remain primarily the defence organization, in the political field, of business and property.[5] Playford was at one with the Establishment on the preservation of a conservative political structure and a conservatively ordered society. He relied on the help of the Adelaide financial community. His party was dependent on Establishment finance, and successful management of the non-Labor forces required their co-operation.

Electorally however Playford's survival depended on the small farmers of the party. (The ratio of country to city seats was 2 to 1). Farmers dominated the Assembly ranks of the Liberal Country League and nearly all of the cabinet was drawn from 'the yeoman proprietary'. The Liberal Country League in the Assembly never contained more than 3 of a possible 13 members elected from the metropolitan region. The 9-member cabinet of 1962–5 contained 1 representative from a metropolitan electorate. And this at a time when town planning issues were preoccupying the metropolis, which by 1961 contained 61 per cent of the state's population.

Thus electoral, parliamentary and party political arrangements favoured the country, and the economic objectives of the era did not encourage concern with the problems and consequences of city growth. Nor were the dominant values receptive to social welfare considerations.

If price control and economic intervention breached the principles of laissez faire, Playford agreed with the Establishment in keeping welfare provision down. Expenditure on schools, hospitals, libraries and social services all lagged in the 1950s. The Grants Commission noted Playford's 'economising on social services', the provision of beds in public hospitals trailed the average figure for the Commonwealth ... As for the derelicts of the modern industrial state, Playford shared with the Establishment the belief that ... 'charity should be the most strictly private enterprise of all'.[6]

The development of metropolitan Adelaide and its planning problems provides an example of the workings of neo-capitalism and extends analysis beyond the bipartisan interpretation of politics, for problems like pollution, freeways, high-rise low-income housing estates, do not respect such an interpretation. They have existed under both Liberal and Labor governments, partly because economic growth has been a strongly avowed social goal of both parties, partly because both have to some extent been victims of a bureaucratic, technocratic dominance. One significant feature of my account of post-war urban problems is that the sources of oppression, injustice or maldistribution are as often as not in the public sector. And a main cause of these public sector problems is the dominant notion of 'technical expertise'—a latter-day version of the old British paternalism, with much less tender social values and little inclination to consult the public, or the state's clients, about the services to be provided.

So a simple indictment of capitalism will shed only a half-light on urban and environmental problems. Pollution for example is a good deal worse in Prague and Krakow than in some Western cities. It is a problem caused neither by capitalism nor by socialism but by the predominant emphasis in both these systems on economic growth. No other test of social success has had such nearly unanimous acceptance as the annual increase in the gross national product. This is true of all countries, developed or undeveloped, communist, socialist or capitalist. Japan has been deemed a successful society since World War II because of its dramatic increase in gross national product. So also Germany and Israel and, lately, France. Britain, with a much smaller increase, has been perilously close to being a failure. That one must pause to affirm that beauty or fresh air or clean water is worth the sacrifice of some increase in the gross national product shows how effectively our beliefs have been accommodated to the needs of the urban, industrial, bureaucratic system.

State Planning, Private Enterprise Unlimited 1945–55

In the ten years after World War II a small group of enthusiastic individuals sought to persuade the state government of the benefits to be derived from town planning legislation, and the urgent need for it. They received scant attention. But, in the manner of an 'approved contradiction' (a phrase used by Galbraith in a similar context), while the state resisted the introduction of any control over the activities of private enterprise, its own activities, especially those of the South Australian Housing Trust, indulged in a degree of economic and physical planning that has made Adelaide the most 'planned' of all Australian cities outside Canberra since the war.

The first signs of interest in town planning in Adelaide after the war appeared with the formation of the Town Planning Institute of South Australia in 1948. Its first president W. C. D. Veale, an engineer, gave evidence on the institute's behalf before the royal commission on state transport, recommending preparation of a master plan for the metropolitan area. The institute concentrated on trying to persuade the government to introduce legislation enabling preparation of such a plan and on informing politicians and public of the need for it. The planning movement was fortunate to have as an advocate Sir Lloyd Dumas, managing director of the *Advertiser* and a personal friend of the premier. He financed a visit to Adelaide in 1950 by the professor of town planning at Sydney University, Dennis Winston, who wrote a series of articles for the *Advertiser* explaining the evils of haphazard growth and the need for a development plan. Taking advantage of the interest generated by these articles, Veale then led a deputation to the premier and Playford agreed to appoint an honorary committee to report to him on the matter. The commissioner of highways was elected chairman and this committee completed its report in 1952. The government was reluctant to move, but the *Advertiser* continued its supportive campaign and attacked Playford's intransigence, quoting with disapproval his statement to parliament that 'Adelaide had been planned as a city many years ago and all that could be done now was street-widening and other alterations.'[7]

At this stage the few powers that did exist for dealing with metropolitan growth were scattered through a variety of acts all containing conspicuous weaknesses. The 1929 Town Planning Act had vested control of subdivision in local councils, but regulations were minimal and no control was exercised within the City of Adelaide or beyond the metropolitan area. There was no control over the location of subdivision or over premature subdivision. Under the 1923 Building Act, councils could make by-laws regarding the structure, use, condition, density, height, location and appearance of buildings, and could also make zoning regulations. But most of these powers had never been invoked.[8]

Legislation finally introduced in 1954 provided for the establishment of a town planning committee of five members to prepare a plan for the development of the metropolitan area, for subdividers to pay the cost of roads and to set aside 10 per cent of subdivisions for recreation areas, and for no subdivision plan to be approved unless it could be economically provided with water and sewerage. Labor opposition members claimed that 'this Bill is not intended to work nor will it give effect to what it purports but it is rather intended as a sop to the public clamour for town planning'.[9] The bill did appear to have been carefully timed to coincide with the Australian Town Planning Conference which was being held in Adelaide. Despite the professed intentions of this bill, Playford told delegates to the conference that there would be no town planning till his enonomic programme was complete.

Two sorts of opposition to the bill were voiced in the Legislative Council. The most predictable was on the familiar theme of protection of property rights. One Liberal Country League member was upset that 'a man might have a large piece of land that he could easily sell but could be told by the government that he could not sell it because it might be needed for a beauty spot. That is taking away the rights of the individual, and we are here to safeguard people's property rights.' But while Liberals spoke for the rights of property owners to profit from their land, a Labor member spoke about every man's democratic right to control his destiny through the machinery of parliamentary responsibility and attacked the bill as a 'totalitarian proposal insasmuch as it will hand the responsibility of this parliament over to a Committee'. In the light of future events his opposition was most perceptive. Don Dunstan, Labor member for Norwood and future premier, thought it 'significant that the members of the public who are most outspoken against this measure are the speculative landholders ... In South Australia many speculative landholders have reaped a good profit from the public by means of improper subdivisions.'[10]

It was true that, outside parliament, opposition came from the Real Estate Institute and the Chamber of Commerce, who joined forces in a successful endeavour to get the bill withdrawn and delayed until amendments were prepared. The president of the Real Estate Institute submitted a report arguing that if the bill were approved it would result in inflationary tendencies for land in sewered areas and increase the cost of homes. The Institute wanted its own representative on the Town Planning Committee, opposed the section of the bill compelling subdividers to provide sealed roads 24 feet wide, felt that the phrase 'economically and advantageously sewered' was too wide and should be deleted, criticized the bill for making no provision for compensation to owners of real estate. Lack of such provision 'was against the rights and freedom of the people'.[11] Its ally, the Chamber of Commerce, wanted the matter put to a select committee.

Not surprisingly the bill was shelved by the Legislative Council but in diluted form it was reintroduced and passed in 1955, establishing a five-member town planning committee to prepare a metropolitan plan and retaining the important provision that land proposed for subdivision in the metropolitan area must be able to be economically supplied with water and sewerage. Like the 1949 Town Planning Act in Victoria, though, there was no provision that the plan, once prepared, need be acted on. But throughout this protracted struggle to create the more conventional channels for the town planning of private freeholds the South Australian Housing Trust (SAHT), on public land, had embarked on a housing programme which amounted in effect to a major intervention in town planning, closely integrated with the state's economic planning.

In 1949, in need of a large area of land on which to concentrate its activities, the SAHT purchased 5000 acres of farmland seventeen miles north of Adelaide. Just thirty years after Ebenezer Howard, whose garden city theory had been partly inspired by Light's plan for Adelaide, had written to Charles Reade in Adelaide lamenting the concentration of half of Australia's population in five cities and advocating properly planned rural garden towns as the best corrective, the SAHT espoused decentralization by means of new towns as its official ideology and began to plan the country's first new town at Elizabeth. Their new principles were written into the fourteenth annual report (1950) and are worth repeating here for the large social thoughts they contain.

The tendency of large cities to sprawl in a more or less haphazard fashion ever further and further afield, often running out for many miles along arterial roads in 'ribbon development' has been a matter of concern not only to professional town planners but to all who are aware of even some of the innumerable problems created by the necessary provision for water supply, sewerage, transport and other essential services. Unchecked proliferation of suburban areas may solve the immediate housing difficulties of very many citizens but only at the cost of imposing permanent and ever increasing burdens on the city dwelling community as a whole. It is significant that the cost of living is substantially higher in the large cities than in those of smaller population and area.

Undue centralisation of urban life is an evil, and one which, once it has taken place, cannot be reversed. Active steps are therefore required to prevent over-centralisation occurring, and these steps must first take the form of bold and decisive forward planning for the needs of the increasing population of the future.

One of the recognised forms which planned decentralisation may take is the development of new towns ... Such towns, if they are not merely to be 'dormitory suburbs', require some reason for their existence and this must ordinarily be provided by a hard core of industrial or commercial development. The town must, in fact, be to a large extent self-sufficient.

In 1954 construction began for a new town of 25 000 people, designed on the principles of British new towns—neighbourhoods of five to six thousand people surrounded and defined by open spaces, a town centre to include civic buildings, shops, commercial facilities and a pedestrian mall, and initial employment provided at the nearby Weapons Research Establishment. About ten-and-a-half years after construction commenced, the ten thousandth house was completed and the population had reached 42 400. Originally conceived to cope with 'the rapid growth of the population of Adelaide due to natural increase and immigration and the increasing rate of industrial development in the state', a large proportion of Elizabeth's subsequent population was immigrant workers, resulting in a somewhat unbalanced population which has caused criticism of the 'British ghetto' or 'blue collar government town'. But the trust's leaders were aware, as their general manager wrote, that 'the social problems of new areas are very great; when thousands of people pour into a new area it is not easy to weld them into a community. It takes time for natural leaders to appear. Most of the families are young and most of them are not wealthy enough to endow the many social institutions found in older communities ... The Trust has placed emphasis on the growth of such institutions.'[12]

Within the limits of SAHT power and financial resources, then, how successful has Elizabeth been? Its climate and land are relatively poor, and house and street design monotonous; women and children suffer from the surrender to the motor-car and the lack of pedestrian ways and public transport; and it has the permanent built-in shortcomings 'of a low income town on cheap land with few middle class members beyond the minimum required for the town's own service'.[13] Although built by the SAHT, most of its residents chose to come here because they had the option of public housing in other parts of the metropolis. Elizabeth contains its fair share of the sick, handicapped, disturbed or deserted fragments of families, as do all Housing Commission estates. *But* the SAHT builds a third of all new houses in the state, which gets the houses themselves a better social reputation, then rents and sells them, without any means test, to all comers. So Elizabeth has as many volunteers attracted by its jobs, or its superior houses, as captives held by its rental houses. Its society is strengthened by large numbers of highly skilled workers, by their competent ambitious families, and by a scattering of resident doctors, teachers, technicians, and small business proprietors.[14]

In terms of distributive justice, costs of journeys to work and equality of access to some of the non-material goods of urban life, Howard would have been content with this application of his theory. The irony of the achievement was that the SAHT had been established in the thirties as the principal instrument of R. L. Butler's industrialization programme, had developed in the forties under the strict 'anti-planning' auspices of the Playford government, but yet produced in the fifties Australia's first new town. This contradiction is more apparent than real. The new town was an example of state planning to improve the living conditions of the productive workers (and happy workers, the argument goes, will be more productive ones) while in no way disadvantaging the economic interests of private enterprise.

Slow Progress of Adelaide Plan 1955–65

Between 1955, when the act authorizing preparation of a town plan was passed, and 1965, when the Labor Party won its first election in thirty-two years, one man leading a small committee struggled to roll the stone of town planning up the hill of government resistance to any interference with private enterprise. Stuart Hart was appointed town planner and chairman of the Town Planning Committee in 1956. Qualified as an engineer and planner, Hart was only thirty-three when he arrived in Adelaide from his job as deputy planning officer for Scotland's Fife County Council. He was given no encouragement by Playford and was warned of the opposition with which he would be confronted by the Surveyors Institute, Real Estate Agents Institute, Chamber of Commerce and Adelaide City Council.[15] His cautious recommendations in the sixties must be seen in the context of his initial experience in Adelaide and of his knowledge of the causes of the demise of town planning in the twenties.

The situation confronting him in the late fifties was that of a public uneducated in planning principles, a government uninterested in applying them, and an immediate crisis in speculative land subdivision, especially along the hills' face. Therefore his first concern was to try to protect the hills. Several foot-hills subdivision plans were refused approval by the Town Planning Committee, on the grounds that they could not be economically sewered and provided with water. In strict legal terms, however, Hart did not have the power to refuse subdivision on these grounds, because they did not apply outside the metropolitan area. Thus when one subdivider (Skye Estate Ltd) appealed to the Full Court to squash the Town Planning Committee's decision regarding a 180-acre subdivision on the upper levels of the Adelaide hills, their appeal was upheld.[16] Hart had lost his first battle, but his committee's first report tabled in parliament at the same time requested more extensive powers to deal with such cases. So did the fourth report in 1959, by which time the situation had become critical.

One of the greatest costs the community has to bear in a rapidly expanding city is the provision of public services. By limiting development to areas where services can be applied easily and cheaply, services can keep pace with development ... At present the Engineer-in-Chief's authority extends only to the defined metropolitan area ... As the bulk of subdivision is now taking place outside the defined metropolitan area, the area should be extended as a matter of urgency. The Engineer-in-Chief reported on ten applications involving 1,232 allotments adjoining the metropolitan area that, if the land had been within the area he would have been unable to certify that it could be advantageously and economically sewered and reticulated with water.

From October 1957 to October 1959 applications for approval of subdivision plans had increased 79 per cent and the rate of creation of building allotments was twice the actual requirement. This led the minister to express public concern on 3 November 1959 at the growth of speculative investment in land subdivision. But the number of applications for approval increased considerably in November and December and property owners made it clear that they would brook no delay in or interference with their profit-making activities. They formed the South Australian Landowners Protection League and in September 1959 their secretary, a land agent himself, protested strongly against the 'increasing, costly and unnecessary delays by the Town Planning Office in processing subdivision applications'. A public meeting of landowners was arranged to protest against 'injustices; in the Town Planning Act and regulations'.[17] Here was another defeat for Hart, who, in the absence of the necessary powers, had been using delaying tactics on undesirable subdivision plans. The trouble arising from this probably accounts for what was later described by Stretton as Hart's 'impeccable cooperation' in processing plans to carve up the hills' face in the sixties.

By July 1960 the Town Planning Committee felt the situation to be so crucial that it produced an interim report urgently recommending a system of rural zoning based on the economic provision of public services and the extension of the area in which the engineer-in-chief's certificate applied. The report also regarded as essential the retention of the open character of the hills' face as of equal significance to Colonel Light's provision of parklands. The hills are crucial to Adelaide both as a backdrop and as a containing wall for this almost naturally linear city which is growing at each end, its sides flanked by hills and sea. But a town planning act amendment bill introduced in October 1960 to extend control of subdivision plans to all areas was shelved and the planners repeated their by now monotonously regular theme in 1965 in their report on objections. 'Premature subdivision continues, unsatisfactory living conditions are being created and the cost of providing public services to these areas will be extremely high. *Urgent action is necessary.*'

Meanwhile in 1962 the committee's main task, its *Report and Plan for the Development of the Metropolitan Area of Adelaide,* had been released. It presumably represented the town planner's judgement of the best his unpromising government might consider acceptable. Hart may well have been a 'scrupulous democrat' when he arrived in Adelaide. Brief experience with the city's political realities would have taught him in any case that scrupulous democracy was the only possible approach to adopt. For with an unsympathetic government, an apathetic public, and an actively hostile collection of vested interests the only course likely to succeed in changing government attitudes was public clamour for town planning. The 1920s' experience also suggested to Hart that planners

> can never expect . . . to be too far ahead of public opinion . . . on reflection, perhaps the lesson of the repeal [of 1929] is that town planning is one-tenth bright ideas and nine-tenths of sheer hard work putting those ideas into effect over what may prove to be a very long period of time.[18]

Accordingly much of his time was spent talking to citizens and citizen groups, councils and industrialists, about the advantages of town planning. In ten years he delivered over 350 talks, which works out to one-tenth of 1 per cent of the population—the smallest number that Hart believed needed to be convinced and vocal before any politician would act. This approach demands close attention to citizens' preferences and keeping close to present trends, and is of necessity fairly conservative since it depends on the articulation of needs and ideas by largely uninformed citizens. This conservative approach was inevitably, then, built into the 1962 plan, as one commentator observed:

There can be little doubt that the plan was documented to be politically acceptable to the government of the day, a government which had shown little enthusiasm for planning. Understandably directed toward acceptance and subsequent legislation the plan became for the most part an extrapolation of current trends.[19]

Specifically it espoused the 'preference for single family dwellings' and therefore allowed for continuing residential densities even lower than Canberra's, averaging 5·8 persons per acre. It argued that 'there is little valid evidence to support the view that the metropolitan area could or should be limited, either in the size of the population or the area of the land built on' and therefore accepted that 'the development of the metropolitan area will continue'. On the one hand it agreed that 'the desirability of greater dispersal of the population over the state is widely accepted'. On the other hand it decided that in assessing future population 'the possibility of organised decentralisation has been excluded and a forecast is made only on the basis of social and economic trends'. The committee also accepted the increasing use of the private motor-car and therefore proposed several major freeway systems in preference to large-scale public transport improvements.

Yet within its self-imposed but realistic limitations, the positive proposals were sensible and humane enough.

The type of expansion most desirable for metropolitan Adelaide is in the form of metropolitan districts varying in size from 50,000 to 100,000. Each would be self-contained with industry, commerce, recreation, and educational facilities. Individual identity can be achieved by separating each district by strips of open development —large institutions and recreation areas— and each district should also be served by fast means of transport with the central area. It is essential that easy access to open country or beaches be achieved from each district.[20]

The committee was clear as to the mechanisms of power needed to implement its proposals. It would require additional measures to control land subdivision more effectively, a unified system of zoning to govern the use and development of land, new measures to ensure that land for essential public purposes (highways, schools, open spaces) be available at the right time and place, and a more effective way of obtaining land for public open space. But political limitations faced not only implementation of the plan but shaped its very proposals, as Hart recorded at a later date.

A statutory planning authority is . . . faced with grim reality and cannot indulge in theoretical academic exercises. A development plan must be acceptable and workable; and to that end judgment must be based on what can or cannot be done within the prevailing economic, social and political situation.[21]

What, then, was done?

When it received this plan the Government was quicker than usual in deciding to do nothing rash. It published the Report and Plan the next day and next year amended the Act to allow a further year for objectors to object. It considered the Plan's traffic proposals for three years, then ordered another survey of metropolitan transport needs, which took three further years to carry out.[22]

Meantime the assistant town planner, Hans Westerman, resigned to take a position in Canberra, observing on his way out that the difference between Canberra and South Australia was that Canberra possessed a blueprint upon which it *would* act but that South Australia had a blueprint upon which it might or might not act. Whether it did or not was no reflection on the effort invested by Hart, which according to the *Advertiser* leader writer on 26 November 1964 was nothing less than a 'quiet revolution'.

> A decisive breakthrough is occurring in the ability of town planning supporters to secure enforcement of the main provisions of the town plan for metropolitan Adelaide. It is a 'quiet revolution' with no abrupt disintegration of some stubborn administrative sound barrier, and no obvious change yet in the cautious attitude of the state government. Rather it is due to the gradual conversion of many hundreds of community leaders in business, industry, the professions and local government to the view that, subject to necessary amendments, the town plan is basically a matter of common sense ... The new outlook on town planning in the community is a personal tribute to the town planner and his belief in the ultimate power of reason ... What he has said has made enough sense to enough people to swing the tide his way. As a story of patient persistence it probably has few equals in South Australian public life.

This was a fitting epitaph to the stage planning reached in the twilight days of the Playford era, and an anticipation of the new dawn of the Labor government elected in 1965, the first for thirty-two years.

Technocratic Triumph 1965–70

Between 1965 and 1970 the long campaign to introduce town planning came to fruition with the passing of the Town Planning and Development Act of 1967, the creation of the State Planning Authority and the production of the Metropolitan Adelaide Transportation Study (MATS) in 1968. These were the years of the technocrats, in that the land-use and the transportation planning had been left to the technical experts, and the fruits of their work were released to the public in 1968. No one was more surprised than they themselves at the intensity of the hostility with which their MATS plan was met, for until then there had been very little active public interest in the planning process. This section explores the nature of the planning that emerged in the 1960s and the nature of the opposition to it, and the final section examines some of the effects of that opposition since 1970.

Neither the legislation introduced by Playford in 1954 nor the amended legislation of 1955 mentioned long-term planning objectives. The 1955 act, which created the Town Planning Committee to prepare Adelaide's development plan, was given no guidelines by parliament for the future development of Adelaide, and members of both houses entered into almost no discussion about where the city was going and why. The completion of the plan in 1962 still brought no parliamentary discussion of planning or of road construction programmes of the size envisaged in the 1962 plan—a proposed ninety-seven miles of freeways. There was no expressed attitude on roads and their relationship to the city, the people or land use. Rather there was a general belief in their inevitability and their economic worth in terms of the state's progress. Discussion revolved around zoning regulations and subdivision with no broad analysis of either community planning or problems of community disruption, noise, congestion and pollution. The inevitability of a motorized society was a matter of ideological belief. As one Liberal member argued, 'encouragement is an admirable thing but coercion into using public transport is another matter. [That] would be a deplorable misuse of power. Time and again we have seen bureaucratic controls stifle free enterprise.'[23]

Yet changing modes of transport are possibly the most powerful and insistent of the forces shaping the city. The professor of architecture and planning at Adelaide University argued that the proposed ninety-seven miles of freeways constituted the single biggest change in the metropolitan area in the whole 130 years of Adelaide's history. In recent years all major Australian cities have undertaken transport studies and the controversy thereby triggered is one that inevitably develops when communities face up to the real costs of the motor age and the rising demand for individual mobility. In Australia the spread of cities since World War II, following widespread car ownership, has taken place in the almost complete absence of co-ordinated planning apart from very general zoning regulations. Such zoning has been the responsibility of local authorities whose aim has been to attract as much development as possible, preferably private rather than public because of ratable values. (Public institutions pay no rates on their land.) This has resulted in commercial and industrial expansion along main highways, and tentacles of mixed uses (factories, junkyards, shops, houses, used-car lots, service stations and takeaway food outlets) decorated with garish advertising, eventually inhibit the very mobility that first attracts the businesses. But poor accessibility and congestion is not the whole of the traffic problem, as the Buchanan report, prepared for the British government in 1964, recognized.

> The penetration of motor vehicles throughout urban areas is bringing its own peculiar penalties of accidents, anxiety, intimidation by large or fast vehicles that are of scale with the surroundings, noise, fumes, vibration, dirt and visual intrusion on a vast scale. Included in the last item is the proliferation of establishments serving or served by the motor vehicle.[24]

The freeway proposals of the MATS plan, ordered by the Liberal government in 1965 and completed just after its return to office in 1968, paid no attention to these problems and ignored the impact of the proposals both on the people and on the visual integrity of the city. So we need to describe the political arena in which it was decided to conduct a transport study, and the ideologies of those responsible. This will indicate why there was no integrated conception of city and regional planning on humanistic lines. The lack of interest shown by members of parliament over the period 1950–70 is part of the problem too. Why was there a lack of ideas in both parties? Is parliamentary democracy suitably structured to be able to discuss the problems of urban development?

These problems are traceable in part to the structure of Adelaide's politics. The inertia since 1955 can be explained partly by the abrogation of responsibility to public servants and in particular to the Town Planning Committee, later the Joint Steering Committee of MATS, and still later the Metropolitan Transportation Committee, and partly by the thirty-year influence of Playford's paternalism over many members. Playford's ideology had social effects as significant as those resulting from the transfer of responsibility to public servants with their ideology of 'technical rationality'. But first, a look at some other relevant factors impinging on the consciousness of parliamentarians of both parties, limiting legislative possibilities, and helping to explain the lack of a far-sighted planning philosophy.

The largest single industry in South Australia and the major contributor to post-war industrial growth is the motor vehicle industry. The General Motors-Holden's and Chrysler plants absorb the products of many factories producing vehicle components. Other manufacturers produce omnibus and commercial vehicle bodies, fork-lift trucks, garage equipment, trailers, caravans and a wide range of vehicle accessories. Repairs too are an important part of the car industry, which, in all, accounts for 30 per cent of the total value of production and employs 39 per cent of the workforce in South Australia.[25] In a state lacking in industry and natural resources the presence of firms playing such a large part in the financial structure of the state cannot be ignored. The 1962 plan acknowledged this.

In the future industrial expansion is assured by certain developments of key significance. The most important is the new steel making plant of B.H.P. Ltd. and a large scale expansion program by G.M.H. Ltd. . . . which will encourage further linked industries . . . This is the background against which the future urban economy of metropolitan Adelaide must be considered.

As an important source of employment a transport programme geared to the motor industry is understandably something not only motor companies but trade unions would endorse, and the Liberal minister for roads and transport and minister in charge of town planning from 1968 to 1970, Murray Hill, emphasized this: 'This state depends a lot upon the motor car industry . . . I know the great benefit to commerce and industry in this state that the motor car provides.'[26] The Labor party has been and still is curtailed by the employment factor in this balance.

R. Jensen argued in 1969 that

in attempting to counter development and transportation proposals for Adelaide a powerful vested interest exists which appears to see in the urban freeway the furtherance of the interests of business, commerce and industry. Not the least of those 'vested interests' are politicians who, through deference to highway engineering expertise and the 'economic equilibrium of the state' view proposals for state economic expansion as sacred cows not to be interfered with . . .[27]

The important 'vested interest' that he failed to mention is that of the unions in protecting workers' jobs. And to date this is the only consideration affecting the actions of unions in the transport industry, unlike, say, the Builders Labourers Federation in New South Wales, which has developed an ethic of 'social responsibility' for the work it does.

Another relevant factor in the thinking and activities of politicians is the multitude of responsibilities held by local, state and federal governments in town planning matters, which readily lends itself to 'passing the buck' and disclaiming responsibility for any task which is not easily categorized. In South Australia there are fifty-five government departments, ten of which have duties and responsibilities for aspects of planning and city development. Local councils also have responsibilities, especially in connection with roadworks, sewerage and rubbish disposal, and the commonwealth, as a revenue provider, has some responsibility. The clearly defined responsibilities of each department in theory mean that in practice no one for example is responsible for measuring decay and the physical and social impact of the car on the city environment.

Two of the most powerful agencies of planning administration in South Australia are the State Planning Authority (SPA) and the Highways Department. The SPA was created by legislation passed by the Dunstan Labor government in 1967 after a protracted struggle in the Legislative Council where the chief protagonist against town planning legislation was the real estate agent Murray Hill. The Planning and Development Bill introduced in February 1966 was to replace all previous town planning acts and to give effect to the 1962 plan's general intentions. It created the SPA, which was to be chaired by a director of planning (former town planner, Stuart Hart). The SPA could buy and develop land, recommend planning areas; prepare development plans, prepare, recommend and administer planning regulations, redevelop land, give interim development control of local government areas while planning regulations were being prepared, administer a planning and development fund, and set up advisory committees and public reports. It also set up an independent planning appeal board to 'safeguard the interests of the individual'. Its membership comprises a legal practitioner as chairman, a local government representative, a representative from the Australian Planning Institute and a businessman. There were provisions for land to be reserved for future public use, for interim controls and for uniform rules about zoning and subdivision. A flexible arrangement between the SPA and local councils was intended to leave councils some freedom to decide their part in planning their areas but not the freedom to do no planning at all. And the bill gave the 1962 plan official status as Adelaide's development plan.

It took nine months to get through the lower house. The Legislative Council then proceeded to deal with it brutally and quickly. Murray Hill, who led the hostile opposition, wondered 'to what extent town planning should be permitted'. He himself had a conspiratorial interpretation of the upsurge of public interest in the matter. He believed that 'a forceful group of planners in this state is endeavouring to mould public opinion in an attempt to have the principle of town planning accepted', but he was not convinced

> that most people are prepared to accept, or even want, such planning . . . [the planners] realise and acknowledge that town planning is not particularly popular with the people unless the climate for its acceptance has been created. I believe that these people have formed an association and they are endeavouring to establish that climate . . . At its meetings the association attempts to mould public opinion . . . However I think many people are still cautious about

the results that will ensue if we are not careful in controlling the degree of power to be given to the town planning authority under this measure.[28]

Hill said he spoke for the little man, the businessman and the alderman. Planning would, he thought, adversely affect ordinary people's lives, industries' prosperity and local governments' powers. There was some inconsistency in Hill's denial here of the right of planners to try to influence public opinion when in 1970 as minister for transport, he purchased some five hundred copies of the *Sunday Mail* containing a metropolitan development questionnaire, in order *apparently* to influence the result. As the *Advertiser* politely observed, 'the most charitable view . . . is that [Hill] is so wedded to the MATS plan that he saw nothing wrong in whipping up public support for it by ordering papers by the hundred, and, as he says, distributing them among his friends so that they could have their enthusiastic say as well.'[29] Hill also opposed the power of the SPA to purchase, subdivide and develop land. This was an 'insidious form of socialism', and Hill was 'definitely opposed to any legislation of a socialistic kind'.[30] In spite of all this, the act that finally emerged was surprisingly intact. Appeals arrangements were made slightly tougher for planners, some statutory planning delays made more lengthy, some planning initiatives made more the preserve of the local authorities, and a couple more businessmen, one from the Real Estate Institute, were added to the SPA.

An examination of the values and ideas of the people in both the SPA and the Highways Department suggests the bias that occurs when so much decision-making devolves from parliament to such bodies. These two agencies illustrate de facto goals and professional bias almost free from public scrutiny. The values of the agencies that determine the shape of the city need to be understood, and they are revealed on the most immediate level by looking at the composition of the bodies responsible for that planning. The Town Planning Committee was chaired by Stuart Hart, who was the only member qualified as a planner. His earlier training though was in engineering. Of the five members of the committee, only two were not engineers. W. C. D. Veale was the chief engineer and town clerk for the City of Adelaide and favoured freeways as instruments of efficiency. He was on many issues a humane planner who did think about people. He insisted for example on a garden in the south parklands that was named after him being something the old folk could really enjoy and not a sterile architectural exhibition. But he was not qualified as a planner and both he and another committee member J. D. Cheesman were members of the Adelaide Club. J. W. Murrell was the chief engineer in charge of sewerage with the Engineering and Water Supply Department and member of four engineering societies. His concern was with the efficient provision of services. H. H. Tyler was neither planner, architect nor engineer, but town clerk of Enfield. His position demanded prime concern with efficiency and precision. In short, the Town Planning Committee was oriented towards planning in terms of technical efficiency.

The committee's 1962 report stressed the need for co-ordinating all forms of transport to ensure the most economic and efficient movement of people and goods. The traffic system recommended was the extension of public transport services, including some new railway lines, and the construction of 97 miles of freeways and extensions to existing roads. The Joint Steering Committee was set up by the Liberal Country League government to follow up these transport proposals. It comprised the commissioner of highways as chairman, the town planner, the railways commissioner, the general manager of the Metropolitan Tramways Trust, and Veale. Under them MATS was set up and they were responsible for overall direction and making of policy decisions during the study. Their assistants or deputies gave technical advice through the Technical Advisory Committee. Among the two committees were six engineers in a membership of ten. Four of these had town planning diplomas; one had accounting qualifications. The deputy town planner first qualified as a surveyor, and the other two members had mathematical backgrounds. The consultants employed by the Joint Steering Committee (De Leuw, Cather & Co.) were engineering consultants who further biased the final result by their specialized technical interest in planning. The fact that the goals and objectives of the study as well as the formulation of the recommendations were established in conference with the Joint Steering Committee made little difference given the similarity of outlook of both groups and the complete affinity of professional interests. Hart was perhaps the one exception to this. On his return from America in 1964 he reported that

> freeways carry, and attract, large volumes of traffic and as each new one is opened, capacity volumes are soon reached creating a demand for more freeways. The congestion on freeways at peak hours and the decline in public transport are causing public concern. Building more freeways is clearly not the most efficient or economic way of meeting the needs of the expanding metropolitan area.[31]

But Hart significantly was not the chairman of the committee. Moreover his ardour for these large battles had been dampened by his earlier defeats over protection of the hills' face, so he was unlikely to take a strong stand against a freeway programme.

One observer of the American city planning process has concluded that 'highway engineers tend to think that the setting of highway

routes should be a technical endeavour. Others, including city planners, often complain that highway engineers are inclined to handle
the side effects of route location—which may be as important as
intended effects—as peripheral matters'.[32] It is generally assumed
that public servants are, or should be, objective and politically neutral.
But to treat problems without reference to ideology simply means
the acceptance of the dominant ideology and consequently of the
relations of forces they express or justify. The idea of political
neutrality demands that individuals have no values and make no
choices. But no planning information, as Stretton has pointed out in
relation to transport planning in Australia, is more political—and
moral or immoral—than the traffic planner's choice of what to feed
into his computer.

> If a traffic planner quietly leaves pedestrians, school journeys,
> residential noise and adjacent property values and amenities out
> of his test programme, and if he includes direct compensations
> but not true replacement and relocation costs, or if he leaves out
> everything that can't be quantified simply because it can't be quan-
> tified, and announces his result as 'an optimum transport system'
> —then . . . he has deliberately chosen to plan for some classes and
> individuals against others and probably for a general increase in
> his city's real inequalities.[33]

The South Australian Highways Department confined its terms
of reference to 'technical' considerations to such an extent that objections were met before they were heard. One of the victories for
technical rationality was the proviso of the Metropolitan Transportation Committee to people living along the proposed Noarlunga
freeway route that those wishing to present a submission must do so
in the form of an alternative freeway. That is, the committee would
only allow one solution—the freeway solution—and the only question
to be resolved was where it was to go. In December 1969 the Town
and Country Planning Association learned that the committee would
be taking evidence on the alternatives to the Noarlunga freeway. The
association sought to give evidence on noise, air pollution, alternative
land-use patterns, and the inadequacy of the MATS plan to cope
with these problems. It was told that none of these things were
relevant to the inquiry and permission to appear before the committee
was refused.[34]

The main sources of road finance are state motor vehicle taxation
and driver's licence fees, commonwealth grants, and property rates
imposed by municipal councils. The main bulk of highways money
comes from allocations under the Commonwealth Roads Act. Costs
considered in the allocation of this money are

construction, reconstruction, property acquisition and maintenance. Benefits considered [are] community benefits arising from reduced time, accidents and vehicle operating costs, including saving in private travel time. It [is] not considered acceptable to measure in monetary terms such things as [are] difficult of a monetary evaluation, including disruption to community life associated with road works.[35]

Yet this may be the largest of the social factors associated with freeways.

Transportation is an essential element of urban development which should be integrated with people's needs for it and with a planning process responsive to those needs. But this is not possible when allocations to the Highways Department make it independent of parliamentary control. The transport minister Hill realized this, together with the advantages of the plan to the motor-car and real estate industries, and attempted to have the plan ratified as a 'service plan'. The freedom and autonomy available to the Highways Department in the control of the most powerful force reshaping the city is freedom from public scrutiny, financial self-sufficiency and effective insulation from opposition through its monopoly of 'technical expertise'.

The SPA is not an effective counterbalance to this predominance of engineering values in the government agencies responsible for Adelaide's transport planning. The chairman of the SPA is the director of planning, Hart, three top public servants are automatic members —the director of the Electricity and Water Supply Department, the commissioner of highways and the surveyor-general. The remaining seven members are 'appointed by the Governor'—one nominated by the minister of housing and one by the minister of transport, one by the Adelaide City Council and one from each of a panel of three names submitted by the Municipal Association of South Australia, the Local Government Association, the Chamber of Manufactures, and the Real Estate Institute. So four and possibly six could have engineering backgrounds, and two, possibly four, even five, could have interests in property which could be considered undesirable. An analogy drawn by one commentator shows the major area of concern about the SPA.

> If a mouse conservation association contains cats, we may be suspicious of its effectiveness, even if we believe them to be high minded cats. If the mouse organisations have no representative, our suspicions will be increased. If the end result is a decrease in the mouse population our suspicions will be confirmed.[36]

This, he concludes, is the situation on the SPA: no formal representation for conservation groups and a history of decisions in favour of subdivisions. Other bodies with vital interests in the by-products of the freeway routes—education and housing authorities for example —had no official representation in the discussion of the largest and most dramatic plan to reshape Adelaide, a plan requiring $436 million for highways and $105 million for public transport and anticipating that the trend in declining public transport would continue. Of the money spent on highways, $280 million was for freeways.

These were bleak years in the record of Adelaide's stock of ideas and intended actions in urban planning, illustrating that no matter how long awaited and fought for, planning *per se* is not necessarily a good thing. But they produced fertile results in a healthy citizen backlash of distrust for planning or, rather, a distrust of leaving it to the so-called experts, which has resulted in major urban policy changes over the past four years (1970–4). How did it happen then that what looked like one of the most unassailable power structures in Australia has proven over the last few years so fertile for intervention?

This general problem of social and political change has no general theoretical answer. Whether change comes, and how it is brought about, depends on particular historical circumstances. When Hart came to Adelaide, he perceived that only by massive public demand would the state's conservative rulers be persuaded to accept some modicum of planning. His single-handed public education campaign matured at just the right time to reap its just harvest. By the late sixties, as never before, a strong dose of citizen indignation needed to be injected into the body politic to counterbalance the predominance of the engineers and the conservatism and neglect of the politicians. Demographic changes also meant that such protests could be politically effective. Playford's industrialization programme had increased the population in the rural electorates just outside the metropolitan area. They could swing the parliamentary balance in favour of the Labor party, as had happened in 1965. And Liberal premier Hall's handling of the MATS plan helped bring this about again in 1970. And few things annoy and stir people into action as much as an eight-lane freeway pointed in their direction.

Opposition began among individuals and groups whose professional or personal interests were threatened. But the more the MATS plan was debated, the more did the public and some politicians perceive the issues and implications involved. And opposition was strengthened by Premier Hall's handling of the matter. When the plan was released in August 1968, his government insisted that it would not commit itself to MATS until it had been studied and objections heard for six months, and it had been debated in parlia-

ment. Yet in February 1969 he issued a ministerial statement to the
effect that the government endorsed all the general principles of
MATS, including the expressways and freeways. All this in spite of
mounting articulate press and public hostility, in spite of 966 sub-
missions and 24 council reports (between August 1968 and February
1969) and despite an urgent motion by Sir Arthur Rymill, a member
of his own party in the Legislative Council the previous week that
MATS should be considered by parliament before the government
accept any substantial portion of it.

Rymill, chairman of the Bank of Adelaide, member of the Adelaide
Club and of one of the Establishment's oldest families, and a large
rural and urban property owner, argued that the MATS plan had
'the attitude that no one counts except the traffic engineer and that
no considerations count other than traffic engineering . . . sweeping
geometrical curves have been drawn over the plans of the metropolitan area and no part of the plan has sought to avoid things that
might be in the way of these geometrical curves'.[37] He also attacked
the proposed imbalance between public and private transport, and
the freeway rationale itself: 'People who say these freeways are traffic
generators have been scoffed at by the [Highways] Department. Many
of us know they are. When we make them we are only building up
fresh trouble for ouselves.' He ended by pointing to the financial
absurdity of the proposals and urged the government to drop the city
and suburban freeway schemes and recommend satisfactory alternatives. But the minister for transport, Murray Hill, opposed Rymill's
motion on the grounds that MATS was a *service* plan, not a develcp-
ment plan, and therefore did not have to be debated by parliament.

In August 1969 opposition leader Don Dunstan moved that the
plan be withdrawn and referred to the SPA for reassessment on
grounds of financial feasibility, inadequate public transport provisions
and unnecessary destruction of homes and other properties. His
criticisms were threefold. The first was that MATS was based on the
false assumption that the private car was and would continue to be
the only acceptable form of transport. Secondly he questioned the
desirability of freeways because they dislocated people and businesses,
eroded the real property tax base and distorted land use. Finally he
pointed out the social injustices of the freeway proposals, the fate of
'that section of the people who must always be served by public
transport. If we are to have a constantly declining public transport
system, and the forecast in this plan is for just that, a large section
of the population will be inadequately served'.

Outside parliament, opinions were polarized in a predictable way.
Support for the plan came from those organizations which had a
vested interest in the car industry or stood to gain from the increased

road expenditures. The Adelaide City Council supported it because 'it will greatly improve traffic conditions in the City of Adelaide'.[38] The council had appointed a special committee to report to it on MATS. The committee recommended support because the plan 'aimed at maintaining and enhancing the vitality of the entire metropolitan area with particular emphasis on the C.B.D. [central business district]'. But, as Stretton observed, the concentrated study, research and consultation which the council undertook on behalf of the retailing and business interests contrasted sharply with the 'studied ignorance' of the effect of road and rebuilding programmes on the city's poorer residents.

The Royal Automobile Association defended MATS on the grounds that 'Australia is one of the most highly motorised countries in the world and . . . people who own cars expect to be able to use them.'[39] The Australian Federation of Civil Engineering Contractors strongly supported MATS. No wonder then that the public detected a certain conspiratorial air on the part of private enterprise in the issue. For it did appear from statements issued that 'only the engineers for highway construction freely support the MATS plan', and 'solely from a technical point of view.'[40]

Physical and visual destruction of the environment, anticipated reduction of property values, increasing traffic and volume of noise, bad effects on residential areas and the inadequacy of the concept of the 1962 plan were the major areas of opposition to MATS. Opposition came most consistently from local MATS revision committees, the Town and Country Planning Association, the Royal Australian Institute of Architects, the Australian Planning Institute, public statements by Labor members of parliament, local residents' meetings and private statements in letters to the *Advertiser*. The Town and Country Planning Association submitted a lengthy critique, concluding their objections with the statement, 'We also believe that the inclusion of the professed objectives of the report and the errors which show public transport at a disadvantage reveal an attempt on the part of the MATS planners to mislead the government and the public, and promote the inevitability of a freeway solution.' Their recommendations urged rethinking of what planning involves. 'Planning is not another name for gazing into a crystal ball, even one linked to a computer. Planning means setting sights on some desirable goal and so ordering the forces of change so that that goal is attained.' They criticized the 1962 plan for its extrapolation and reinforcement of present trends with no evaluation of social priorities. 'Transport', their submission concluded, 'important though it is, is not the pre-eminent factor in planning. Human values should have the dominant priority.'[41] The MATS plan was somewhat dishonest in its rhetoric of concern for social values.

Though the planners claimed to have accounted for social values they did not claim to have based their work on any social research at all. They offered no restorative land use or economic or social replanning of the territories which their routes disturbed or fragmented. The land they actually took they would pay for; with that (they thought) public responsibility ended.[42]

One writer was able to question MATS' engineering expertise, the emphasis on the motor-car, the destruction of the environment and the social values involved through a poem he entitled 'A Sentimental Bloke—with apologies to C. J. Denis'.

> When I first heard about the MATS
> I thought—My Gawd, they've all gone bats
> 'Oo do they think they bloody are?
> God 'isself 'cos they drives a car?
> They're makin' such a 'spensive fuss
> Wen wot we wants is a flamin' bus
> An' a few more trains and a subway too.
>
> But these poor b's ain't got a clue
> 'Stead o' usin' brains, they got them Yanks
> 'Oo when they seen the Torrens' banks
> Where some kids fish an' others play
> Said, "There's the track f' y' new freeway.
> That useless creek an' them scrappy trees
> Wavin' about in the mornin' breeze
> Will be transformed into concrete piles
> With curvin' roads stretchin' out f' miles.
>
> Fair dinkum! I ask you, give us a go
> What do they think they bloody know?
> Our kids need schools an' open space
> Not freeways smog an' rat-race pace.
> Where do their kids fish an' play
> In the concrete mess of the U.S.A.?
> Their kids, they never sees the stars
> 'Cos o' all the muck from motor cars.[43]

An article in the *Advertiser* in October 1968 by John Miles entitled 'Public clamour intensifies' had noted that 'the sound waves arising from the proposals, which are estimated to affect directly 2500 properties and 5000 more indirectly, are loud and continuing . . . the resultant public clamour is deeper in intensity than the reaction to any other report in the state's history.'

It's worth noting that the issues that had been most concerning the planners—premature subdivision on the metropolitan fringe and on the hills' face—had never generated any public concern or fierce opposition. But tearing down people's homes (in a society with a higher proportion of owner occupiers than any other), whether for highways or slum clearance or anything else, did. The ferocity of public opposition to motorway planning probably owed more to this than to Hart's years of 'educating', or any other influence. Adelaide is a beautiful city, particularly the inner suburbs. The highway engineers were proposing to lay much of this beauty to waste. Their highways were designed not to link the main subcentres of the city with each other but, like Melbourne's, to pour traffic into the centre, thereby generating pressures which would lead to further destruction.

By July 1970 it was clear that Adelaide residents were not prepared to take the MATS plan on trust. Public meetings about the plan drew attendances of hundreds, and editorial comments in the newspapers had a much more critical tone. In that month Hall's Liberal Country League government fell, officially on the issue of the building of the Chowilla or Dartmouth dams. While the opinion of one columnist, that 'for every one who voted for Dartmouth now there were a dozen who voted for MATS never' can not be proved, there was a clear division between the parties on this issue. Labor promised in election brochures to 'withdraw and revise the MATS plan' and 'require the S.P.A. to produce a plan which not only integrates public transport with other transport, but also one which is financially possible and reduces property destruction to an absolute minimum'.

One of the first actions of the new Labor government was to appoint as a consultant S. L. Breuning, an American and chairman of Social Technology Systems in Boston. His report was submitted to the government in November 1970. It emphasized the need to provide the user with a service as good as or better than his car, but with great reductions in the social disadvantages. Its emphasis was the reverse of MATS. Instead of assuming that the use of public transport would decline, its first priority was to improve it and increase its usage. Instead of emphasis on freeways, the need for them is described as 'questionable'. In March 1971 the government officially adopted the philosophy of action suggested by the Breuning report.

The issue is much larger than merely deciding the best roads to build for private motor-cars. The question is whether unrestricted use of private cars is detrimental in the long run to the city as a place to live, work and play. But the freeway issue is also a good illustration of the complexity of most urban problems. Freeways are partly a 'capitalist conspiracy'. Oil, motor, rubber and spare-parts companies are obvious beneficiaries. So are highway engineers. But that raises the connected problem of the role of 'technical experts' in the planning process and the question of their political and social accountability. Workers in the car manufacturing industry are quick to protest to any government that takes any action (from changes in tariff policies to cut-backs in freeway construction) that threatens their jobs. And the Royal Automobile Association had a large part of the public behind it when it argued that people who own cars—that is, four out of five Australian households—expect to be able to use them. Having been led to believe that they live in an affluent society, they want to behave as they have been led to believe affluent people (in Los Angeles for instance) do. Yet also (and this is not a capitalist plot), since Australians have massively chosen to live at very low densities (Sydney, with a third of London's population, occupies the same area), they cannot get to all the things they want to visit without considerable reliance on the private car. To abolish cars would mean rebuilding Adelaide. At 150 persons per acre you can walk to a lot of places. At 70 persons per acre you can bus or cycle. But at 6 persons per acre, in a very hot country, you need a car too.

Popular Revolt and Changes in Urban Policy since 1970

To the handful of city planning reformers urging legislation from World War II onwards, the situation must have looked fairly intractable. Ten years after such legislation had been passed in New South Wales and Victoria (1945 and 1944) Playford had strangled their hopes in his message to the 1954 conference. When Hart had been appointed town planner in 1957, he had found a public uneducated in planning principles, a government uninterested in applying them, and a collection of vested interests actively opposing them. Yet Adelaide is now, of all Australian cities, the most advanced in its planning aims and achievements.

I have shown how, in the field of transport planning, citizen indignation has wrought a major change in urban transportation policy in Adelaide. The citizen backlash of distrust for planning or, rather, a distrust of leaving it to the so-called experts (which in Adelaide in the sixties had meant engineers dominated by 'technical rationality') engendered by the MATS plan, has spilt over into other areas of urban policy since 1970. In at least two major areas, urban redevelopment and decentralization, South Australia's latest policy-makers have reversed traditional assumptions and provided an example for the rest of the country, but only because they have been roused by public indignation and participation and more recently by union initiatives. Four developments since 1970 illustrate this new trend in participatory planning. Two of these projects—the plans for a new town at Monarto and a regional centre at Noarlunga—were the product of government initiative. The other two—the happy outcomes of conflicts over the Hackney redevelopment project and the City of Adelaide's redevelopment activities—were responses by the government to public protest.

Hackney is an old suburb in Premier Dunstan's electorate just across the parklands from the city. The area is made up of nineteenth-century cottages, a CSIRO (Commonwealth Scientific and Industrial Research Organization) research unit complete with sheep pens, a caravan park, church, pub and car park. Despite the deceptive appearance of many of its houses, Hackney is not a low-income area. Household incomes have not been surveyed but the occupations suggest a wide range, and the area average is probably as high as the metropolitan average. Thirty-one per cent of the area's inhabitants are pensioners, 12 per cent work in administrative and clerical jobs, 8 per cent are professional and managerial, 20 per cent are self-employed tradesmen, 11 per cent are unskilled males, and unskilled females comprise 14 per cent, with university students providing 4 per cent.

In 1967 it was decided by the SPA that this was an area ripe for redevelopment of a kind that was 'economically feasible' for the state government. At that time, when no one else was much interested in the matter, Rolf Jensen, the professor of architecture and planning at Adelaide University and author of *High Density Living* (1966) was the state's 'expert' on redevelopment. He headed the five-member subcommittee of the SPA that submitted a report to the Liberal government in 1968 on the Hackney North Comprehensive Redevelopment Area. The Liberals weren't interested and shelved the matter for two years, during which time the SAHT and the local council (St Peters) acquired some houses in the area.

Jensen is a well-known advocate of high-density living in general and high-density redevelopment in particular:

World opinion is now showing a clear trend in favour of a considerable program of urban renewal and high urban densities, and the problem now is to ensure that this work is undertaken in the soundest possible way so as to constitute a real and permanent solution to urban growth.[44]

Dunstan was sympathetic with these views: 'The suburban villa and the motor car ... constitute the greatest planning problems we have to deal with ... I would like to raise my voice against this as the dominant form of housing.'[45]

The proposals for Hackney involved compulsory acquisition and total clearance of the fourteen-acre area and its 250 residents to make room for high-density residential redevelopment to accommodate 1000 people. The SAHT was to be responsible for five acres, private enterprise for nine acres of the project. These plans, submitted to the new Labor government of 1970, received Dunstan's approval. The outstanding feature of the preparation of the proposals was the unsatisfactory professional and technical competence and perhaps dubious integrity of the technocrats. They miscounted the population by not counting caravan-dwellers, hospital patients and resident staff in the caravan camp, hospital and hotel. The understatement was of the order of 25 per cent. They grossly overstated the 'redeveloped' population—they assumed every bedspace occupied every night of the year, because they didn't try to find out occupancy rates for the types of housing they proposed to build. That overstated the expected population by about 25 per cent. They had a survey of *what* the residents hoped to do *if* compulsorily removed. They miscounted the responses with full pro-bulldozer bias, then represented those responses as *desires to move*, in their reports to government.

What followed was a political embarrassment of the first order to Dunstan and a lesson to all Australian governments espousing theories of high-density living, that they are out of touch with the values and needs of most 'ordinary Australians' and especially with the needs of families. The St Peters Residents' Association took up arms of behalf of the 'victims' of the Hackney proposals and created so much disaffection in the area that there was a substantial drop in Labor support. So much so, in fact, that the day after the local government elections of 30 June 1972, for which the Labor mayor of St Peters found he had lost too much support even to bother running for re-election, Dunstan perceived the political threat to be so great as to call for a drastic policy reversal. No matter how Machiavellian the motives, his concessions to public indignation were major. The new philosophy and approach to urban renewal were expounded six weeks later to the Royal Australian Planning Institute conference in Brisbane.

> Inner city redevelopment [does not mean] the wholesale tearing down of existing communities simply to replace them with an asphalt desert and high rise blocks of flats ... the existing communities [should not be] displaced, but augmented; not bulldozed, but added to; not compartmentalised, but given the opportunity of achieving the social and economic cohesiveness that should exist in an urban city region ... Further, such redevelopment should mean progressive planning, involving on the one hand the community of the area, on the other ... the new settlers.'[46]

Dunstan himself pointed out that the lessons to be learnt from this experience were of fundamental importance to any government involved in residential redevelopment.

> They relate chiefly to communication. It is essential to maintain at every point in the planning process a close involvement with and by the residents ... Their participation and agreement must be secured at each decisive point. If this is not done, the result can be more socially disturbing [and, he might have added, politically

ruinous] than the very situation that redevelopment should be endeavouring to alleviate.[47]

A special committee comprising residents of the area as well as planners and bureaucrats was set up by state cabinet to review the project, develop a detailed programme for the renewal of the area in co-operation with the residents, and ultimately to implement this programme. The large social thoughts written into their approach are unprecedented in the history of urban redevelopment in Australia.

Urban renewal ... not only involves the integration of all the elements which comprise any effectively planned new urban development, but also requires the evaluation of the existing structures ... These are not only physical, e.g. the different uses of the land, the condition of buildings and traffic patterns. Of equal importance are the economics and social characteristics of an area and how these are related to its physical features. It is necessary, e.g. to assess the interconnections between rates and rentals and the condition of buildings and to be aware of what services are housed by these buildings and how the people living in the area assess them. Less tangible but of great significance are the social experiences the area provides—whether it is neighbourly, convenient to friends or relatives, and offers valued services such as a good doctor.

The implications on all these factors of any renewal proposals must be taken into account in developing and evaluating them. The process is therefore a complex one requiring a range of skills and experiences. The adverse consequences of renewal programmes developed without recognition of this complexity, as has occurred in some of the inner suburbs of Melbourne and many overseas cities, are striking evidence of the essential need to attempt to develop any renewal programme within a framework which recognises all the physical, social and economic factors.[48]

The Hackney trauma made one thing certain: nothing of the sort would ever be allowed to happen again in a Dunstan administration. Social democracy would be, and would be seen to be, responsive to those concerned. The 'victims of progress'—those ousted by new highways, new cities, urban renewal—would, in South Australia at least, be consulted at the earliest possible stage and then kept in touch.

Dunstan reversed his own government's policy on urban renewal after public protest. Unsolicited, but acting on good advice, he reversed the previous Liberal government's policy on metropolitan growth which had been written into the 1962 plan. The decision by the government early in 1972 to limit the growth of Adelaide to 1·3 million people, and to make this practical by building a new town at Monarto (fifty miles east of Adelaide) to cater for growth beyond that, is a major breakthrough in attitudes to metropolitan growth. It was the first commitment of this kind by any Australian government, state or federal. Since December 1972 the new federal Labor government has committed itself to planned decentralization and has been generous with federal financial support for Monarto. But the Murray New Town Act passed by the South Australian parliament in 1972 was the first departure by any state government from the 'acceptance of present trends' line of thinking embodied in the statutory plans prepared for each Australian capital in the fifties and sixties.

Meanwhile, as happened twenty years ago when it built the country's first 'new town' at Elizabeth, the South Australian Housing Trust is continuing the planned decentralization policy that it has espoused since 1950, this time south of the city on land it purchased in the fifties (at Noarlunga, now the fastest-growing district of metropolitan Adelaide).

Means have already been established to encourage a two-way flow of information and ideas between the public and the planners—people can drop in on the planners to contribute ideas, get information and examine plans in preparation; the planners have already held a series of meetings in the Noarlunga district; the formation of informal community groups has been encouraged, to consider specific problems (facilities for youth, environmental issues); and the planners have maintained contact with students and staff of the local high school and with planning students at Adelaide University and the Institute of Technology. This is a new development in the planning process in Australia. Previously citizens have only been allowed to experience the process of formal objections to a nearly finalized plan. By contrast, in the case of Noarlunga, meetings between planners and public preceded the start of physical planning. 'Participation' at Noarlunga could be cynically described as laying a foundation so that those who complain in the future can be told, 'Your opportunity to complain was in the past.' Three hundred came to the first meeting, more like forty to other meetings. And the planners are understandably nervous at the possibility of public disapproval of their medium-density housing experiments. Will they demand 65-foot frontages and no 'substandard substitutes', as past history suggests Australians are conditioned to expect? (Only the trendy artistic and professional elite enjoys medium-density living in Paddington and Carlton, and they are not the SAHT's clients.)

That remains to be seen. Other aspects of the new centre look promising. The location, twenty miles due south of Adelaide, has all the positive environmental attractions that Elizabeth lacked. It is less than a mile from the Onkaparinga Estuary where the SPA is purchasing land for an 880-acre district park, and it is within easy reach of beach and hills. Like Elizabeth it is adjacent to a railway line and has the dual advantages of being separate from but rapidly connected with the old city. Employment promises to be somewhat less industrial and more diversified than at Elizabeth and, because the SAHT's housing programme will provide 30 per cent of the district's population increase the trust will be able to co-ordinate the location and timing of a significant part of the population with the early growth of the centre and avoid some of the difficulties of the pioneering period of new cities.

The importance of consulting with citizens about changes in their city was again impressed on the government in matters relating to the character and development of the City of Adelaide (the city square mile, and the mainly residential area across the river in North Adelaide). In 1965 H. C. Bubb became city engineer and later 'town planner' of the City of Adelaide. Like Jensen he favoured high-density living and hoped to replace much of the run-down terrace housing in the city with high-rise development. Bubb's main concern was to build up the tax base of the City of Adelaide. Rates in Adelaide are based on rental values of properties. Therefore he set out to promote redevelopment at high densities to get higher rents on sites and collect higher rates. Applications for permission to renovate or destroy and rebuild the small cottages scattered around the city square mile were refused. Instead they were allowed to deteriorate beyond a 'state fit for human habitation' and were then legally resumed and demolished by the council. Thus over the space of a few years several hundred small cottages disappeared, replaced temporarily by car parks.

There was not much that the poor, inarticulate and powerless residents of the inner city could do about this. But when intentions were announced to bulldoze a residential section of North Adelaide that housed some of the state's most prestigious, wealthy and educated citizens to make way for a shopping/high-rise/parking complex, the local indignation led to the formation of the North Adelaide Residents' Association, which then set about reforming the Adelaide City Council itself.

This was done by electing sympathetic representatives from the North Adelaide ward to the council and persuading a few more councillors to their cause, including the new lord mayor. These activists not only managed to stop the bulldozer in North Adelaide but also persuaded the council to put city development under interim development control. (Historically the council has always had sufficient influence, usually through its connections in the upper house, to get itself excluded from the provisions of all planning acts. This applied to the 1967 act, but it was written into that act that if the council chose to, it could apply to the premier to adopt interim development control.)

This it did in 1972, though rather than be placed under the control of the SPA, which this entailed, the mayor asked Dunstan to delegate authority back to the council. Dunstan refused, but it was agreed to set up a City of Adelaide development committee of seven members, four to be government appointees. The upper house amended this to three, with three city councillors, and the lord mayor as chairman. The government appointees were Hugh Stretton, academic and author, R. D. Bakewell, head of the Premier's Department, and Newell Platten, architect and planner. The council's representatives were J. Roche, multi-millionaire, manager of the Adelaide Development Company and owner of forty acres of land in the city and more along the hills' face, R. Bowen, director of L. J. Hooker, and J. Chappel, architect and small landowner in the city.

The council appointed consultants (Sydney-based Urban Systems Pty Ltd) to draw up a master plan for the city, and appointed its own 'client committee' to instruct them. The client committee was in practice the tough-minded town clerk who disapproved of public participation and open (to the press) planning and fought with the consultants monthly on the issue. Their report was submitted in September 1974. It recommends replacement of the present regime of very discretionary planning that describes rather than measures performance requirements (a system that works well under its present enlightened administrators but didn't work too well before that) with a more rigid regulatory code. The trouble with defining such a code though is that in allotting certain areas for certain sorts of development *every* property owner in that area can then claim maximum expectation and hence compensation for that land should the government or the SAHT want to acquire it. Leaving such decisions to discretion on each occasion avoids the expensive compensation problem but makes the planning more vulnerable to the vicissitudes of political change.

The Urban Systems report also recommends that, to maintain a social mix in the city, 10 per cent of its housing ought to be public housing. Well before this the SAHT had begun building new terrace and old-folk's housing in the city and it has begun a programme of buying existing housing in the city and old inner suburbs as part of a long-term policy of holding a 'class share' of inner locations for low-income tenants. (There are also new arrangements for the welfare agencies to get their clients into trust houses and these take as many as half of each week's vacancies. Also a programme has begun to buy old city boarding-houses to conserve cheap beds for solitaries and transients there.)

Unions traditionally have not involved themselves in matters other than wages and conditions in Australia. But in the past few years there have been some important exceptions. In Sydney the now famous (or notorious, depending on whose side you're on) Jack Mundey and his builders' labourers have imposed over forty green bans on development projects since 1971 which residents' groups and environmental activists have thought undesirable. Less well known but no less effective have been the activities in Adelaide of the Plumbers and Gasfitters Union providing further evidence of community distrust of leaving planning to the 'experts'.

Their first activity was on the issue of the demolition of the 130-year-old Australia and New Zealand Bank in the centre of the city in 1971. They could not stop it being knocked down but they did inform the developer, Mainline Corporation, which had the option on the site and planned to replace the bank with a speculative office tower, that no plumbing would be installed in that tower if it went up. This step was taken after widespread community opposition (led by professional aesthetes) had been expressed to the destruction of this beautiful old building. Eventually the state government intervened to resolve the conflict by purchasing Mainline's option, for $700 000.

Since then, other bans have been imposed, all at the request of residents affected by proposed development projects, and most of which have concerned the preservation of open spaces (in suburbs which don't have much), from encroachment by office towers (in Unley), supermarkets, (in Highbury) and factories (in Norwood). Bob Giles, the union's state secretary, is the inspiration behind these actions. Like Jack Mundey he grew up in the bush, left school early and joined the union, and became a full-time union official ten years ago in his late twenties. His interest in environmental problems began in the early sixties with a concern about street lighting in his neighbourhood, and has developed, through reading he did when associated with the Town and Country Planning Association, into an original and thoughtful environmental and political philosophy. A member of no party but a communist with a small 'c', Giles's profound dislike of bourgeois society and his concern for ecological problems has led to bans on a proposed restaurant on the hills' face and a gambling casino at Wallaroo. He acknowledges that a minority of the union understands what he is saying but he sees his role, and that of the union, primarily as an educator, especially of the future generation. Only as a last resort does his union impose bans, an action that he confesses is not perfectly democratic—but then, neither is Australian society.

It has been clear for some time that planning cannot succeed unless it has the human as well as the material resources for its execution. There are two crucial components of the 'human resources' problem. Above all else perhaps we need political commitment by the states' and nation's rulers to the concepts and practices of planning. *Nothing* can be achieved without their co-operation and active support. If nothing else, the history of these past seventy years has taught us that. But we also need a community aware of and willing to participate in the issues, debates and decisions, and a political process whereby they can. So there is a need for *redistribution of power*, not just of resources.

One of the preconditions for future innovation and change is that political structures must be 'open'. Adelaide's have been at two main points. The state Labor government has been responsive, though it remains to be seen how far this 'revolution' will go beyond rhetoric and good intentions. Also the Adelaide City Council has been vulnerable to public protest and involvement. Perhaps, too, Adelaide has been receptive to pressures for change because of the imaginative and respectable leadership of the academic, author and activist Hugh Stretton. He has been on the board of the SAHT since 1970 and played an important part in the Hackney and City of Adelaide reforms and the Noarlunga innovations.

With a responsive government operating in what resembles a small 'city-state' environment, Adelaide's activists have achieved changes not only in planning policies but in the nature of the planning process, which now incorporates citizen involvement in its early stages. But Adelaide has been unique in its combination of people, opportunities and events, beginning in the late fifties with Hart's public education efforts, helped on the way by the provocative MATS plan, and culminating in the early seventies with imaginative leadership, an aroused populace and a responsive government.

To make democracy work in the world and on the time-scale of today, 'special burdens' must be carried, not only by 'highest elected officials' but by citizens also. By and large these burdens have no place at present in the political philosophies of Western nations, but they are beginning to flourish in Adelaide. That, however, is no cause for complacency, for that was also the situation in 1920. At that time property owners had little difficulty in defeating radical planning proposals, which they saw as a direct threat to the bases of their wealth. Since then, a changing pattern of interests among some sections of the business and property-owning communities, involving environmental considerations (for example in Rymill's opposition to MATS) as well as recognition that profits can still be made under the umbrella of state developmental planning (for example the favourable attitudes of V. E. Jennings and G. J. Dusseldorp, two of the largest developers in the country, to land nationalization), has contributed just as much to the recent good changes of opinion as have the rebellious feelings of 'the people'.

Neo-capitalism is alive and well and merely adjusting the interests of Jennings and Dusseldorp to make them both now in favour of nationalizing land. This is clearly not in the interest of pure land speculators. But this changing set of interests within the capitalist class creates a situation which an alert grass-roots movement may well be able to manipulate to their own advantage, as has been the case in Adelaide, to introduce a more radical style and conception of city planning involving a new emphasis on community welfare, social equity, and protection of the environment.

But much of what is good about planning in Adelaide now is the result and responsibility of a few intelligent individuals in positions of power and/or influence, in the Labor Party, in state departments and utilities. As Louis XIV recognized (*après moi, le déluge*), this arrangement does not guarantee that present policies will be continued if the current men of power and goodwill lose the former, or the latter. Moreover recent achievements have still largely been generated by manipulating *physical* planning, by employing nice anti-freeway and anti-high-rise consultants in place of the nasty traffic engineers. No structures have been established through which planning might become a process. It is still essentially a physical, land-use affair.

Adelaide still needs a metropolitan government and a policy committee with planning powers and considerable influence over areas like education, health services, industrial location, transport, pollution control. It needs a clear statement of objectives both in total or mean form (high employment, rising average incomes) and in distributional form (more equal access to hospitals, schools, housing), and regular published figures monitoring progress towards these objectives. The policy committee would appraise progress and formulate urban development policies, showing their implications for all services (not only the land-use planners), and it would publicly advocate the action required of state government, private developers, public utilities and other outside bodies. Finally, there should be some means for relating this metropolitan planning process to regional or state-wide planning. So far, none of this is happening.

7

Melbourne: Capitalism, Crude and Uncivilized

> Under the present capitalist system such meagre planning as
> has been attempted has been frustrated at every level by
> private ownership . . . and by the influence of such owners on
> public authorities at all levels—by speculation and profiteer-
> ing by property owners and by corruption of public officers
> and politicians in connection with them.
>
> R. and M. Crow 1969[1]

> The national hobby of land speculation must be controlled
> if land use is to be controlled and planning ideals realised.
> This is no longer a radical dream, except in Australia.
>
> N. Clerehan 1972[2]

Property and Class Power, State Power and City Planning

Marxists have criticized industrial society for converting mediaeval
concepts of property, regarded as claims to a benefit of some kind,
into capitalist concepts of property, regarded as the exclusive and
unlimited possession of things that give power over the labour of
others. But many have failed to notice that under social democratic
governments property is again changing its character. Access to
housing, retirement pensions, education, medical care—needs which
used to constitute good reasons why people sought property—now
depend increasingly, in 'welfare states', on rights assured and distributed by communal action in ways that differ from those governing
transactions in the open market.

Ownership of land, which was simplified during the nineteenth
century into something close to unlimited personal possession, is
again becoming an increasingly complex, communally regulated
bundle of rights—rights to occupy, to develop for various purposes,
to lease, sell or inherit, pay taxes at differing rates, secure capital
gains, vote in elections, and so on. It is no longer possible to understand what is happening in urban, industrial, bureaucratic societies

without careful study of these new forms of property or rights.[3] These developments are creating new forms of power—powers such as those of planners who regulate land uses and development rights or of housing authorities looking after the poor. These powers cannot be adequately explained in traditional Marxist terms, but new forms of oppression arise from the use of them. For example many contemporary injustices are due to the exclusion of minorities from rights accorded by the state to majorities through social services originally introduced by social democrats. Other injustices grow from the social values of the new technocrats who wield state power through welfare agencies like housing commissions and development agencies like planning authorities. Still other injustices result from the possibilities for corruption inherent in these new powers, for example the opportunities for those involved in planning decisions at state and local level to use their foreknowledge to engage in land speculation,[4] and their vulnerability to bribery by property owners with interests in particular zoning decisions.

Post-war planning problems in Melbourne stem partly from the enduring political power of property owners—exercised formally through parliament and informally through personal connections between businessmen, bureaucrats and politicians—but also from the use, and abuse, of the new state powers exercised by technical experts and bureaucrats. The enduring influence of the older property-power nexus was evident in the defeat by the Legislative Council of the Greater Melbourne Bill in 1951. Opponents of the bill included urban and rural property owners like pastoralist and company director Sir William Angliss, founder and chairman of Olympic Tyre and Rubber Company Sir Frank Beaurepaire, Australian Mutual Provident Society director Sir Frank Clarke, and Sirs George Lansell and Arthur Warner, each directors of numerous companies. They argued that the government had no mandate for 'this revolutionary proposal' and that a Greater Melbourne council would be 'a sort of socialist octopus—whose chief disadvantage will be its intense centralisation'.[5] Their influence on urban problems is evident in the unlimited growth of the central city, the decision to make Westernport Victoria's 'Ruhr', the proposals to allocate $1400 million for freeway construction, and the neglect of social and welfare services in the 'deprived' western suburbs.

Their power is not the only determinant of the nature and direction of urban development, nor does it provide an adequate explanation of all urban inequalities. But in previous accounts of the process of urban development the question of power has been ignored. For example the first extensive account of urban growth in an Australian city, by the Urban Research Unit, *Urban Development in Melbourne* (1973), identifies five main 'actors' in the process but does not probe the class bias of that process by locating the five actors in the class structure and assessing which has most power. In their account, developers and residents are given equal weight and there is no suggestion of the manipulative powers of large landowners and speculators. Their profit-motivated interest in urban growth has been disastrous for aesthetic planning and egalitarian considerations. But the state power exercised by technocrats has been equally disastrous in different ways. Witness the redevelopment policies of the Victorian Housing Commission or the freeway proposals of the *Melbourne Transportation Study*, produced by a committee of engineers. What follows then is a closer look at the origins and outcomes of some of these planning problems. But first an outline history of statutory planning since 1944, its limitations, and the potential for corruption inherent in and associated with such planning in a capitalist society in which ownership of land has become one of the most fruitful sources of wealth.

Post-war Politics and Statutory Planning

The chronic instability of Victorian politics up to 1955 was outlined in chapter 3. This was one reason why so little was achieved in city planning despite the many probing inquiries into the problems. In the immediate post-war decade, from the passing of the first town planning act in 1944 to the preparation of the plan for Melbourne by the Board of Works (MMBW) in 1954, there were ten governments in which every coalition was tried with the exception of a Labor and a conservative Liberal government. Within that unstable situation the prospects for purposeful city planning in the immediate post-war period looked dim. They did not improve in 1955 when the long reign of the Liberal Party under Henry Bolte began.

Bolte had never lived in the city until he entered parliament at the age of thirty-nine. He 'made no contributions to party philosophy and was little concerned with social welfare or with the implications of urban development. He was, after all, a country member. Not raising his eyes above the narrow gamut of his rural preoccupations he dealt with practically no other matters except finance . . . He started as he finished, a Victorian chauvinist.'[6] He was, as his original backers had believed, 'a very talented small-town horsetrader who would repay their patronage by keeping a conservative government in power and allowing them and their friends to develop their business interests with a minimum of government disturbance.'[7] Neither Bolte's ready accessibility to business leaders nor the Liberal Party's responsiveness to its big business backers were conducive to a radical, equity-orientated style of city planning; nor were the economic objectives of the post-war period. Bolte's priorities were never in doubt: 'We are concerned about water pollution, but it is not as important as a $100m.

industry . . . Pollution of minds is a more important problem than air or water pollution'.[8]

Victoria in the Bolte era provides a classic example of the development in Western economies which has been called 'neo-capitalism', the unification of business with administration and politics and the management of the state's political and administrative apparatus in the interests of business and industry. Given their view of the existing economic system, it is easy to understand why governments in Western industrialized countries should wish to help business in every way, yet do not feel that this entails any degree of bias towards particular classes or interests. For if the 'national interest' is inextricably bound up with the fortunes of capitalist enterprise, apparent partiality towards it is not really partiality at all.

In post-war Victoria these links between business, government and administration were both formal and informal. They were informally sustained by Bolte's personal circle of friends and backers—company directors and financial figures like Sirs Reginald Ansett, Cecil Looker, Charles McGrath, Thomas Ramsay, Maurice Nathan and Ian Potter —who sometimes toured Europe in the company of Bolte seeking to attract overseas capital to invest in Victoria.

Formal or institutionalized examples of the influence of businessmen on public policy-making bodies are numerous. Victoria's fourth university committee had a majority of business interests and was chaired by Sir Thomas Ramsay. The State Electricity Commission is run by three commissioners, T. P. Scott (retired general manager of National Mutual Life Association), Sir Roger Darvall (former general manager of ANZ Bank Ltd and director of BHP Co. Ltd) and a civil engineer. The Melbourne Underground Rail Loop Authority is headed by R. Roscoe, merchant banker, director of Chase-NBA Group Ltd. Its other members include T. P. Scott, W. H. B. Daddo (deputy chairman of Repco Ltd—manufacturer of automobile components), K. A. Allen (president of the Melbourne Chamber of Commerce), Councillor C. I. Beaurepaire (director Olympic Tyre and Rubber Co. Pty Ltd, Olympic Consolidated Industries Ltd, Olympic General Products Pty Ltd), G. F. W. Brown (chairman Victorian Railways, director Rocla Industries Ltd) and Robin Boyd, who was replaced on his death by Bill Gibbs (general manager of GMH Aust. Ltd) who recently has been appointed to head the Victorian Railways.

It may be that businessmen who enter the state system may not think of themselves as representatives of business in general or even less of their own firms or industries in particular. But businessmen involved in government or administration are not very likely to find much merit in policies that appear to run counter to what they conceive to be the interests of business, much less to make themselves the advocates of such policies, since they are almost by definition likely to believe such policies to be inimical to the 'national interest'. This chapter illustrates their influence on urban development and urban planning problems.

Partly in response to commonwealth initiatives, and partly in belated response to the movement for town planning which had existed since World War I, Victoria passed its first planning legislation in 1944. The Town and Country Planning Act empowered municipalities to regulate their land uses and created the Town and Country Planning Board (TCPB) to advise the minister for local government on planning matters. The failure of most municipalities to use these powers necessitated stronger state initiative. Thus the Town and Country Planning Act of 1949 appointed the MMBW to prepare a planning scheme for the metropolitan area. The completed scheme was published in 1954, approved by the MMBW and put into effect as an interim development order in 1955, and placed on public exhibition so that objectors could object. Four thousand did, and the determination of their objections was not completed till 1958. The plan's main objectives were summarized in a later assessment: to accommodate an expected future population of 2·5 million; to control, but not necessarily halt, outward expansion by a rural zone; to encourage the growth of district centres of shops and offices in the suburbs; to encourage redevelopment of the inner suburbs; to improve relationship of residence and work-place; and to provide an effective highway system.[9]

As planning schemes go, this was a cautious one, reflecting the political sensitivity of the issue. It was a 'trend plan'—that is, a plan that started with projections of current situations into the future and attempted to harmonize public and private development with these trends. Such planning assumes that many factors are fixed and not ranges of alternative figures within which particular choices are partly or wholly matters of policy judgement. The plan for Melbourne made no attempt to restructure metropolitan development. Rather, development trends evident at the time were used as the guide to the allocation of future urban zonings. No limit was put on the city's ultimate population size but, at the time, the plan was considered adequate for the likely growth demands of at least thirty years. In the few areas where the scheme was intended to counter existing trends or encourage new forms of development, it did not succeed. The attempt to check the decline of population in the inner areas by comprehensive redevelopment has not stopped the decline in population of those areas. There has been no public development of district centres to ease pressure on the central area, and almost no co-ordination of the private retail dispersal that did occur. The eventual location of these shopping centres usually required a variation to the zoning proposals of the 1954 plan, indicating the inability of statutory planning schemes to sponsor development directly.

The planners' aim to improve the home/work relationship did not materialize, though substantial areas in the south and east were reserved for industrial purposes and plenty of industry has since located there. But overall the length of the journey to work has increased.[10] For unrestricted development does not wait for the tardy processes of statutory planning to catch up with it. The 1954 plan's underestimation of the rate of growth and areas needed to accommodate it was recognized by the board in its 1958 report, *The Problems of Urban Expansion in the Melbourne Metropolitan Area*, which recommended immediate release of further zoned areas. In 1962 a report was prepared setting out additional zonings for another 250 000 people within the planning area. In 1967 the zoned area was extended up to the 320 square miles sought in 1962, and the 1954 scheme, so modified, came into effect as the approved planning scheme in 1968.

Meanwhile new moves were afoot, related to the old problem of the need for more co-ordination between the public utilities and the planning authority. The MMBW had 'no official links, and imperfect working links, with the other utilities and departments. So railways, trams, buses, power, gas, education, housing, hospitals, harbours and industrial promotion all studied their independent crystal balls and planned their works ahead into the different metropolitan futures they saw there.'[11] It became apparent in the early sixties not only that planning for a population in excess of 2·5 million would be needed but also that some reassessment of overall goals might be necessary. Accordingly in 1966 the minister for local government called for a general review of the planning of the metropolis. In letters to the TCPB, the MMBW, and the Town and Country Planning Association, he asked them to consider the most desirable shape and nature of the urban community of Melbourne in the future, the most suitable method of planning and regulating the future growth of the metropolis, and the most suitable authority or authorities to carry out such planning and supervision.

As suggested by the title *Organisation for Strategic Planning*, the TCPB report concentrated less on the desirable shape of the future metropolis than on defining the critical issues of planning policy and the most suitable authority to formulate and carry out that policy. It argued that planning must be a state responsibility and that the government should not yield these responsibilities to any separately elected body, for such a body 'would be competing with state parliament itself'. It therefore recommended a new state planning authority, or reconstituted TCPB, plus a council for the co-ordination of regional planning. On the shape of the future metropolis this report was brief but adventurous. It recommended linear growth by corridors of metropolitan towns, thus implicitly rejecting the principles of the new MMBW plan. The TCPB report was based on the belief that governments should not force citizens into settlements of unwelcome shape or density. But its authors did hope to direct growth into three radial corridors of metro-towns, and warned that such a plan could be a 'speculators' guide' and would need to be accompanied by some action to restrain the price of new corridor land and compel its development without speculative withholding. But any of the methods for doing this are anathema to Victorian freeholders and likely to be killed at birth by the Liberal and Country Party majority in state parliament. And without such action, any plan that tries to reserve land on the perimeter for open space and rural conservation can do more harm than good, chiefly by creating an artificial land shortage that forces up the price of available land.

Compared to the TCPB's report, that of the MMBW, *The Future Growth of Melbourne* (1967), gave much more consideration to the shape of Melbourne. It examined the same three basic patterns— growth corridors, controlled outward growth, and satellite cities— and came up with recommendations for a mix of these: corridor growth, with some limited satellite city growth in the north and west to 'balance' development of the metropolitan area, and some 'filling in' and 'filling out'. The report favoured low-density expansion into the countryside, but thought there could be medium- and high-density redevelopment of most of the pre-1929 metropolis, to include 300 000 additional jobs there and residence for 500 000 people on 8000 acres at a net density of 130–160 people per acre.

The chief protagonist of the board's 'balanced growth' plan at a forum held after the release of the two reports in September 1967, was Sir Bernard Evans, who at the time held the two key positions of chairman of the Melbourne City Council Building and Town Planning Committee and vice-chairman of the MMBW Planning and Highways Committee. He had strong reasons for supporting a radial corridor plan. Himself a resident of the wealthy eastern suburb of Toorak, he started from the premise that Melbourne's growth hitherto had been lop-sidedly to the east and south and argued the MMBW's case for a 'balanced' Melbourne. By this he meant that there should be planned development to the north and west so that the central business district would be centred in the metropolis. He pointed out that it was reasonably developed for trading, and best use could be made of it by western development aided by the new Lower Yarra Crossing (Westgate Bridge).[12]

In the survey and analysis accompanying its 1954 plan the MMBW had written,

In the west . . . the country is flat, windswept and barren. The soil heavy and tenacious, the rainfall low and generally the area is more suited for industrial than residential use. The north, while more attractive than the west, has not the same appeal as the east and south. It is not surprising, therefore, that . . . two-thirds of the population increase has settled in the eastern and southern districts. This trend expresses a strong desire which cannot be ignored.[13]

Yet little more than a decade later the MMBW itself, with its planning committee under Evans's leadership not only 'ignored' these factors in its planning but did not even mention its own earlier analysis or explain why it no longer operated or was no longer important.

How did the 1967–71 MMBW-Evans radial corridor plan to the west and north come to overthrow the whole direction of 1954 MMBW planning? What sections stand to gain by an intensive subsidized drive to develop an urban corridor due west to Melton or satellites at Melton or Sunbury? Firstly and obviously, developers and would-be developers who own land in this direction and expect to profit from the plan. Evans had interests in land west at Altona. Secondly there is a specialized need by established manufacturers or potential manufacturers in the west to attract top executives and technical staff to work in their plants. Ever-increasing commuting distances and deteriorating transport however have meant an increasing impediment to the movement of executive and higher-skilled workforce to the west. Remedies advanced do not contemplate this elite actually coming to live among the low-paid migrant industrial workers. The industrialists envisage relief coming from two directions —from the Westgate Bridge speeding travel time from east to west and from some little separated 'Tooraks' at Hoppers Crossing, Werribee, Melton or Sunbury. As C. A. Wilson, general manager of the Lower Yarra Crossing Authority explained to the 'Deprived West' Seminar in May 1972,

> Industry in the west will be far more accessible from the southeast. This can be expected to provide a much greater potential labour force pool, with a wider range of skills. This will encourage a more diverse range of industry in the west, and accelerate industrial development which, despite cheaper land prices, has been deterred by the inattractive labour force situation.[14]

On the form of authority best suited for metropolitan planning the MMBW, like the TCPB, nominated itself for the job, but conceded that specialized authorities for the satellites and redevelopment areas would be needed. The immediate result of these two reports was the Town and Country Planning (Amendment) Act 1968, compromising between each set of recommendations. The bill had four main objectives, the last of which was the most important: to provide a tribunal to hear and decide town planning appeals, to make better provisions for co-operation between local councils on planning schemes involving more than one council area and to provide for the establishment of a state planning council and for the extension of the metropolitan area. The area administered by the MMBW was trebled and the board was made the responsible authority for planning this area, but it was brought more tightly under the control of the minister. The TCPB, the State Planning Council and state cabinet deal with strategic planning, regional planning is carried out by authorities set up for the purpose, and local government handles local planning.

In Adelaide the planners had to work hard educating the public to demand more and better planning through political channels. Victorians were not as pampered by their planners and not much interest was expressed in their policies till the late sixties when rapid growth of the single-centred city was creating problems obvious to many laymen. By then, those who expressed an interest were dissatisfied with the planners' efforts. In February 1972 the MMBW arranged the first public discussion of its revamped plan, *Planning Policies for the Melbourne Region*, published in 1971. The public was charged $2 a ticket to participate. They complained at the plan for a future city of 5 million people and criticized it as a 'first generation plan'—an elaborate but unsatisfactory pattern of land-use restrictions, red, pink and green areas on a map that can always be changed by someone who makes enough noise. They also abused planners for failing to tackle the problem of land speculation.[15]

By late 1972 radical alternatives were being proposed by concerned groups of citizens at the hearing of objections into the planning scheme. The president of the Town and Country Planning Association (R. A. Gardner) argued that Melbourne should develop in a 76-mile linear corridor stretching from the city to Trafalgar in Gippsland. The 6-mile-wide corridor could house 2·3 million extra people that the board expects Melbourne to have by 1997. A super-freeway would run down the centre alongside 125 mph trains. A joint submission by the Victorian Chapter of the Royal Australian Institute of Architects and the Royal Australian Planning Institute criticized the absence of maximum population levels, considering the idea of indefinite growth of the Melbourne Metropolitan area ('Melbourne Unlimited', as an *Age* editorial referred to it on 20 February 1973) as unacceptable. The institutes claimed that the present plan failed to compare alternatives or to present a rational argument to support its strategies and that its policies concentrated on physical aspects of planning and did not take social planning and its costs and benefits into account.[16] These formal objections to a formal plan illustrate only the tip of an iceberg. Since 1968 public opposition to many aspects of government policy in relation to the city (freeways, high-rise public housing, terrace demolition, overbuilding of the central business district, and environmental pollution) has been gathering momentum and forcing changes on a reluctant government. A more vigilant press, reinforced by a more concerned public, has detailed some of the questionable dealings which appear to be inseparable from the statutory planning process.

In October 1972, following reports in the *Age* on land transactions totalling $350 000 by the chairman of the MMBW, implying misuse of information gained through his position as a local councillor and member of the MMBW, a board of inquiry was appointed to look into these dealings.[17] The inquiry found no culpable conduct. But in 1973 alerted journalists noted further matters for concern. In February of that year a company of which one of the chairmen of the Town Planning Appeals Tribunal and his wife were sole directors and shareholders was reported to have made over $700 000 on a city property sale. The deal went through after the company had lodged an objection to plans for the $19 million redevelopment scheme of the Nauruan government. The grounds of the objection made it impossible for the Nauruan government to proceed unless it purchased the land owned by the company.[18]

In the same year the MMBW announced that it would ask the state government to slow down Melbourne's growth. This happened after it had heard all of the 'objections in principle' to the 1971 scheme, most of which were opposed to unlimited metropolitan growth. This tardiness was not surprising, though, given that for fifteen years under Premier Bolte the state's watchword had been growth of industry and population. In making this statement, the MMBW's chief planner explained that restraints on growth would require a firm government planning policy direction. In the past, overall restraint of metro-politan growth has been regarded as beyond the scope of land-use planning, but by 1973 it was emerging as a

> desirable objective ... Planning has been administered as a check-and-balance system, whereby the public interest, as interpreted by the planning authorities, has been used as a restraint on the operations of the self-interested participants in the urban property market ... From rather tentative beginnings planning has become part of the apparatus of urban government with increasing (but cautious) legislative backing from the State. But the effectiveness of planning remains dependent on the degree of political support for its various objectives.[19]

That, historically, has been Melbourne's problem. It has proved very difficult for the planning authorities to restrain the operations of 'the self-interested participants in the urban property market'. The ideology of the developer is one of straight-forward profit maximizing, and where the constraints applied by planning authorities increase his costs without offering a complementary increase in selling price, he will try to avoid them. He can do this by either operating only where they do not apply, by resorting to the statutory procedures open to him to appeal against them, by taking some form of political action, or acting in some less socially acceptable way. This does not make developers peculiar in a capitalist economy. Planning authorities have tried to regulate their behavior to more socially responsible ends. But their success has been minimal because their aims must be backed by concrete political support, and this is unlikely when the philosophy of the dominant political party respects and defends the right of the individual to do what he likes with his own property.

This conflict between the best planning intentions and the harshest political and economic realities is illustrated in more detail in the next section, in the overdevelopment of the city centre, and the plans to industrialize Westernport and to build $1400 million worth of freeways across the metropolis.

Freeways

Writers of the Left assume, almost to a man, that freeways are a conspiracy of the Right. Thus I. Illich argues that

> highways, like other institutions of the right, exist for the sake of a product. Auto manufacturers ... produce simultaneously both cars and the demand for cars. They also produce the demand for multi-lane highways, bridges and oil fields. The private car is the focus of a cluster of right wing institutions. The high cost of each element is dictated by the elaboration of the basic product, and to sell the basic product is to 'hook' society on the entire package.[20]

This simple argument overlooks the role of the car as an extender of opportunities to travel, visit friends, escape into the peace of the bush and to save time which can be used for other, more creative activities than travelling. The Illich argument (which is typical of most writers of the Left who nevertheless nearly all drive cars) also makes one very large assertion, that car owners (four out of five Australian households) are simpletons seduced by filthy capitalists into buying cars they do not really want. It follows from Illich's argument that transportation planning which allocates most of its funds to freeways is a huge capitalist conspiracy and that consumer demand for more roads is completely unjustifiable. He would therefore be inclined to see, in the appearance of anti-freeway pressure groups in Australian cities in the last few years, the beginnings of or foundations for an anti-capitalist revolution. He would be wrong. The recent rebellious reactions of 'the people'—in reality some small but effective pressure groups—against freeways, environmental pollution, high-rise redevelopment, are not signs that capitalism will soon need an undertaker. Those residents' action groups who have taken up arms against urban inequalities have done so in an effort to be the civilizers, not the grave-diggers, of capitalism. They are concerned to point out the injustices of a transportation policy devoted to freeways, in that such a policy discriminates against those who do not and can not own cars: the young, the old, the handicapped, the very poor, housewives and so on. They are increasingly concerned about environmental and resource problems associated with the private car, and in making these important points, noisily and publicly, they have provided an essential counterbalance to the engineers who dominated the original formulation of transportation policy in the sixties.

The preparation of the Melbourne Transportation Study (MTS) was a more or less independent event in the development of metropolitan planning. It was prepared under the supervision of the Metropolitan Transportation Committee (MTC), established in 1963 by legislation to advise the government on the planning, development, co-ordination, control and improvement of Melbourne's transport facilities. The composition of the MTC, like that of the steering committee that guided the Adelaide MATS plan, was dominated by engineers. An American consulting firm comprising predominantly engineers was hired, and the resulting proposals were very similar to those of MATS. Of a total proposed expenditure of $2616 million, $1675 million was to build 307 miles of metropolitan freeways and a further $546 million for highways, totalling $2221 million on roads, and leaving only $255 million for public transport.

Volume 3 of the MTS states that the plan should be a 'demand plan'. To the committee the question of the accumulation of all the individual consumer demands of all the individual car owners added up inescapably not only to a freeway system of several hundred miles but to a system which funnelled traffic right into the centre of the city. The plan 'forecast' the necessity of all-day parking in the city and calculated 'balancing' the supply to the demand, block by block. To make this workable, a ring freeway in a tight loop around the central business district—which would destroy thousands of inner suburban houses—was 'necessary' to avoid 'permanent peak-hour traffic chaos'.

The methodology of the predictive aspects of the MTS is trend planning, which is in a sense non-planning, a product of *laissez-faire* policies which cater for the rich and the strong and ignore the poor and the weak. Car manufacturers and oil companies, and finance and hire purchase companies have fourteen full-time paid lobbyists in Canberra protecting their interests. Car owners and drivers have influential state motor organizations, in Victoria the Royal Automobile Club of Victoria, looking after them. Those without cars are unorganized and unrepresented. Yet one of the stated objectives of the MTS is 'to maintain a proper balance between public and private transport'. To achieve 'balance', a much greater investment would have to be made in public than in private transport. But the study proposed six-and-a-half times more spending on freeways than on public transport. The MTS must be explained in terms of the ideology of the 'technical experts' responsible for it and the political arena in which it was decided to undertake such a study. Liberal politicians have always been receptive to car, oil and steel manufacturers.

Public reaction to the study was similar to that aroused by MATS in Adelaide. Those organizations with a vested interest in the car culture (from manufacturers to consumers) or who stood to gain in other ways from increased road expenditure, like the Melbourne City Council, and engineers with their technical approach to the issue, all supported the proposals. The Royal Automobile Club journal issued an eight-page report praising freeways on the grounds of increased safety and reduced travel time. There was no mention of their environmental and social impact. Sir Bernard Evans defended the MTS in the face of growing public opposition in 1971. He addressed the MMBW planning and highways committee on the eastern leg of the ring freeway,

> Your committee and the Board's engineers have been working on this project for almost eight years. We have spent $1.5 million on acquiring properties and having consultants and engineers work on the project—the whole thing is ready to go ... [but] all sorts of people are crawling out of the woodwork to criticise the scheme unnecessarily.[21]

But the financial and engineering criteria expressed by Evans and used by the engineers of the MMBW and Country Roads Board did not impress some sections of the public. Opposition appeared in articles from some churches, inner suburban residents' associations, the Town and Country Planning Association and finally from public transport users' very own pressure group, the Commuters Campaign. These diverse groups were not united on the degree to which freeways were a bad thing. Some groups objected to *any* freeways, others wanted routes more carefully chosen to minimize social, community and environmental destruction; still others wanted a transport policy of *genuine balance* between public and private modes. Most agreed that the inner-city freeway system, which would involve destruction of eight acres of city parkland and a hundred trees, must not be built. A fast and efficient public transport system would keep the city alive. Government response was slow. In July 1971 the minister for public transport emphasized that government action depended on public demand: 'If such demands are not made funds go elsewhere'. He argued that while car owners readily provided funds for road building, there was no public transport users' association to express their needs. 'Only through positive demands will the government stop neglecting public transport. In part this is already taking place and it is encouraging when organisations throughout the community . . . take the unprecedented step of demanding better public transport.'[22] In August 1971 the cost of the proposed freeway system leaped to $3000 million. The Commuters Campaign followed this announcement with a protest against the social and financial costs of the plan, criticizing its 'misallocation of limited public resources'. They recommended bigger car parks at local railway stations, a complete overhaul and upgrading of public transport and a re-examination by the MTC of the basis of the 'demand' for people's travelling habits. The secretary of the campaign wrote to the press expressing support for the new Liberal premier Dick Hamer

> in his abhorrence of the network of freeways near the inner areas and trust [that] his view prevails over those who would otherwise give credence to the idea that the state government is more closely attuned to the interests of the petrol companies, metal and car manufacturing corporations and highway construction bureaucracy rather than the interests of the community.[23]

Public transport users, though, were not the only source of community opposition. Residents from those areas directly threatened by freeway construction, particularly the educated and articulate members of the inner and southeastern suburbs, were vocal. The United Freeway Action Group, the Carlton Association and the Committee for Urban Action (a coalition of inner-suburban action groups) each distributed well-argued literature and campaigned for public transport. Strong opposition was voiced by residents of the wealthier eastern suburbs affected by the proposed eastern leg of the city ring road. Responding to this pressure from a Liberal voting area the government decided in October 1971 to scrap the eastern leg of the ring route, and Hamer ordered the TCPB to examine the project from 'angles other than traffic engineering'. The *Age* described this major switch in approach as 'a major defeat for the M.M.B.W. and its chairman, who were ardent supporters of the scheme.'[24]

Subsequent reports from the TCPB, the Town and Country Planning Association, the Country Roads Board and the Committee for Urban Action all condemned the proposed freeway system and in December 1972 Hamer announced that the proposed network would be halved by scrapping 150 miles through built-up suburban areas. Three months later, just two months before the state elections, and

in the context of the new federal Labor government's expressed
hostility to funding state urban freeways, the premier issued a statement on the Melbourne freeway network. Freeways would not be
built in inner areas where their construction would involve substantial loss of established housing and disruption of existing communities.
This victory for grass-roots political action suggests that for reasons
of survival and self-preservation both capitalism and bureaucracy, in
certain circumstances, are flexible.

City Centre and City Council

In 1898 Beatrice and Sidney Webb described the Melbourne City
Council (MCC) as

> a most 'respectable' body of wealthy men; three or four being
> contractors, others interested in real estate, others were leading
> solicitors and merchants ... there are no 'parties' in the council
> and not a suspicion of philanthropic sentiment: they are there in
> the main to improve the value of city property by economical and
> wise corporate action and indirectly to provide clean and well-
> lighted streets for the mass of the citizens.[25]

Nothing much has changed in the seventy-odd years since that observation was made. A more recent observer has labelled the council
'a cosy collection of club-land cronies'.[26]

The MCC has done little to ensure that the city is developed in an
egalitarian manner. It has allowed land and office speculation and
development to override planning considerations, favoured high-rise
redevelopment of inner areas under its jurisdiction at the expense of
low-income terrace-house dwellers, supported the MTC's freeway
plans because they would enhance the prosperity of the interests in
the central business district (neglecting again the destruction of inner-
city housing and local communities), failed to respond to the pleas
of citizens' organizations like the Town and Country Planning Association for a city on a human scale, and neglected the interests of the
residents of the city area while pampering those engaged in profiting
from the property boom. The franchise, structure and powers of the
council explain this bias.

The area under the MCC's jurisdiction is divided into eleven wards,
each of which elects three councillors. The six non-residential wards
of the central business district elect eighteen (absentee rate-paying
businessmen) councillors, who call themselves the Civic Group and
claim to be 'above' party politics. In effect they form the non-Labor
party which automatically gains a majority on a council which
exercises considerable powers free of interference from any state
government, for the Melbourne and Geelong Corporation Act of 1938
exempted the MCC from the operation of the Local Government Act,

which means that the council cannot be reformed without its own consent. Thus 29 per cent of the voters (in the six central business district wards) elect half the councillors while the remaining 71 per cent in the other five wards elect the rest. Labor is further disadvantaged because the council and its committees sit during the day and the occupations of the Labor councillors (mainly school-teachers and public servants) prevent them from getting the necessary time off to devote to council business and to sit on the important committees like the building and planning committee.

What effect has this council had on city development? Who has gained most from the kind of development that has taken place? Would this have been very different under a Labor administration? Some recent figures indicate who is investing in and profiting from land and office speculation, and those collecting these profits have not collected any of the costs of this overgrowth of the city. In 1971 it was announced, in celebratory tones, that land values in the central business district had increased 800 per cent in three years, that sites were now selling at $100 per square foot and that in the past twelve months twenty-six permits had been issued for multi-storey office and shop complexes.[27] In June 1973 the MCC released a report which revealed that land prices throughout the city had doubled since 1968 and that 'the great economic expansion' had 'forced out activities not capable of meeting rising land values and rents'.[28] Earlier in the year the council's Strategy Plan consultants (Interplan, an American firm with local architect Peter McIntyre as a director) issued a draft report which forecast a $33 million over-supply of office space by 1975. R. P. McIntyre, president of the Royal Australian Institute of Architects, is also associated with R. P. McIntyre Developments, a company which owns shares in Asmic Pty Ltd, a large property owner and speculator in the central business district which made $5 million profits between 1970 and 1972 on three city properties.[29]

These speculative activities have been encouraged by the MCC partly because each new building increases council revenue. For example the 26-storey AMP tower pays $165 000 in yearly rates, whereas the buildings that had formerly occupied the site returned only one-ninth of this. No Australian researcher has provided the equivalent for our cities of Oliver Marriot's excellent book on London, *The Property Boom* (1967), but the identity of our property investors is no mystery.

> Life offices are by far the biggest investors in city land. The property boom has drawn huge sums of insurance money from the share market into the hands of real estate agents . . . When looked at in terms of city land ownership in Melbourne the big life offices rank as follows: A.M.P., National Mutual, Colonial Mutual Life, and T. & G. Insurance.[30]

Australia's largest institution, the Australian Mutual Provident Society, added $81·4 million of property to its assets in 1971, real estate then absorbing 28 per cent of AMP investment funds. National Mutual put 29 per cent of its funds into real estate, raising the group's total property holding to $168·5 million.[31]

While the insurance and development companies have clearly gained from the property boom, planning authorities have worried about how to cope with the added strain to the road and transport system this boom in speculative office building created. E. D. Borrie's *Report on a Planning Scheme for the Central Business Area of Melbourne* (1964) pointed to the declining employment in the central business district in manufacturing (reduced by 46 per cent) and warehousing (34 per cent) since 1951 and the increase in office employment. The MTS showed that 31·5 per cent of the 154 000 workers in the central business district travelled by private car. Melbourne's transport services have encountered the same disabilities as those experienced in Sydney. The journey to work is getting longer and more expensive and the loss on the railways for 1972–3 was forecast at $37 million. Yet, as in Sydney, there has been no suggestion that growth in the central area should be limited or redistributed.

When in 1970 the MMBW proposed a planning amendment to reduce allowable plot ratios in the city, it was 'greeted with horror by city developers and architects'.[32] The Institute of Architects, the Melbourne Chamber of Commerce and city development firms attacked the MMBW. One city real estate agent and property developer argued that if the amendment was adopted 'it would reduce the size of buildings by ten to fifteen per cent, effectively writing off $100 million in city values.' Within three days property owners had formed the Building Owners and Managers Association 'to represent the owners and managers in the many spheres where collective thought and action would be beneficial to their interests'.[33] Their first task was to investigate the question of plot ratios in the city. The MMBW did not pursue its amendment.

Property owners form a small cohesive group which is able to act swiftly and decisively when its interests are threatened. The majority of city users—non-executive office workers, shop assistants, cleaners, shoppers—have no say in the pattern of development. The council is run by and for businessmen and property owners for whom the city itself is a commodity to be transacted in the market-place. City users gain little from these transactions—there are more shops, yet less choice of goods since only certain kinds of high-turnover retailing can survive rising rents. Taller buildings shoulder to shoulder cut out sunlight from people using the streets. Old pubs where beer was cheap and workers could drink in working clothes give way to trendy taverns where beer is expensive and dress 'respectable'. Open spaces and free meeting-places dwindle and people's attitudes about the city change. It is no longer a place to stroll, browse, shop, meet friends and take in diverse colours, shapes, smells and sounds. It is a place to flee from as soon as consumer transactions are complete. The sounds and smells are no longer pleasurable but oppressive and harmful. Given a choice, citizens have preferred more trees and fewer cars in their cities. Melbourne's citizens have not been asked. They do not compete, as pluralist democratic theory would have it, on equal terms with property owners for a say in city development. The latter monopolize the MCC and state parliament and nullify the efforts of the more progressive liberal views of Premier Hamer, whose statements on the future of the city are well intentioned and more in tune with recent changes in public awareness and opinion.

As minister for local government in 1971 Hamer wrote to the MCC asking it to set up a city planning department to make a blueprint for the central city area. He proposed

> a colourful living city with a wide variety of activity working twenty-four hours a day: maximum separation of pedestrian and vehicle traffic: a car parking policy related to public transport into and within the city and to circulation of pedestrians and cars: and an overall strategy to provide for harmonised retail, commercial and office functions as well as theatres, hotels and restaurants. The last thing we want is a city of concrete canyons hedged with mono-lithic office buildings and populated only in office hours.[34]

But the resistance with which the MCC is able to confront the best of planning intentions was indicated in 1972 when it was revealed that the Council had been withholding for more than a year a report it had commissioned in 1970 on city residential planning. Town planning consultants Loder and Bayly submitted their report to the council in June 1971. It recommended that building in 'conservation areas' should be limited to two storeys, that the council should set up a special demonstration project for a planned environment, and that large-scale demolition was unnecessary. It also warned of the threat posed by uncontrolled rising car ownership levels to the amenity of the inner suburbs. All efforts to have the document released for public discussion were rejected by the council's building and planning committee.[35]

But we need to ask whether the development of the city would have been very different if the Labor Party had been running the council. Two matters suggest that it would not have. The first is the example of the Labor Party in office in New South Wales, both in state government and on the Sydney City Council. The next chapter argues that the experience of Labor in Sydney was just as disastrous for the social and distributional consequences of urban growth as the rule of the crude Victorian capitalists. And this for two reasons. Firstly Labor failed to understand the equity or distributional implications of single-centred, unrestricted city growth. Labor also shared with the Liberal Party the belief that economic growth was the most important social goal and regarded the property boom as an exhilarating manifestation of that growth. There is no evidence that the Victorian branch of the Labor Party was more enlightened in this respect than the New South Wales branch. For when criticism began to emerge in Melbourne of freeways, destruction of the environment, dehumanizing of the city, it came not from the ALP but from small groups of residents in areas specifically threatened by proposed freeways, pipelines, refineries, and destruction of inner-city terrace housing by the Victorian Housing Commission's high-rise, high-density redevelopment programme.

Inner Suburbs and Housing Commission

Seldom has a public authority become as controversial as the Victorian Housing Commission (VHC) has over recent years. The VHC, brought into existence towards the end of the depression years by the missionary zeal of Christian social reformers, began with the objective of 'slum abolition'. But in the post-war years slum abolition became 'slum clearance' which became in the 1960s 'block demolition' and included pulling down structurally sound hotels, shops, houses and factories. These operations were never properly planned, even from the point of view of physical co-ordination of other basic services like roads, schools, kindergartens, community centres, welfare services and shops. So two main criticisms of the VHC unfolded. It was depriving low-income groups of housing and an environment they did not want to leave, providing unacceptably rigid and unsatisfactory rehousing at high densities, and in the process more affluent workers were gaining from the own-your-own flats that private enterprise built on very cheaply acquired clearance sites, two-thirds monopolized by one firm.[36]

The high-rise redevelopment policy of the VHC did generate many problems. It was expensive, block clearance was an inefficient way of dealing with poor housing, was disruptive of local communities and was of dubious benefit in alleviating the social problems that the commission was originally created to solve. At first glance, then, this issue would appear to fall into that class of problem in which 'the enemy' is the public authority and the problem is caused by the technical incompetence and impoverished social values of the technocrats. That is part but not the whole of the story in Victoria.

Why had the policy been embarked on in the first place? Which sections of the community stood to gain and in what ways from high-rise inner suburban redevelopment?

H. W. Viney argued in 1967 that the idea of the inner core with net density patterns of 200 people to the acre arose

> from the pressures of ten years ago to retain a central business area to protect the heavy investment in the golden mile and arrest the movement out to the suburbs. Despite the continuing movement outwards property values in the city have not fallen and the business community whose very survival depends upon an accurate analysis of trends and patterns of behaviour have quickly adjusted to the situation by the movement of Bourke street to the Suburbs.[37]

In the fifties and early sixties the commercial interests of the 'golden mile' did favour higher densities to bring back the middle class to the inner areas, boost city revenues and revive a declining central business district—the conventional wisdom about inner-city redevelopment in the United States in the fifties. It would be fair to speculate that these commercial interests exerted strong pressure on official policies for the inner areas, urging the use of VHC slum-acquisition powers to create higher densities. This was confirmed by the current president of the Town and Country Planning Association who in the fifties was executive director of the City Development Association. The CDA was formed in the early fifties. Its members included the leading banks, insurance companies and property owners of the golden mile. Their aim was to promote the city centre and to campaign for policies to cater for its needs. The CDA urged the changing of permissible building heights from the limit of 132 feet to the present plot-ratio formula, the establishment of a traffic engineering department in the city council, a freeway programme, and more city-centre car parks. They were also concerned about residential redevelopment of inner areas, lamenting the loss of population and recommending government acquisition of large tracts of these areas for redevelopment, for middle- to high-income earners, by private enterprise.[38] The CDA was a predecessor of the Civic Affairs Division of the Chamber of Commerce which was formed in 1969 to investigate the problems of the inner suburbs.

As Viney perceived in 1967, there has been a change of attitude by big corporations, and a policy of redevelopment at lower densities has gained ground in recent years. The big retailers pioneered the exodus from the city to the suburban centres. The banks and company head offices are more concerned with ease of access by car for their important customers than with attracting throngs of people to the city. The oil, steel, rubber, spare parts and motor industries all support a radial freeway system centering on the city, but high densities in the inner areas would overtax the capacity of the freeway system. So the new policy of these diverse business groups supports freeways right into the city, massive increase in parking there, and redevelopment at lower densities in the inner areas. This new approach is outlined in a booklet by the Melbourne Chamber of Commerce, *A Proposal for the Establishment of a Civic Affairs Division within the Chamber to Deal with the Problems of Inner Area Redevelopment.* Listed among the initial supporters of this move were Imperial Chemical Industries, Ansett, Dunlop, Mobil Oil, Jennings, Hooker, McEwans, Waltons, the National Bank and the ANZ Bank.[39] Their group formed to tackle the redevelopment problems of 'the half dozen suburbs largely in a state of decay' around the city. They advocated increased parking in the city, an inner-ring road and 'an extension of residential development schemes based on private enterprise and government acquisition and clearing of land'.

Like any other activity of government, urban planning can be good, bad or indifferent, and it can distribute very different costs and advantages to different people. A policy of comprehensive redevelopment is a good illustration of that generalization. As practised in Victoria, that policy distributed immeasurable social and economic costs to the original communities who were displaced and relocated, social and psychological costs to those rehoused in the VHC's high-rise family flats, yet great advantages to those developers (especially A. V. Jennings) who built on cheaply acquired clearance sites, and to those middle-income earners who were able to buy these flats.

Since 1968 a well-organized protest movement has made it difficult for the VHC to clear areas with the speed necessary to keep up with production from its concrete building components factory. Building unions have placed bans on the clearance of areas for redevelopment by private enterprise. Inner-suburban councils began to refuse to co-operate with the commission. And local residents have resisted efforts by the VHC to clear their areas. In May 1971 the VHC announced that it was phasing out high-rise redevelopment. It is a sobering thought for the residents' action groups who believed that they alone were responsible, by their persistent protests, for the change in official redevelopment policy, that that change coincided with the changing interests of some of the state's powerful commercial and industrial corporations.

The inner suburbs are still a battleground, but the problem has changed somewhat. In the urban environment there is no escape from the rigours of scarcity. As the populations of Sydney and Melbourne each approach three million their richer citizens increasingly value the amenity and accessibility of the inner suburbs. They simply use the market system to satisfy these preferences, raising property values in inner areas and forcing poorer tenants out as landlords see opportunities for higher profits from renovating and renting or selling to these higher income groups. They have formed associations like the Carlton Association to protect their new areas from 'undesirable intrusions' like freeways, Housing Commission high-rise housing, developers' bulldozers, and so on. Their conservation activities are timely and appropriate, and the new social mix has contributed economically and culturally to the inner areas. But the trend of displacement of poorer residents is disturbing and calls for some government action to preserve a 'class share' of housing in these areas, as the Housing Trust has been doing in Adelaide and the federal government in the Glebe in Sydney. The alternative is cities that in the future will be even more segregated than they are now, with the poor living at great distances from the city centre in amenityless western suburbs, powerless and neglected.

The Deprived West: Locational Inequality

The city of Melbourne was located where

> forty miles of basalt and delta plain met forty miles of valleyed hills and sandy beaches. As the poor spread thickly over the plain and the rich thinly over the hills and coast, neither love nor justice ever had much chance. Realism won without trying. To its topography Melbourne may owe a good deal of its past and present unkindness to its poor ... It has had the ill-effect of segregating the city severely.[40]

This segregation and inadequate provision of health, educational and other social services by a state Liberal government which gets no votes from the west is the most recent issue to gain publicity in Melbourne planning. For in this 'twilight zone' extending west from Footscray to Werribee and Melton and south to Altona and Williamstown live upwards of 300 000 people. Twenty per cent of them are younger than ten, 40 per cent under twenty. It is a significantly younger population than any other area of the metropolis. It is also a strongly migrant population.[41] In parts of West Sunshine and St Albans migrants outnumber Australians six to four. In the suburban western sector of the 1966 census 36·1 per cent of residents were migrants. In the whole of Melbourne the migrant population is 9·9 per cent.

It is a population lacking workers in professional, managerial and administrative jobs. People in these occupations work but do not live in the west, as the 1966 census indicated. Kew, five miles east of the city, was then home for 317 doctors and dentists. Footscray, the same distance west of the city, could attract only 37 doctors. In all the western suburbs—Altona, Footscray, Keilor, Melton, Sunshine, Werribee and Williamstown—only 100 resident doctors and dentists were to be found. In Camberwell, six miles east of the city, with one-third the population of the western suburbs, there were 422 doctors in 1966. In the case of teachers the same pattern is evident. Kew had 763 resident teachers, Camberwell 2089, and the whole of the west 1661. Two of every three teachers working in the west live elsewhere. The principal of Altona High School noted in a report to the local council that teachers obviously preferred to spend up to 100 minutes twice a day in travelling rather than live in or near Altona.[42]

> Down the map of this metropolis of two and a half millions the founders of its latest university drew one straightish line. Children born west of it have a chance in twenty-two of reaching a university. East of it, a chance in seven. Where 50,000 families occupy one block of five rich suburbs, their children have a chance in four, and the other three chances—of success without education—are fairly comfortable too.[43]

In November 1970 the member for Melbourne West in the Legislative Council argued that the west was the victim of political discrimination. He said the reason for poor education facilities was that the area was represented in parliament by the Labor Party. He listed education, hospitals, rail services, pollution and an inadequate police force as the worst of the west's problems.

The first stirrings of consciousness from the people in the area came in May 1972 when five hundred of them attended a seminar called 'The Deprived West' organized by the Sunshine Lions Club. Papers were given to the seminar on hospital care, primary and secondary and preschool facilities in the west. A Sunshine councillor pointed out that the industrial output of the western suburbs in 1967–8 was $846 million, twice that of the next highest region. But the value of new houses and flats for the same period was only $23 million, the lowest for the Melbourne region. Later in the year the president of the Australian Council of Trade Unions Bob Hawke called for the formation of a joint committee to control industrial development in the west. He argued at a seminar on industry, transport and employment in the western suburbs that industry had been allowed to prosper in the west regardless of the social and economic needs of the people and that the environment had been 'systematically eroded and demolished through the mistakes of industry and pollution connected with economic activity'.[44]

The Lower Yarra Crossing Authority (LYCA), the Western Industries Association and the 1971 MMBW Regional Policies Plan all advocate subsidized development of land in the west. They have not advocated subsidies for better community services. The LYCA, a group of companies and individuals formed to build the Westgate Bridge (to improve travel time from places of residence in the east to places of work in the west and from the west to the central business district) and backed by government-guaranteed loans, 'naturally supports any new development in the western area which will enhance its own financial stability. Every effort must be made to develop large residential communities that will depend on the crossing for their link with the CBD'.[45] The LYCA is naturally anxious for Westgate Bridge tolls to pay for the bridge construction. Powerful interests support the promotion of industrial development and growth in the west—the central business district interests behind the 'balanced growth' 1971 corridor plan of the MMBW and industrialists concerned to utilize the cheap land in the west ($12 000 per acre compared with $40 000–$90 000 in Notting Hill and Waverley in the southeast) and therefore to attract an abundant labour supply close at hand. 'Industrial growth of the type envisaged requires people; and already many of the industrialists in the area complain that there are shortages in the supply of local skilled and unskilled labour'. Hanover Holdings therefore were proposing the development of 700 acres at Altona (400 acres of which is Crown land that they are requesting the government to release to them) 'to provide the population that would in turn encourage further industrial development in the Laverton Altona sector'.[46] Of the 2000 acres of industry at Altona, some two-thirds is owned by large industrial corporations—Dow Chemicals, British Petroleum, Colonial Sugar Refining.

With those kinds of pressure to 'develop' the west, and their influence on the state Liberal government, it is not surprising that the western suburbs decided to form into a region to bypass the state government for direct aid from Canberra. Eight western councils formed an interim committee in January 1973 to approach the federal government for $200–$500 million for education, hospitals, parkland, drainage, sewerage and better public transport. Their aim is to bring facilities in the west up to the standards of the eastern and southeastern suburbs.

Under the new federal Labor government it is likely that they will succeed. The federal minister for urban and regional development Tom Uren referred to the west as a 'wasteland'—'There is squalor, educational and social starvation'—and announced sweeping changes to be made. 'If Cabinet approves the concept then the western suburbs of Melbourne—probably the largest deprived area in Australia—will have remodelled schools, new hospitals, controlled industry, sewerage, play grounds and a host of other amenities this area has lacked for years'.[47]

These were not hollow promises. Twelve months later through its area improvement programme the federal government had allocated $3 million to the western region of Melbourne and $5 million to Sydney's western suburbs. These regionally based programmes of assistance to local councils in areas deficient in urban services and facilities are not given for specific projects. Rather the local communities are asked to identify their needs and can obtain grants for projects ranging from studies that will further urban and environmental planning to acquisition of parklands, open space, landscaping, drainage programmes, public education activities on urban issues. Projects funded under the scheme so far include $20 000 to the Sunshine Council for the employment of two migrant officers to work with migrant and community groups, $100 000 to the Altona Council for the development of local beaches, and in Sydney $60 000 for the establishment of three community television centres. The long-term aim of the area improvement programme is to encourage the regions to present their own cases to various public authorities in the three different levels of government, based on their own agreed priorities and strategies.

Industrialization of Westernport

The Bolte government's decision to promote industrial development in Westernport Bay was made, the agreement with British Petroleum signed, and the enabling bill rushed through parliament without time for it even to be read by members. The fate of Westernport indicates the priorities of the Bolte government's decisions concerning the state's development, and the interests behind it. The history of land transactions in the area over the past ten years provides one of the best available examples of the way statutory planning powers are exploited, and the objectives undermined, both by individuals using positions of influence within councils and by big companies using political leverage at state government level. Space forbids detailed elaboration here, but interested readers should turn to appendix 1.

The agreement between the state government and British Petroleum was followed by one with Esso-Hematite (Westernport Development Act 1967) and another with BHP subsidiary Lysaght's (Westernport Steelworks Act 1970). In March 1969 the Westernport Regional Planning Authority (WRPA) was formed to prepare and implement a planning scheme for the area. It comprises two councillors from each of the six shires in the region and a full-time director. Members of the authority are not restricted from voting on matters affecting their own property, and meetings are not open to the public. No provision was made for representation of residents, or for qualified architects, biologists or conservationists. There is no provision for representation for future residents—workers and unions. Conflicts between the WRPA's professional officers and the councillors are settled by councillors making their decisions 'in camera'.

Of the twelve councillors on the authority in 1971, at least six were known to be involved in land dealings in the area. Other landholders included BHP, Esso, BP, and the Gas and Fuel Corporation. BHP and East Coast Development Pty Ltd also owned land on French Island, in the middle of the bay. In 1970 the authority received a commissioned report from R. M. Buchanan, a Sydney chemist, on the feasibility of using French Island for most of the industry to be located at Westernport. Buchanan was a director of East Coast Development Pty Ltd. Also in 1970 the WRPA received a draft report prepared by Plant Location International on the feasibility of rezoning certain areas at Westernport for industrial use. This report, which recommended the rezoning of thousands of acres of rural land around the bay, was referred to the authority's Industrial Development Advisory Committee whose members included BHP, BP, Esso, Lysaght's, Nylex Corporation, Dowd Associates and Commonwealth Industrial Gases. They all had financial interests in land and industrial activities in the area. Heavy speculation followed for the next six months before the director reported to the authority on the findings of the consultants.

By then, local residents were objecting to the fact that the future of the peninsula was in the hands of American consultants, the WHPA and a combine of industrial speculators and that they were not able to see the consultants' reports.[48] The Save Westernport Coalition (of local and state environmental action groups) did manage to see a copy of the American report, however, and revealed its contents in a pamphlet, *The Shame of Westernport* in July 1971. It concluded that *people* had been ignored in the pages of statistics,

> people are simply 'the labour supply', to be moved as close as possible to the industrial area while simultaneously being robbed of all its recreational possibilities . . . The most urgent study of all —the relationship of the scheme to the welfare of the city—has not even been undertaken . . . It is doubtful if, in recent years, any large city anywhere has been asked to hand over such an enormous recreation area to so few people.

Yet, despite mounting local opposition, the WRPA voted in July 1971 to zone a 5000-acre belt of farmland for industry.

Conservationists, local action groups, some local councillors and over 1400 individuals decided to oppose the rezoning, and the Westernport Peninsula Protection Council raised several thousand dollars for a 'fighting fund'. Yet Bolte still argued that the industrial zone would be 'a big lift for Victoria. I can see it having the biggest tonnage of any port in Australia.'[49] Later that year the government overrode objections by the Hastings Council and granted large rate concessions to the $1000 million Lysaght's steelworks. Such heavy-handed government and WRPA action provoked increasing local protest. A Save Westernport rally attracted 2000 people. The Peninsula Conservation League and the Institute of Landscape Architects called for a freeze on development until an independent review of plans for the heavy industrial complex was carried out, and they submitted a 25-page critique to the WRPA. By August 1972, 28 400 people had signed a petition calling for a freeze on development pending ecological, economic and social surveys. It was not just the nature of the plans for Westernport that angered residents; it was also the planning procedure. Not only was the industrial plan drawn up first with the ecological study to follow at some point in the distant future after the industrialists had taken what they wanted, but also the land-use planning was done in great secrecy, excluding local residents yet including the industrialists.

In February 1973 the state government announced a freeze on the development of heavy industry for two years during a $1 million environmental survey. This decision was made under what many observers regard as a more enlightened premier, Dick Hamer.

> He does not play down the threat that both industrial fumes and industrial wastes are now imposing on the atmosphere and waters in and around Melbourne. He is palpably very concerned about parks, the devastation created by freeways, and the need for more 'lungs' in the ever spreading outer suburbs where Sir Henry was inclined to allow speculators and 'developers' to run riot.[50]

But this decision was more likely influenced by the fact that the popularity of the minister for local government, whose electorate lies on the peninsula, and of the government in general in this usually Liberal-voting area was seen to be somewhat precarious in a pre-election period, rather than by the enlightened views of the party's leader. For those views must contend with the more self-interested views of the financial community which supports the Liberal Party. The extent to which the crude capitalist operations of the past in Victoria can be civilized by one 'enlightened' leader and a host of middle-class conservationists and environmental activists is difficult to assess.

Popular Revolt and Liberal Reform

The tacit Boltean assumption had been that bread, circuses, freeways and large new industries were adequate political baits with which to meet the electoral challenges of the late sixties. That the public did not fully agree is evident in the abundance of citizen's action groups that emerged in the late sixties in opposition to a number of urban planning issues: the VHC's high-rise inner-suburban redevelopment, the social and environmental destruction of the freeway programme, the industrial development of Westernport, the neglect of the western suburbs, other more specific environmental issues and the general encouragement of growth at whatever cost. What are the interests of residents' associations, what methods are open to them, how effective have they been in influencing urban planning policies, and what potential do they have for influencing the future shape of the urban environment?

A survey in 1972 of eleven inner-suburban residents' groups indicated that their members are predominantly middle class and professional and that most organizations are defensive, often narrowly self-interested in their aims,[51] which are usually intended to 'preserve the present character of the area'. Most of the groups were formed in response to threats to their areas from VHC slum reclamation and comprehensive redevelopment, or from the MTS freeway programme. The Carlton Association, formed in 1969, is typical of most of these groups in all but size, being by far the largest with 1200 members. (The next largest, Fitzroy, has only 200 members.) Carlton is an old and picturesque inner suburb, once working class, close to Melbourne University. It is steadily being 'gentrified' by middle-class professionals and groups of university students who appreciate its locational and aesthetic advantages.

The Carlton Association's aims are to promote and develop the social, educational and cultural well-being of the residents of Carlton, to press for the comprehensive planned development of the area, to maintain its historical character and to co-operate with kindred associations when desirable. It has subcommittees dealing with architecture and town planning, community services, education, environment, an underground railway group to prevent any increase in rates for the new underground, a freeway action group to keep the proposed F19 freeway out of Carlton and an urban renewal action group to look into the VHC's plans for Carlton.

Activities of residents' action groups have ranged from publishing and distributing pamphlets outlining and criticizing government policies to public demonstrations, meetings, petitions, protest letters and visits to cabinet ministers, and the enlistment where possible of union co-operation to place bans on certain development projects. All groups have shown great respect for property rights and for respectable democratic procedures. They have not allied themselves with any particular political party. Some have stood and been elected as independents in opposition to the old Labor machine politicians in local councils. Their politics are opportunistic. They form alliances with Liberals, Labor politicians or unions, if this will further their aims.

How successful so far have these diverse issue-oriented groups been in influencing government policy? The case studies discussed in the previous section indicate that they have only been successful in areas where they have directly threatened the political power of the ruling Liberal Party. For example campaigns against VHC redevelopment had little impact until the Chamber of Commerce and other central business district interests decided that it was no longer in their interest to support high-density inner-suburban redevelopment. The affected residents of the inner suburbs, which all return Labor members to parliament could otherwise have gone on complaining, till the whole area had been redeveloped, with no effect. Similarly the freeway programme was first modified in 1971 because opposition had arisen in eastern suburbs like Malvern where the Liberal vote could have been affected, and the freeway programme was only halved a few months before the 1973 elections and after the new Labor federal government had indicated that it would only advance money for public transport policies. The recent freeze on heavy industrial development at Westernport can likewise be seen as a pre-election response to widespread opposition in the usually Liberal-voting electorates on Mornington Peninsula. Environmentalists have been successful in persuading the government to divert its proposed outfall sewer from Carrum (inside Port Phillip Bay) to Cape Schanck (outside the bay), in forcing the oil companies to put their pipeline around the bay instead of under it, and in persuading the government to introduce an environment protection bill creating an environment protection authority in 1971. But seven Liberal cabinet members, all living in bayside electorates, voted against the oil pipeline. After three years in operation and the resignation of several junior members of its staff, the director of the Environment Protection Authority finally resigned in disgust at the political interference that had hindered it in carrying out its duties effectively.

It would seem, then, that whatever Hamer's environmental intentions, the Liberal party and government can stand up to the large corporations only when its own power is directly threatened. Recently the government announced that it would put brakes on the population growth of Melbourne and that plans for a city of five million people were no longer acceptable. Observers have noted with pleasant surprise Hamer's genuine concern about waste disposal, water pollution, freeway destruction of green spaces, old homes and other irreplaceables.

> The new Hamer-Thompson administration is not indifferent to the mass of Melbourne voters who lack powerful industrial companies, stock exchange seats, nation-wide organisations or racing fraternity credentials to support their approaches to Ministers in Spring Street. All this is very new in Victorian politics since the early fifties.[52]

But neither is the Hamer administration indifferent to the powerful industrial companies. They cannot afford to be. One sceptical observer has accurately noted that 'the Victorian government appears to set up departments and authorities at the drop of a hat'.[53] It has yet to be shown that the Liberal Party is willing or indeed able to contravene the wishes of its largest financial supporters. At the moment it seems to be procrastinating with inquiries and surveys to avoid the inevitable confrontation between Hamer's stated ideals and Liberal Party political realities.

But that is not the only conflict of interest involved in the environmental conservation issue. The conflict over the construction of the Newport power station illustrates the point that issues are not always so clear-cut as to be a straightforward battle between 'the people' and 'the filthy capitalists'. Some kinds of conservationism are a civilized adoption for the city as a whole of the standards of tidiness, good house-keeping and aesthetic taste that any good landowner or householder would adopt within his own domain (keeping towers off Black Mountain for instance). But beyond that, conservationism tends to demand *more*, not fewer, economic resources, and must not unthinkingly be equated with anti-growth philosophies. Eliminating pollutants from exhaust fumes *reduces* miles per gallon; the alternative to the Lake Pedder reservoir in Tasmania is *more* expensive water sources; and the alternative to the State Electricity Commission's proposed power station at Newport, just a few miles from the city of Melbourne, is more expensive power generation and more expensive power for the final consumer. In September 1974 the Victorian government confirmed its intention to go ahead with the $145 million project despite a ban by six vital unions on the construction of the station at the mouth of the Yarra. Hamer said that the government was satisfied that Newport would not contribute to pollution around Melbourne. The six unions (the Amalgamated Metal Workers Union, the Building Workers Industrial Union, the Plumbers Union, the Federated Engine Drivers and Firemen's Association, the Electrical Trades Union and the Furnishing Trades Union) and the Australian Conservation Foundation are convinced that the station will dramatically worsen Melbourne's air pollution problems. But their spokesmen admit that the unions are solely concerned with environmental damage. Hamer is concerned that on any other site the cost of the station would rise to $400 million and that electricity users should not have to carry the burden of such additional charges. The station is to burn mainly natural gas piped from Esso-BHP's deposits in Bass Strait. Sir Roger Darvall, one of BHP's directors, is also a commissioner of the State Electricity Commission, so it does appear, to those looking for a conspiracy, that the SEC is run jointly by engineers, whose sense of social responsibility is not all it should be, and agents of capitalism in the guise of commissioners. Again we have an issue that combines all the elements of post-war planning problems: bureaucratic pig-headedness and narrowness of vision, the vested interests of capital, but also the vested interest of 'the people' in the products of state and private capitalism, in this case cheap power.

Rohan Rivett has argued that 'the odds are not so heavily in favour of the moneyed or the ruthless as they have been throughout Melbourne's past ... The battle is going to be far less lop-sided this time than ever before. Because today many citizens have really begun to care.'[54] But caring is not enough. Dissatisfied citizens need resources of various kinds with which to pressure governments. The resources available to residents' groups so far have included the occasional support of strategic unions able to ban undesirable developments; the availability of a whole range of professional skills (legal, architectural, planning) and access to and knowledge of the bureaucracy by these professionals; advocacy journalism like that of Ben Hills and others on the Melbourne *Age*; and increasingly environment-conscious residents and students with flexible time and ideas that have been inventive, resourceful and colourful. But there is potential class conflict within the protest movement between middle-class professionals, who are increasingly taking over the inner suburbs, and the older working-class residents, between owners and tenants in the inner areas, and even, in the case of Newport, between some unions and a majority of workers. Furthermore, deep-seated cultural values present obstacles to change, in particular of attitudes to the institution of private property and to the imperatives of economic growth. These values have only recently begun to be questioned. Premier Hamer has publicly questioned the unlimited growth of Melbourne. But the relatively secure political position of the Liberal Party in Victoria has made it less receptive to change and has forced environmentalists to fight rearguard battles against *faits accomplis*. Their success depends more on the threat they are able to pose in specific cases to Liberal power, which is not always a weapon available to them; on their ability to take over, reform or influence local councils; and on their ability to make so much noise that they persuade the federal government to move in on the issue, as has recently happened with public transport, office building in the central business district, and the deprivation in the western suburbs of urban services and facilities.

Of one thing we can be certain: eight-lane freeways and Westernport-type 'planning' schemes increasingly politicize the community. But although perceptions of urban problems are quickening, so too are the problems.

8

Sydney: Development without Improvement

[The Cumberland County Plan] could certainly have been a
better and more radical plan; but then it would have had
little hope of being carried out under our system of representative government where so many shades of opinion have
their influence on public policy.

D. Winston 1957[1]

Urban Growth and Locational Inequality

Planning can fail for more reasons than the resistance of property
interests and the dominance of the profit motive in a capitalist society.
Sydney's post-war planning failure illustrates two of them—the per-
vasiveness of the 'growth ideology' and the sheer difficulty of devising
methods to cope with the complexities of a large and rapidly expanding metropolis. Part of the latter problem has been the failure by
planners and politicians alike, until very recently, to recognize that
urban development does have significant effects on income distribution, whether deliberate or accidental, and that the process of
indefinite, single-centred growth of cities produces real income transfers from poor to rich, some of which are brought about by the
activities of the public sector.

Most large locational decisions made in a city affect income distribution. As the spatial form of a city is changed—by relocating
housing, transport routes, employment opportunities, sources of
pollution—so also is the price of accessibility, or the cost of proximity
if you live near a polluting industry, for any one household. Decisions
made in the public sector of an urban system can be made with
redistributive effects in mind, for if real income is defined as command
over resources, real income is clearly a function of location and
accessibility to open spaces, health and educational services, shops
and jobs, entertainment and transport facilities. Many of these
resources are located by the public sector, so it is important to
recognize that 'the redistributive aspect of general governmental

functions is far from trivial and increases with city size'.[2] Yet few criteria have been developed for determining the location of public activities. Public finance concepts have been largely spaceless and location theorists have neglected the problem of public facility location.

For twenty years the New South Wales Labor government, a government supposedly concerned with the redistribution of income in the interest of a more egalitarian society, allowed government departments and public utilities to make locational decisions with no thought about, or in ignorance of, their class distributional effects. So while one area of their social policy aimed to improve welfare services for poor inner-city residents, decisions like those to build the eastern suburbs railway (to improve the journey to work for the rich in the east) or the Warringah expressway (to do the same for the rich on the north shore) imposed heavy costs on the inner-city working class. For both these decisions involved destruction of workers' homes close to the city and forced their inhabitants to relocate twenty miles out where they could afford land or qualify for entrance to a Housing Commission estate.

At the first meeting of the Cumberland County Council in November 1945 the Labor minister of local government Joe Cahill stressed an important principle.

> The scheme [for metropolitan Sydney] must be considered as a whole—not a collection of arbitrary prohibitions and restrictions. I stress this because it is the Government's intention that town and country planning shall be democratic and that, under skilled guidance, the people themselves shall join in the planning to the greatest extent possible. We will not have planning imposed from above.[3]

In the words of the premier, W. J. McKell, the most significant feature of his government was its determination to work on the lines of a master plan. There were to be no more 'bits and pieces reforms dictated by the expediency of the moment', no more 'jabs and stabs at public works, all disconnected, often overlapping, never fitting together into any general pattern', no more 'merely haphazard development in industry, in the growth of cities and towns as huge jumbles of confusion.'[4]

McKell had a vision, not unlike that of the federal Labor party at the time, of a better post-war world, an integral part of which involved a social reformist approach to city planning. Slums would be abolished, outer areas would be zoned for residential, commercial and industrial development, land would be preserved or resumed for parks and recreation areas, foreshores protected and sites reserved for public buildings, educational and cultural centres, and legislative authority would at last be given to town planning.[5] Here was a government prepared, or so it seemed, to give to planning the prestige and support without which it could achieve nothing.

Yet twenty years later a Liberal minister for local government and highways, P. H. Morton, addressed the Town Planning Jubilee Conference in Adelaide on the failure of planning.

> One serious failure has been the inability of government and planners to generate public enthusiasm and sympathy for the cause of planning. This is a serious handicap for we live in a democratic state where things can only be done if the people approve. Like other states, New South Wales has encountered problems with cumbersome administrative procedures ... The problem of how to plan efficiently and quickly while still affording sufficient protection to the individual citizen is a very real one. I regard the indifference of some planners to the rights of the individual as another serious failure.[6]

When a Liberal talks about the rights of the individual, he is usually talking about the rights of those who own property to profit from it. When he talks of freedom and democracy and argues that people should be able to do as they want with their own property, this generally means rich people should. But planning regulations do sometimes affect small home owners as well as big property interests, and do sometimes unintentionally cause land prices to rise by creating an artificial shortage that penalizes first home buyers but enriches speculators. And when planning does have this effect, opposition to it cuts across the party-political spectrum and enlists the support of that 75 per cent of the electorate who are, or are becoming, or want to become property owners. This situation may provoke two opposing responses, depending on prevailing social values and the political situation. Planning may be abandoned because it is interfering with market forces, or it may be strengthened by the introduction of mechanisms to allocate social space independently of ordinary market forces—say, by the nationalization of development rights or by betterment or capital gains taxes on land speculators. Morton's explanation of the failure of planning in Sydney is illustrative of the Liberal viewpoint but inaccurate. What is important here is the general consensus that planning had failed.

The Cumberland plan seemed anachronistic and inflexible in the context of Sydney's rapid post-war growth. Admitting this inadequacy, the state government disbanded the original planning authority, the Cumberland County Council, in 1963 and replaced it with a different kind of authority. What then had gone wrong? Unlike the 1954 Melbourne plan and the 1962 Adelaide plan, which were both born into politically hostile worlds and conceived with those constraints in mind, no such obstacles surrounded the birth of the Cumberland plan.

McKell's Labor government viewed town planning as a key to making their post-war world a better place to live in. McKell himself had been personally committed to the planning cause since the slum abolition movement of the thirties.

A. J. Powell has argued that the shortcomings of planning under the Cumberland County Council (CCC) were technical, that planning methods remained static and inflexible.[7] The CCC's chief planner on the other hand believes that its main weakness was the 'lack of direction of planning at government level'—that is a failure in political support.[8] Although Labor governed in New South Wales from 1941 to 1965, its personnel obviously changed in that time. McKell moved out of state politics in 1947 and J. J. Cahill, premier from 1953 to 1959, died at a critical period in the evolution and testing of planning methods and intentions in 1959. But it would be no more enlightening to explain the weaknesses of planning in Sydney in terms of personality changes or technical shortcomings than to see it purely in terms of a capitalist conspiracy.

This chapter explores the role of each of these elements, along with some of the more pervasive and deeply rooted problems of urban, industrial, bureaucratic societies in order to suggest, in the last chapter, what hope there is for future change or improvement. This next section describes the evolution of land-use and transport planning and analyses the failure of efforts to decentralize and to control land prices. The following one looks at two more failures—the overgrowth of the city centre and the planning process at local government level —and the final section deals with some citizens' recent responses to what they consider to be public and private planning failures, and looks at the emergence of new cross-class alliances in a 'popular front' demanding 'grass roots' planning.

Cumberland County Council and Cumberland Plan

The first significant incident in the history of the Cumberland County Council was the insistence by local government interests that they should be given control of metropolitan planning. The Local Government (Town and Country Planning) Amendment Bill introduced in 1945 was primarily concerned with the preparation of a statutory land-use plan for the County of Cumberland, an area of 1750 square miles around Sydney embracing 39 local councils. Its preparation was to be the responsibility of a town and country planning advisory committee, but defenders of local government challenged the committee's role as principal author of the plan. The Local Government Association pressed for the establishment of a second-tier local government body to prepare the plan, and the bill was amended accordingly. The creation of the ten-member CCC (one member from the Sydney City Council and the other nine elected by contituencies of from five to twelve local councils) was indicative of the influence that local government could exert in the Legislative Council.

A number of defects in the legislation were pointed out during the debates, some of which perhaps should have been recognized as salutory warnings. This was particularly true in regard to the effect of planning regulations on land values, the difficulties in ironing out zoning inconsistencies, the problem of financing planning schemes, and the issues of compensation payments and betterment taxes. It was evident to some that neither the government nor the community could afford to finance the kind of schemes envisaged unless drastic alterations were made to the fiscal priorities of the government. Foremost in their minds were probably the costs of slum removal, roadworks and the acquisition of land for public open space and the removal of incompatible land uses.

Some of the reasons for the eventual demise of the CCC can be traced to the original legislation. The metropolitan planning authority, because it was a local government body, had to rely on the support of the minister in its efforts to co-ordinate the activities of other state authorities. But the minister was advised by the planning staff of the Local Government Department and the town and country planning advisory committee, neither of which was on very good terms with the CCC because they had been deprived of fuller planning responsibilities by local government opposition to the original legislation. A further weakness in the CCC was the tendency of councillors to take a parochial rather than metropolitan viewpoint. One Campbelltown councillor who did take the broader view was not re-elected by the councils he represented. Other councillors simply ignored the wishes of the CCC and permitted commercial ribbon development along country road frontages. For although councillors in principle supported the CCC, in practice each council was reluctant to restrain development and resented curbs on possible future growth of their municipalities.

Hence the CCC encountered gradually mounting suspicion from several quarters in its early years, followed eventually by outright hostility. The first adverse reaction came late in 1946 after the CCC had introduced an interim plan. This was a mild form of restraint sufficient only gently to check some of the worst and most obvious excesses of unbridled sprawl, one of which was galloping land subdivision on the fringe of the metropolis. The affected councils began to chafe. However, the first real shock came with the presentation of the Cumberland plan in 1948. It had a green belt the aim of which was correctly interpreted by the affected councils as a permanent check on urban expansion in their areas. They were not pleased. Nor were councils in the established areas unaffected by the green belt, for the plan had boldly designated large tracts, consisting partly of prime building land, as a network of parkland which criss-crossed the metropolitan area.

Though the government had created the CCC, it had not undertaken to underwrite the cost of its planning proposals. To publicly earmark for park purposes such large tracts of land, without knowing how it was to be acquired, was perhaps a mistake. The state government did ultimately agree to help finance the land acquisition programme, but not until three years later, by which time large areas of the proposed park system had been sheared off to placate irate landowners. For just as local councils resented restraint on the development possibilities of their areas, property owners did not accept that what had traditionally been regarded by common consent as a basic freedom could be withdrawn for the benefit of the public interest.

There were other equally grave problems that the CCC had to contend with in the first six years of its existence before the Cumberland plan was finally given legislative authority in 1951, not least of which was the uncertainty surrounding both the acceptance (because of local government hostility) and the financing (because of the federal Liberal government's refusal to assist on the ground that it was not a matter of Commonwealth concern) of the Cumberland plan submitted to the minister in 1948. This uncertainty had several unfortunate results. Firstly, as Winston noted, development in this period, although nominally subject to the interim control powers of the CCC, more often than not had to be allowed to go ahead since there were no funds to pay compensation nor was there any certainty that there ever would be.[9] Secondly the hesitancy with which the state government reacted to submission of the plan in 1948 led to the resignations of most of the experienced staff, who were not replaced. Finally, the years of uncertainty had adversely affected any status that the CCC might have enjoyed in the hierarchy of public authorities concerned with metropolitan development. 'The optimism of the early years was never recovered.'[10]

Nevertheless the planning scheme adopted by the government in 1951 has been described as 'the most definitive expression of a public policy on the form and content of a metropolitan area ever attempted'.[11] Winston summarized its aims as 'co-ordination, consolidation and conservation'. The Cumberland approach could be described as idealistic, compared to the very pragmatic attitudes adopted in the case of Melbourne and Adelaide. Town planning was based on a few broad concepts concerned primarily with the future form and structure of the metropolis. It contained three broad proposals for giving effect to its aims. Firstly, to improve people's journeys to work, a good deal of employment should be decentralized to outer industrial zones, and shopping and office centres in the suburbs. These should be linked by expressways and improved railway networks. Secondly the new centres should become focal points of recognizable districts, separated from each other by open space, and given some sense of identity by local planning schemes. Most importantly the whole metropolis should be enclosed by a green belt. The plan showed a pattern of zoned living areas sufficient to provide for a total population of 2·35–2·4 million, a capacity for increase of 700 000 people. This increase was envisaged as being spread over twenty-five years and was based on the best demographic advice then available.

How effective were the provisions of the plan in achieving its objectives, and how well did it fare in the political arena? Most of the planners' ambitions were frustrated. The prevention of sprawling urban development was probably the most significant achievement of the Cumberland plan in the fifties, although other methods might have achieved a similar result, such as making the availability of services an essential requirement for subdivision. The programme of open space acquisitions, although reduced from its original ambitions because of lack of funds, did preserve some two hundred acres of foreshore lands around the harbour and significant tracts of parklands in the western suburbs, but this did not win popularity with the local councils involved, who resented the loss of ratable land and the prospects of meeting the costs of development and maintenance of the parklands. There was some improvement in the living and working relationship in regard to manufacturing and retailing employment, but there was no restraint on the build-up of employment in central and inner areas, which accounted for 37 per cent and 18 per cent of metropolitan employment in 1966. District centres did develop in accordance with the pattern proposed by the plan, many of them on railway routes, but these centres have been predominantly retail. At best, it can only be said that without county planning the concentration of employment would have been worse than it is.

Two of the most formidable obstacles to the successful implementation of the plan were the expansion of the city centre and the quality and quantity of local government planning. Most local councils were reluctant to complete local planning schemes, preferring to exercise the discretionary control over private developments which was conferred by the County Planning Scheme Ordinance. And under the Labor-controlled Sydney City Council the old city centre continued to grow without limit, increasing traffic problems and land prices.

Although many of the difficulties experienced by the CCC in the fifties were administrative and political, some were undoubtedly due to technical shortcomings in the plan itself. The primary weakness of the plan lay in its underestimation of future population growth and the consequent inadequacy of residential and industrial zoning. Immigration, together with changes in demographic structure and insufficient funds to allow the extension of services into new areas, generated considerable pressure on the limited amounts of land in the living area zones and contributed to rising land prices.

Because of the manner in which the planning scheme had been approached, it was a plan based on assessments of future needs rather than estimates of potential resources. The plan was based on a framework of major public utilities, but very few of the required works were carried out because neither federal nor state or local government has been willing or able to finance long-term planning either from current annual revenue or through loan funds. So little eventuated throughout the fifties or early sixties of the plans for a county road system, electric railway extensions, an overall pattern of county open space, the elimination of slums or satellite towns beyond the green belt. Shortage of funds was not the only reason for the failure of these plans, for none of them was within the direct control of the CCC, which had to rely on the co-operation and goodwill of other government departments and authorities, and this was not usually forthcoming, their attitudes towards the CCC varying from indifference to hostility.

> The railways took no notice at all of the new planners and refused to build their new lines. The Housing Commission defied the zoning —but the plan didn't provide land of the kind the Commission wanted. When the water and sewerage refused to dive under the green belt it was partly because the planners were doing nothing effective to get settlers to jump over it. The damage these utilities did to the plan was helped on by their choice of locations to do it from—they steadily expanded their own offices in the old city centre.[12]

Departments of Transport, Lands, Industrial Development, and the Maritime Services Board consulted or ignored the council as they saw fit. As R. D. Fraser observed, they used the plan to protect their interests when it suited them, but were not prepared to engage in direct encounter to uphold the plan: 'The C.C.C. would find that at the height of a struggle to maintain a proposal a government authority would have surrendered independently to the opponent.'[13]

Ultimately, of course, major issues were determined in cabinet, where the council's views needed the support of the minister for local government. And the minister's views on the issue were shaped by the planning staff of his own department and by consultation with the advisory committee. What strength the CCC had 'stemmed from its role as custodian of the important elements of the Plan, the provisions of which the Minister had the power . . . to change'.[14]

On two particularly important issues during the fifties the minister did choose to exercise this power, thereby creating a rupture between the state government and the CCC which never healed and which contributed to the eventual dissolution of the council in 1963. The first of these was a proposal by Caltex to establish an oil refinery on Kurnell Peninsula, an area zoned as open space. In January 1953 the minister, supported by the advisory committee, overrode the CCC's objections on the grounds that the development was regarded as of great importance to the well-being of the state's economy.

The second issue, one which epitomized the evolving problem of reconciling the decision-making functions of the government, public authorities and the CCC, involved the pressures which began to build up from 1953 onwards for the rezoning of certain parts of the green belt. As a result of the county plan, the amount of land in broad acres that could be acquired cheaply at non-urban values was by 1957 greatly restricted. This had long been a bone of contention between the Housing Commission and the CCC, resulting in 1954 in the release of 10 000 acres from green-belt zoning. From that time on, to preserve and maintain the green belt became the major preoccupation of the council.

Early in 1958 a proposal was put forward by the Housing Commission to establish a satellite town at Minto for 60 000 people. The CCC refused to release the land for urban development on the grounds that the commission should concentrate on vacant areas still within the existing living areas. The commission replied that this land was only in small parcels and that it was too expensive. The issue was referred to the Town and Country Planning Advisory Committee with the request that it recommend to the minister for local government a suitable compromise aimed at meeting the needs of the Housing Commission while preserving the basic intentions of the county plan. Meanwhile the CCC set about an overall review of the green-belt zoning, providing for the release of 11 500 acres, which it submitted to the minister in October 1959. The advisory committee's recommendation for the release of over 30 000 acres was not communicated to the CCC for comment upon likely implications. It was submitted to the minister in December 1959 and his endorsement meant in effect that the advisory committee was the effective county planning authority. At this time the premier, Cahill, died. He had been a staunch supporter of the CCC since its inception. In the resulting reshuffle of portfolios, the ministry of local government went from J. B. Renshaw to P. D. Hills, a former mayor of Sydney not noted for his concern with planning, as Cahill had been. It was unfortunate that at the same time as the plan was under fire from the Housing Commission a swelling band of real estate subdividers and developers began to doubt the ability of the council to continue to protect the green-belt zoning and were taking up options on large tracts of land in the green belt. Also local councillors, property owners and businessmen of the fringe municipalities (Sutherland, Liverpool, Baulkham Hills) were growing increasingly restive about what they felt was the 'stranglehold' the green belt had on the future growth of their districts. This local feeling was impressed upon state members of parliament, who in turn put pressure on the minister for local government. Hills had been hailed as a man of action and gave the impression of wishing to justify his reputation. The long-drawn-out controversy over the green belt gave him an opportunity.

This issue emphasized the administrative weaknesses in the overall planning system (and the dependence of planning on sympathetic politicians like McKell and Cahill). The conclusion was therefore drawn that a body was needed that could deal with government departments and ad hoc authorities on an equal footing and that had positive and direct lines of communication to the minister and hence to cabinet. The State Planning Authority Act of 1963 marked the legislative and political working out of this line of planning thought.

It has often been argued that the green-belt issue caused the downfall of the CCC.[15] It would be more accurate however to regard the green-belt releases as a symptom of more basic problems involving the composition and powers of the CCC. Wedged uneasily between the local and state government hierarchies, it was seen as a rival political body in a contest it had little hope of winning, for 'no state government could be expected to put its central powers into the hands of a crowd of part-time municipal councillors, but the County Council could not do its duty except by usurping some of the government's central political responsibilities'.[16] The state government seemed to want those goods which the planners expressed concern with—from efficiency, order and amenity to slum eradication and improved communities—but it divorced town planning from most economic and social planning, leaving industrial and regional development to a branch of the treasury, and housing and transport to their own autonomous departments.

The CCC never enjoyed much popularity. At various times there had been signs of unrest at the restrictive effects of planning on the land market and at inequities suffered by landowners because of resumptions. In the state election campaign of 1956, town planning and local government emerged as important issues. The Liberal Party promised to abolish the CCC on the grounds that it was a centralization of power detrimental to local government and that it operated against the legitimate interests of private property owners. It was a theme repeated by the Liberal-Country Party coalition in successive election campaigns. The problems raised by the existence of the CCC obviously tried the patience of the minister for local government, Hills. The CCC

was not susceptible to the kind of direction that a minister or government seeks to wield. Its meetings were open and most of its documents were available to the public. It publicised its aims and intentions and, when the occasion demanded, its disagreement with the Minister. All the Minister could do to influence the Council was to suspend or amend its plan by overt public action; he could not *direct* the Council to do anything.[17]

On the other hand, in exercising his power to suspend the plan in cases involving matters of principle, the minister had seriously diminished whatever status the council had held as an authority with powers over metropolitan development. Change was inevitable. But the form of the change was not. That became the subject of intense debate in the early sixties.

As the weaknesses and anomalies of the CCC became more apparent, there were increasingly frequent statements by both parties that metropolitan planning should be the direct responsibility of the state. The premier's 1962 election policy speech foreshadowed the abolition of the CCC and the setting up of a state planning authority whose primary responsibility would be to co-ordinate development programmes of public authorities in the metropolitan area and throughout the state.

State Planning Authority and Sydney Region Outline Plan

The State Planning Authority Act came into effect in 1963 to co-ordinate all aspects of planning by public bodies, under the direction and control of the minister. The most important amendment to the original bill was to increase local government representation on the SPA to five members, creating an authority comprising a full-time chairman and deputy chairman (the former chief planner and chief clerk of the Local Government Department) and ten part-time members—five from local government (the lord mayor of Sydney, two nominees of the Local Government Association and two from the Shires Association), four public utility representatives (the commissioner for main roads, the under-secretary of the Transport Department, the assistant under-secretary of the Local Government Department and the secretary of the Water Board), and the final member selected from a panel of four submitted by the professional institutes (planners, architects, surveyors and engineers). Significantly none of of the 'civilized spenders',[18] housing, health or education, were represented. This indicated the continuing failure of the Labor Party to recognize the distributional importance of decisions made by these authorities. Also the continued separation of urban planning from both regional and economic planning indicated their lack of an overview of the planning process. There was no definition of the SPA's relations with the decentralization and industrial development section of the Premier's Department, and fiscal support for state development and resources planning continued to be directed by the treasury rather than the SPA.

Five years after its foundation the authority produced the *Sydney Region Outline Plan 1970–2000 A.D.*, a broad strategic sketch rather than a statutory plan, reflecting the current American preoccupation with 'goals', 'objectives' and 'flexible strategies' compared with the older British tradition of 'utopian' master plans. Although a Liberal government had won office in 1965, the 1968 plan reveals less subservience to this new political reality than to some of the older ones, like the pressures that celebrated the continued overgrowth of the city centre and the apparently untouchable autonomy of the older state departments and public utilities each with their own separate developmental plans. Plenty of Sydney people, notes Stretton—planners, politicians and others—'like to regard their centralised overgrowth as natural, unavoidable, an international phenomenon'.[19] This celebratory tendency certainly appears with monotonous regularity on page after page of the 1968 plan. Planning of the region, we are told,

> should be directed towards ensuring that, in a world where administration, decision-making, and economic activity are increasingly concentrated in large city complexes operating on a world scale, Sydney shall retain its pre-eminent position as Australia's greatest city, commercial centre and port, and as a city and port of world status and importance.[20]

Bearing in mind the importance of location to the real income of people living in a large city and the constraint of Sydney's 'cruel topography', which provides a strictly limited supply of pleasant land within reasonable reach of the magic of the old city, the most important question to ask of the 1968 plan is how its proposals affect the distribution of wealth in the Sydney region. Does it accentuate, or try to make amends for, existing differences between the rich, nestling around the harbour shores and spread across the good land on its northern and southeastern side, and the poor, stretching across the hot flat western plain and steadily being forced out of the inner suburbs by the recent middle-class influx? Where does it propose to locate the extra 1·75 million people expected in the region in the next thirty years? The diagram illustrating the growth principles shows that development within a forty-mile radius of the city is expected to take a radial corridor pattern, to the west, southwest and northwest. Around Blacktown, Liverpool and Fairfield in the west, on some of the region's most inhospitable land, the plan proposes to accommodate almost half a million people. In the functional language of the plan this looks like a logical piece of urban infilling. The reality is that half a million people must live in areas that suffer from the worst aspects of Sydney's climate, on poor land, with poor existing services. Since the other two growth corridors offer better land, and remembering the way land is distributed in a market city, it is inevitable that only the poor will go west. 'In this corridor, and the inner half of the Campbelltown [southwest] corridor, and the fattening-all-round of the whole western perimeter, the Outline Plan thus accepts a gross increase of segregation without any public expression of regret or misgiving.'[21]

Where a few of the middle class are expected, southwest at Campbelltown, the SPA has spent $10 million acquiring land for a town centre, university, teachers' college, hospital and other public purposes. No such civilities are proposed in the fifty square miles west from Parramatta to Penrith. The plan is long on rhetoric about the need for a new city centre at Parramatta,[22] but short on proposals for diverting investment from the old city centre and expansive on the need to encourage Sydney's 'primacy'. Any diversion of investment from the old centre to the suburbs or new cities, the plan says, 'must be done without prejudicing the role of Sydney as the main commercial centre in Australia and as a commercial and financial centre of increasing world importance'.

Like the Adelaide and Melbourne plans, the Sydney region plan embodied the acceptance-of-present-trends line of thinking, especially in connection with Sydney's unrestricted growth, the physical form of this growth (low-density detached housing), and in its uncritical adoption of freeways as the solution to the urban transport problem. The only clearly defined objective of the plan is the direction and staging of suburban expansion. It pays lip-service to decentralization but proposes no methods of forcing or enticing industry away from Sydney, or offices from its centre. Only 4 of a total of 108 pages are devoted to 'the implementation process', and almost as little space is given to the means for financing the plan, despite acknowledging the impact of land prices on the capital investment needed for adequate servicing. Landowners would, 'under present practice, receive a financial benefit from the zoning of land in the Outline Plan for urban purposes, totalling about $1000 million or more'.[23] The document thus goes on to argue, very tentatively, its boldest proposal, that a charge on the increment in value of 'raw' land 'warrants very serious consideration' as a new source of revenue.

It could be argued that our 'national hobby of land speculation' has been the greatest social disaster and public scandal of the postwar period. Land prices in Sydney have risen dramatically since the war, but particularly over the last five years. In 1970 the average price of a block of land was $7450. By 1972 it was $14 000. In 1974 the average price had reached $20 000, putting it beyond the reach of the poor in general and young couples in particular.[24] The plans themselves have frequently been blamed for this, the Cumberland plan for creating an artificial shortage by imposing the green belt, the 1968 plan for being a 'speculators' guide' by delineating future corridors of urban growth and approximate dates of their release for development, and planning in general for its cumbersome, dilatory procedures. On 12 September 1971 the *Sunday Australian* ran the front-page headline 'Big Developers Bring Off $10 million Land Coup'. The developers, L. J. Hooker Ltd, Stocks and Holdings Ltd, FCA Finance Ltd, and others, explained that they had used the 1968 plan 'as a guide to their successful speculation'. The beneficiaries of rising land prices are a diverse group ranging from the life insurance offices and finance companies to the pensioned couple who would like to sell their half acre to an oil company for a service station or to a flat developer and retire comfortably on the proceeds. As the *Financial Review* perceived in a concerned editorial in 1972,

> almost everyone has been tainted by a self-administered virus of greed fuelled by spiralling land prices which give those who already own property steady capital gains and those who struggle to buy property an even stronger vested interest in ensuring that the spiral will continue. In such a situation, the pressures on both individuals and professional real estate developers to become out-and-out land speculators become intolerably strong.[25]

'Those who already own property' includes 75 per cent of the Australian electorate. In a situation in which they and their families enjoy the appreciation of the capital investment in their own home and land because it is outpacing most other costs and prices, any government is reluctant to make decisive efforts to restrict the potential profits of property ownership. The property-owning electorate as a whole sees itself, or can all too easily be persuaded to see itself, as having a convergence of interest with the big property interests who naturally oppose such efforts.

It was all the more remarkable therefore that the New South Wales Liberal government passed the Land Development Contribution Act in 1970, providing for the collection of 30 per cent of the increase in value of land arising from urban zoning. The minister introducing the bill, P. H. Morton, who has been described as 'a free enterpriser from way back',[26] argued that it was 'not unreasonable that part of the increment in value which arises primarily from the expenditure of public and private funds on essential services should be made available to meet the cost of such services'.[27] This reluctant retreat by a Liberal government from a philosophy that supported almost complete freedom for the individual in respect of his property indicates the unmanageable strains that unrestricted growth had begun to place on public services. But history has shown us that any action that limits the development rights attaching to land sooner or later comes under an unrelenting state of siege. It was not remarkable therefore that the Labor leader of the opposition promised, during a 1973 by-election campaign, to abolish the Land Development Contribution if his party were elected. The Liberal leader then matched this promise and in March 1973 this radical and lucrative revenue source was disposed of.

But the Land Development Contribution Fund had also been accused of contributing to land price inflation because landowners simply passed on the 20 per cent tax to the developers, who passed it on to the final consumers, the home buyers. It does seem from past evidence therefore that efforts to control land prices by various tax devices, whether betterment levies, holding charges on vacant land, or taxes on speculative short-term gains, are counter-productive in that they are passed on to home buyers. Bolder methods are necessary to cope with this problem and a bold federal Labor government is currently experimenting with some. They are discussed in the final chapter.

Decentralization

Decentralization has long been 'everyone's policy but no-one's program'.[28] Like transportation, it has been a volatile political issue heavily influenced by country interests. For the McKell Labor government decentralization had been an essential part of the vision of a better post-war world. Yet when the Cumberland County Council was disbanded in 1963, no positive steps had yet been taken to implement the decentralization policy, and some observers argued that the demise of the CCC was in part at least attributable to this failure to institute policies for growth beyond the green belt. The 1968 plan assumed, rather than planned, that 1 million of the 2·75 million additional people expected in New South Wales by the year 2000 would locate outside the County of Cumberland. There existed no means for ensuring this distribution, and the outline plan suggested none. Why?

There are two reasons for the failure of all governments since 1945 actively to pursue decentralization. The deputy director of the Department of Decentralization and Development, established by the new Liberal government in 1966, expressed one of them in 1971. 'We are out to increase the efficiency of private enterprise and remove inhibitions upon industrial expansion and development generally ... Decentralization can only succeed if we have a sound basis of development here in the metropolitan centre. *Sydney can put on a few more millions*' [my italics].[29] The desirability of continued economic growth in the Sydney region has never been questioned by the Labor or

Liberal Parties. Instead each has tended to compete with the other for the credit of promoting the faster growth rate.

The role of the Country Party and the importance of country interests in state politics provides the second reason for the failure of successive governments to decentralize. The State Development and Country Industries Assistance Act of 1966, which set up the Department of Decentralization and Development, gave the department generous powers and finance to assist industry and local government and the authority to acquire and develop land and construct buildings. Grants and loans totalling $27 million have been made since 1965 to assist over five hundred country industries estimated to employ about ten thousand workers. The department produced a *Report on Selective Decentralisation* in 1969 which criticized the policy of dispersed decentralization and recommended that the government select particular regional centres for concentrated development. The report did not nominate the centres but said that the north coast, northern tablelands, central west, south coast and tablelands, and the Riverina—that is, almost everywhere in the state apart from the far west—suggested themselves as potentially capable of sustaining growth centres. Despite this deliberate cautiousness, political controversy was quick to follow. 'Even if it can arrange the finance', wrote the *Sydney Morning Herald* political correspondent, 'the State Government will have to find a political means of overcoming the hot contest between country towns for selection as regional centres in order to make the scheme practical. Unless it does this it will risk the defeat in elections of its members representing centres which are not selected.'[30]

Needless to say, no growth centres were subsequently selected and two years later J. O'hara wrote two critical articles on the reason for this. Six years after it was elected with a policy commitment to a 'dynamic decentralization drive', the New South Wales government was in 1971 faced with the fact that the $27 million it had given and lent for decentralization had failed to arrest the accelerating movement of population from the country to the coastal cities. 'Bitter parochial rivalries between country centres', together with narrow Country Party concern for immediate political self-interest were, claimed O'hara, paralysing action to combat the drift to the city.[31] While experts had argued convincingly that there was no prospect of a cure emerging from the policy of dispersed decentralization and had recommended concentration of resources to develop one growth centre at a time, Country Party members of the Legislative Assembly had little enthusiasm for promoting development of inland cities for fear that such centres, once urbanized, would fall to the Liberal and Labor Parties. To make matters worse, the change in the State Electoral Act of February 1971, brought about by Country Party pressure, ensures that rural electorates will have thirty-three seats in state parliament no matter how far the population falls. So the failure of the New South Wales government to come to grips with decentralization 'stems largely from the decision of the Liberal Premier, Mr Askin, to leave the shaping of its rural policy to the Country Party'.[32]

The state Labor Party went to the polls in 1971 naming tentative growth centres for six country regions—Grafton-Lismore, Tamworth, Bathurst-Orange, Wagga, Albury-Wodonga and Broken Hill. Although the Liberal Party, since retaining office, has nominated Bathurst-Orange as a growth centre, the persistence of political difficulties was still evident late in 1973. The director of the Department of Decentralization and Development resigned in that month after the minister for decentralization and development had announced that the planning of the growth centre would be switched from his department to the SPA. There were suggestions that the switch in planning responsibility was a political capitulation to wealthy Country Party landholding interests in the Orange district who oppose resumption of their land at October 1972 prices. Sir Charles Cutler, deputy premier and Country Party member of the Legislative Assembly for Orange, as minister for local government is ministerial head of the SPA.

Transportation

The history of transport planning in Sydney since the early forties has been beset with most of the problems already noted in Adelaide and Melbourne in the sixties. This integral aspect of urban planning has been the responsibility of a separate government department (of main roads) which established the primary road system for the Sydney region in the early forties and had its plans written into the Cumberland Plan. The plans of the Department of Main Roads (DMR) placed maximum emphasis on the private car, providing for 200 miles of expressways across the metropolis in six directions, all radiating from and converging on the centre by means of a system of inner distributor roads surrounding the central area. Because of the prohibitive resumption and construction costs involved, only a few miles of these freeways were built under the Labor government. But the building of the Warringah expressway, begun by Labor in the early sixties, was indicative of the party's inconsistent and ill-considered urban policy. The first section of the expressway extending for 1·5 miles north of the Harbour Bridge cost $25 million, half of which went on property acquisition. The land resumed destroyed hundreds of working-class houses, and their occupants were forced to relocate, inevitably much farther away from the city. The beneficiaries of the expressway were the middle- and upper-class north-shore residents. Despite the shortage of funds for freeways, the DMR hired engineering consultants De Leuw Cather in 1960 to review their plans. Their report resulted in the addition of a further 150 miles of freeways to the DMR's plans despite strenuous objections by Cumberland County Council planners, who criticized the report for being biased in its failure to consider public transport alternatives. As in 1948, the DMR's revised plans were adopted in 1968 by the SPA for the Sydney Region Outline Plan, which estimated that 350 miles of freeways would be needed 'if there is to be an efficient main roads system to match the urban proposals in the Outline Plan'.[33] At $7·5 million a mile this meant a capital investment of $2600 million over the next thirty years. But worse was to come in the Sydney Area Transportation Study, ordered in 1970 and completed in 1974. It forecast the same inevitable need for freeways but the cost had now risen to $6000 million. This study was directed by a policy committee comprising nine top public servants from the departments of main roads, treasury, transport and police and one representative of the SPA; was advised by a technical advisory committee comprising engineers, economists and one planner; and was carried out by a study group every member of which was either a highway engineer or transport economist. No sociologists or environmentalists and of course no residents of areas affected by freeway routes were consulted. This was a strictly technical job, shared by the 'technical experts' and the bureaucrats, which was how it had always been done.

Previously, apart from the DMR, transport decision-making had devolved to three other ad hoc committees—the County of Cumberland Passenger Transport Advisory Committee, the Traffic Advisory Committee and the Parking Advisory Committee—all of whom deliberate separately on aspects of the same problems. In the City of Sydney conflicts have frequently arisen because traffic policies designed to relieve road congestion have been nullified by parking policies which encourage the influx of cars, both policies operating to the detriment of public transport. These committees, and the autonomy and influence of the DMR, stand as good examples of policy-making by the bureaucracy.

Ironically the weight of country interests in state and federal politics has been the most important obstacle (until the recent rash of anti-freeway action groups in the community) to the DMR's road programme. In New South Wales 88 per cent of all commonwealth revenue for roads is spent in the country, a tradition stretching back to the Bruxner empire of the thirties. Neither the Labor nor Liberal Party have been prepared to seek substantial changes to this allocation for fear of antagonizing country electorates.

By April 1972, when the climate of public opinion concerning expressways had reached a critical peak, the conservative *Sydney Morning Herald* ran an editorial suggesting that there were 'strong reasons why the Government should hesitate' in its freeway programme to consider carefully some of the social costs involved and their efficacy in achieving the ends they were designed for.

> Experience in overseas cities suggests that there are grounds for second thoughts about the desirability of expressways leading into the city. The danger is that, after destroying valuable residential areas, the expressways will be self-defeating. They will merely encourage more people to drive private motor cars into the city, thereby increasing congestion, pollution and parking problems, and drawing patronage away from public transport.[34]

The editorial pointed out that Toronto, Washington and San Francisco were reverting to development of their long-neglected public transport systems and building rapid transit railways, and expressed hope that the Sydney Area Transportation Study would give 'special thought to the desirability of inner city expressways and to the objections and alternatives suggested by bodies such as Leichhardt Council'.

It remains to be seen whether anti-freeway groups, assisted by the 'professional' objections of conservationists, planners, architects, and the practical support of Builders Labourers Federation green bans on freeway building will be sufficient to resist the powerful 'freeway lobby'—the car and oil, tyre and spare-parts companies, and the automobile users' pressure group, the National Road Motorists Association. That organization represents the drivers of 800 000 cars in the Sydney region, and that constitutes a powerful 'vested interest' of an important nature. For most car owners want and expect to be able to drive their cars when and where they please and for the government to make this possible. Along with property ownership and property rights, car ownership has become an established part of the Australian ethic of private property and individual freedom, and until a majority of car owners are willing to give up some of their 'car rights', the end of expressways will not be a practical political programme.

The problems of transport, decentralization and rising land prices each reveal different sets of vested interests and social values that have posed enduring dilemmas for planners. And solutions to these problems, where they exist, lie beyond the traditional powers of statutory land-use planning. Yet failure to solve them has limited the success of metropolitan planning to date. But local councils, including the Sydney City Council, have had statutory planning powers since 1945. Their failure to use these powers, and in some cases their abuse of them, and the effects of this on the overall impact of metropolitan planning, are the subjects of the next section.

Sydney City Council and Manhattan Syndrome

D. Winston, writing in 1955, listed planning for the City of Sydney as one of the three key planning issues facing the Cumberland Council.[35] But no City of Sydney planning scheme was prescribed until 1971, after two decades in the course of preparation. How can this outstanding example of neglect of 'local planning' be explained?

Notwithstanding weaknesses in the statutory planning procedure, the Sydney City Council (SCC) had consistently failed in the twenty years following the Cumberland plan's acceptance in 1951 to do anything about its planning responsibilities or to allow planning considerations to enter into its decision-making. In the mid-fifties a property or redevelopment boom began. Schemes to limit and disperse central office building have been proposed since 1953 'and regularly murdered by the lobbies of the central investors'.[36] For nearly half a century London has limited its central office development to less than half the densities proposed for Sydney in the 1971 scheme. In Sydney who profited from the redevelopment boom, and why was nothing done about its consequences?

R. W. Archer's study of the development and use of the twenty largest private buildings completed in the city between 1956 and 1966 reveals the beneficiaries. Of these buildings, four-and-a-half were the main offices of insurance companies and another six-and-a-half were owned by insurance firms. The Australian Mutual Provident Society owns five-and-a-half of these. Its investment complements the development operations of Lend Lease Corp. Ltd and L. J. Hooker Ltd, who were completing major buildings at the rate of one each year in the same period. The seven largest insurance companies increased their real property assets from $71 million in 1957 to $399 million in 1965.[37] AMP has been the largest investor, concentrating on Sydney and Melbourne.

For twenty years this redevelopment was not guided by any overall plan to control the location and size of building in relation to the public facilities upon which they were based. Serious congestion problems developed and both the amenity and efficiency of the area deteriorated. The SCC was responsible for improvement in the central business district and for preparing the planning scheme. It has the richest property tax base in Australia. Yet the council was half-hearted in its approach to these responsibilities. This was ironically due to Labor rule in the council from 1949 to 1967 and to the power of the property interests who opposed any restraint on city growth. The long Labor control of the SCC was secured by the (Labor) state government's Local Government (Treasury) Bill in 1947, which enlarged the boundaries of the city to include the Labor-voting inner residential areas. Labor aldermen subsequently elected showed more concern with the welfare problems of these residents than with the rapidly worsening city planning problems.

Although the council began preparation of a planning scheme in 1951 which included proposals for the zoning of the central business district and for the imposition of a floor-space index on city buildings to limit their density, this scheme was never adopted. Following public exhibition of the scheme in 1952, the Pitt Street Property Owners Defence League was formed and the battle began. *Is Planning Stifling Development?* a booklet by S. E. Wilson of the Retailers Association, challenged the 'right' of any section of the community 'to interfere with and damage other people's property causing great capital loss without even a suggestion of compensation'.[38] The council's response to this challenge was to delete from the draft planning scheme which it submitted to the minister in 1959 all proposals for bulk and height restrictions. The scheme was amended by the minister and exhibited again in 1964–5 This time it included proposals for floor-space ratios drawn up by the SPA. Following public hearings of objections, the scheme was again exhibited in 1968 and attracted more objections on the issue of floor space densities. The scheme was finally promulgated in 1971 without establishing controls on floor space. While the Labor council did little to control the boom in private office development, the state Labor government made no effort to decentralize its own activities from the city to suburban or country locations.

What are the costs involved in this overdevelopment of the city, and who pays them? The costs are partly in the lengthening journey to work for a rising proportion of workers and an uneconomic use of resources in catering for peak-period travel, twice a day, to and from the one spot. But besides the mounting proportion of investment that has to go to destruction and replacement before it achieves any additional transport or floor space, there are other consequences of unlimited growth in and around a centre of limited area. Each central activity expands, imposing its own monotony on a bigger proportion of the centre. Fewer types of activity can afford to pay the rising rents. So 'more and more of the artistic, squalid, surprising, wayward, intellectual, picturesque, marginal and shoe-string activities which are a main part of a good city's attraction and diversity are forced out'.[39] As the number of jobs in the centre increases, the proportion of workers who can live on good land in easy reach of the centre decreases, aggravating existing inequalities.

Up to 1967 it was a Labor council that allowed these inequalities of the market city to be aggravated, by their preoccupation with welfare provisions for inner-city residents and by bowing to the demands of city property owners. But this acquiescence to the property lobby was in part a result of Labor's subscribing to the 'growth ideology' that acclaimed the convulsive changes in the central business district as tangible evidence of metropolitan progress. But Labor is not the only villain of this story. In 1965 the Liberal Party won the state election and in 1967 they dismissed the SCC and appointed three city commissioners to redraw the city boundaries. The new council then created controlled one of the smallest city areas in the world, confined largely to the commercial centre. This enabled the right-wing Civic Reform Association (CRA) to gain a majority in the 1969 elections. But in the meantime the business-minded city commissioners in the twenty-two months of their rule approved $300 million worth of development applications on a ten-to-one floor-space index whereas the planners were urging a six-to-one index.

In 1970 the Civic Reform Council commissioned a team of private planning consultants to prepare a strategic plan for the city which was to be completed, strategically, a few months before the council elections of 1971. Who are the Civic Reform Association and whose values did their commissioned plan espouse?

The CRA is a non-Labor group that exists only in the City of Sydney council electorate and has been since its formation in 1921 traditionally backed by the business interests in the city. On its letterhead it describes itself 'Towards a better Sydney—non-political'. The CRA's view of party politics is apparent in this statement from its 1966 annual report: 'The task of the political parties is to provide a good government or vigorous opposition in State or Federal spheres and to leave City Government to those whose *sole* interest is to raise the importance of Sydney . . .' [my italics].[40] The CRA is made up of 'corporate members' (companies with interests in the city) and 'personal members' (individual ratepayers and residents). Their greatest source of finance comes from companies many of whom do not exist on CRA's register as 'corporate members' because they do not wish to be identified as supporting the CRA or being involved in city politics.

An executive council of up to fifty members is elected annually to administer the running of the CRA. Most of these members are involved in finance, insurance, manufacturing, retailing and commerce in the city. Of the forty-two members of the 1972 council, at least thirty were directors of several companies.[41] There were also several prominent members of the state Liberal Party on the CRA executive. Of the twelve CRA aldermen on the present council, only three are directors in large companies, but the proportion of professional people is high. Eleven of the twelve live at north-shore and other upper-class addresses outside the electorate, compared with one ALP non-resident alderman of the eight ALP members of the council.[42]

The *City of Sydney Strategic Plan* was released in July 1971 and adopted by ordinary resolution of council in August 1971. The 'teeth' of the plan—the Development Control and Floor Space Ratio Code and the Parking Policy and Control Code for New Development —were adopted in December 1971. The Development Control and Floor Space Ratio Code sets out the basic floor-space ratios for each precinct and the bonuses of floor-space area to be given to a developer who provides certain public amenities. The amount by which a developer can exceed the basic permissible floor-space ratio 'is scaled to give the developer a financial advantage greater than the cost of the facility he provides, thus creating a powerful incentive'.[43] The Parking Policy and Control Code for New Development gives policy proposals to govern the amount, distribution and regulation of commuter and visitor parking to serve the central business district. It gives the council a guide as to how many car spaces should be provided in relation to the gross floor area of a new building and how many of these spaces should be located within that building.

Like the *Sydney Region Outline Plan*, the *Strategic Plan* talks about 'goals' and 'objectives', 'implementation strategies' and 'action plans' rather than formulating prescriptive statutory planning controls. The aim of the *Strategic Plan* is 'to improve the quality of life for the people who use the city'.[44] Four objectives are recommended to fulfil this aim: to 'foster economic growth by managing, guiding and directing the conservation and redevelopment of the city as a whole', to 'improve access to and ease of movement within the city', to 'conserve and increase the diversity of community activity and services throughout the city' and to 'conserve, enhance and improve the physical environment of the city'.

Can these objectives be fulfilled? Are they internally consistent? Who really gains from the plan as distinct from its rhetorical beneficiaries? How does the plan relate to and affect the metropolitan planning objectives expressed in the 1968 SPA plan?

For George Clarke, head of Urban Systems Corporation (one of the three consulting firms who prepared the plan), successful planning needs some combination of knowledge, power and consensus. Given the short preparation time, 'knowledge' had to be limited to existing data on the city. Given the circumscribed power of the council, it was hoped to encourage other bodies to support the plan. The heavy public relations emphasis indicates therefore that *consensus* was seen as essential, for public, professional and media acceptance, and much emphasis in the rhetoric was placed on public participation. In practice this meant that the consultants approached by letter several hundred organizations (banks, churches, hospitals, government departments, schools, builders, community groups and professional bodies) and 'participation' was derived from general comments by the organizations that the planners had invited to participate. The consultants' summary of 'the needs and demands of the community' was so general that they were impossible to reject—for example to 'improve access to and movement within the city'. In effect the participation programme was a means by which the planners tried to ensure that many interest groups could feel that they had been involved in the determination of objectives for the city. From the planners' point of view they could then point to the participation programme in an effort to legitimize their plan.

There were three main sources of criticism of the plan—the ALP, the local residents' action groups, and professional architects and planners. All made similar basic criticisms attacking the assumptions of the plan. The ALP expressed concern in council that the plan 'merely channelled the obvious current over-development into the central spine without offering any firm policies to control and redirect that overdevelopment to decentralize to outer city areas and secondly that it did not go far enough in ensuring adequate future residential development'.[45] Professional criticism has centred on the economic and transport implications of the plan's workforce prediction of 360 000–400 000 in the central business district by the year 2000. The 1972 workforce was 240 000. The plan expected and accepted that 70 000 peak-hour train travellers would be drawn from the outermost urban areas, Penrith, Campbelltown and Gosford-Wyong, generally thirty-five to fifty miles away. H. Seidler and N. Gruzman have criticized the advantage to developers from the system of bonus floor space and have suggested that developers were influential in formulating the provisions of the plan. B. Mortlock further criticized the system of bonuses in return for 'amenities'. He argued that what was needed was to plan for a comprehensive, publicly-controlled pedestrian network, not to wait and see what developers were willing to provide. J. Paterson has argued that the success of the bonus system depends on demand for premium office space. He anticipated that only owners receiving high rents would be able or willing to subsidize non-office uses in the shape of public amenities.[46]

Overall the strategic plan seems likely to reinforce all those inequalities mentioned earlier that result from over-concentration in the centre of a large metropolis. Workers must live farther out and travel longer distances, the public sector is called on to finance the additional strain on roads and public transport, and the diversity of the city itself is reduced by increasing rents, contrary to the rhetoric of the plan. It must be doubted whether 'the series of strategies and actions' can achieve the stated objectives of encouraging diversity and a better city environment. It may be that the way to retain the city's residential population, to encourage diverse land uses such as retailing, entertainment and tourist facilities, to provide more public amenities and pedestrian and open space and to ease traffic congestion is to *reduce* the floor-space ratio, to encourage lower densities and to disperse the workforce to metropolitan centres.

But the *Strategic Plan* favours bigness. This is indicated by its restrictions on the development potential for small sites, its encouragement of site amalgamation and its implicit encouragement of the provision of premium office space. The plan shares with the large business interests of the city its first objective: 'Foster economic growth by managing, guiding and directing the conservation and redevelopment of the City as a whole.' It maintains the status of the biggest businesses and investors in the city. To a much greater extent than the developers, the established business interests in the city are concerned with the long-run prosperity and economic viability of the city and therefore with improvements to its commercial efficiency and amenity. Despite its reformist rhetoric the CRA council had no intention of restraining the growth of the city, as is evident from the figures for the number of buildings completed, under construction, or given approval since 1971. It spent $51 million on new buildings completed in 1971, $26 million in 1972. In July 1973 there were 49 multi-storey buildings, with an average height of twenty-five to thirty storeys, under construction. A further 96 were proposed, 80 of which had planning approval.[47]

The council's concern with the growth of the city was reflected too in its approval in principle in 1972 of the *Woolloomooloo Redevelopment Project*. Since 1964 the 'Loo, as affectionately known by the locals, had been designated by the state (Labor) government as an area for comprehensive redevelopment. The incoming Liberal minister for local government P. H. Morton was keen for action and in 1968 established a steering committee which decided to hire the SPA as a consultant to the city council to prepare a redevelopment proposal. These proposals, displayed in 1969 but never made a statutory plan, were accepted by the council, and developers began to acquire the land and amalgamate sites. The coincidence of the market features of cheap land, availability of finance and demand by developers resulted within two years in site amalgamations (and hence potential densities, because the SPA's proposals offered floor-space bonuses for site amalgamations) much greater than the SPA had ever envisaged.

In May 1972 the city council was presented with a proposal for the largest private redevelopment project in Australia, worth $400 million. The *Woolloomooloo Redevelopment Project*, a ninety-page document prepared for the owners and developers of the eleven-acre site by a firm of private planners, proposed the construction of approximately eighteen high-rise buildings of an average height of twenty storeys.[48] This would draw an estimated workforce of 80 000 to the eleven-acre area, 68 000 of them office workers. It was estimated that 63 000 of this workforce would come by train, 62 per cent of them during peak hour. The major land uses of the project were office space 56 per cent, retail 23 per cent, luxury hotel motels 17 per cent, as compared with a mere 0·9 per cent of the gross square footage allotted to theatre, cinemas and sports centres. On May 19 1972 the city council granted its approval in principle to this project.

There are several grounds for criticism of this decision. Firstly it ignored the recommendations of the *Strategic Plan* that Woolloomooloo remain an area of low-rise residential redevelopment. In allowing comprehensive high-rise office and hotel redevelopment it was discriminating against the low-income residents of the area in favour of developers' profits and transient demands of wealthy tourists. The density of redevelopment would cause considerable strain on transport facilities and again the public sector would be required to meet the costs (externalities) imposed by private sector development. Finally the office redevelopment ignored the *Strategic Plan*'s recommendation that high-density office development be confined to the city's north-south central spine, served by the underground rail loop.

Faced with a choice between the interests of the existing low-income residents of the 'Loo, the financial interests of a few large property owners and developers and the metropolitan-wide implications of the project on the redistribution of 'real income', the interests of the developers carried the day on the property-oriented CRA council. As the next section shows, the practice of councils favouring the interests of developers and property owners is not uncommon. In fact it persistently undermines the intentions of the best-laid planning schemes.

Local Government Planning: Inequality and Corruption

The reluctant attitude adopted by local government during the passage of the 1945 Local Government (Town and Country Planning) Amendment Act has carried over in the half-hearted response of local councils towards their responsibilities under part XIIA of the act. Although under the terms of the Local Government (Areas) Act of 1948 all councils in the County of Cumberland were required to prepare planning schemes, by 1963, when the CCC was dissolved, only three local planning schemes had been prescribed out of a possible total of forty-two. Most councils preferred to remain in the interim development phase because it allowed development to be controlled with wide discretion.

The record of local council administration of statutory planning powers has not been impressive. 'Local councils exercise development control with scant regard for the metropolitan implications of their decisions'.

> Development, unless judged beyond all possible doubt to be detrimental to the locality (and not always then) is usually regarded with favour by aldermen ... The discretion available under statutory planning carries with it the possibility of patronage, to be granted, delayed or withheld for a variety of good or bad reasons. With a few notable exceptions, the local councils are ill-equipped to exercise these powers.[49]

M. Painter's detailed case studies of planning and development control in six local government areas of Sydney reinforce this assessment.[50] The receptiveness of local councillors to pressures both from developers and from local residents' groups concerned with 'amenity' has persistently undermined the intentions of metropolitan planning. Painter's work shows that the nature of local planning is closely allied with the class character of an area and its stage of economic growth. Thus in Ku-ring-gai, a well-heeled upper-class north-shore area the the council had been predominantly receptive to the 'amenity' demands of local residents, even to the extent of rejecting development applications by prestigious developers like David Jones and protecting streets from use by heavy trucks. Other councils, particularly in those developing outer-suburban areas like Liverpool, could not afford to be so cavalier towards developers and commercial interests. Successive (ALP) Liverpool councils have supported most pressures to convert non-urban land to urban uses, believing these moves to fulfil the major goals of 'city development', expansion and progress. The council's initial draft scheme of 1966 coloured vast areas of the map pink and purple, for residential and industrial uses. And Labor aldermen have been as pliant to pressures for distributive decisions from developers as from battlers.

In councils where the class character of an area is less homogeneous than in, say, Ku-ring-gai or Liverpool, conflicts have arisen between the social and economic needs and demands of different classes. For example in Leichhardt, once a predominantly working-class municipality, the recent influx of the middle class into areas like Balmain and Glebe has led to clashes between middle-class values associated with residential amenity and the interests of industrial land users and of the working class, who are more prepared to tolerate industry in the area in order to live close to their work.

Some of the more spectacular cases of abuse of discretionary planning powers in Liverpool[51] and Bankstown[52] illustrate the influence developers can exert on the planning process. They are not isolated instances. Cases of revealed corruption occurred in North Sydney in 1969 and in Liverpool in 1953 and 1963. Bankstown Council was dismissed in 1963 following bribery charges laid against several aldermen, and the dismissal of the Leichhardt Council in 1953 revealed several varieties of malpractice and corruption, among them the soliciting of bribes for the approval of building and development applications. Most recently, in May 1973, the Randwick Council was dismissed following allegations that the mayor and some aldermen were contravening the local planning scheme by consenting to flat development on land they and members of their families owned. Members of both major political parties have been guilty of misuse of discretionary planning powers, with perhaps the most frequent offenders being ALP members.

The frequency with which abuse of planning intentions by local councils is revealed suggests that local government is not the most appropriate agency to deal with planning matters. The question of what development matters should be left to local councils has never been satisfactorily resolved, partly because it is not easy to decide which decisions have purely local impact as distinct from those which may have metropolitan significance. Local planning schemes are scrutinized and often amended by the SPA on behalf of the minister, but the minister himself is vulnerable to political pressures, and the degree of political support he gives to planning objectives can be subject to party-political ideology or to personal conviction. The initial political support given to planning by McKell and Cahill, for example, was not perpetuated by Hills, the Labor minister for local government from 1959 onwards, and the Liberal minister responsible for planning administration from 1965 to 1972 has been described as 'a free enterpriser from way back'.

Gross inequalities between the resources, human and financial, of different local councils reinforces the argument that, given the present structure of local government, it is not an appropriate agency to administer planning controls. Sydney's topography, and the disposal of land in a free market economy, has resulted in a residential segregation more conspicuous than in any other Australian city, thus reinforcing existing inequalities between different socio-economic classes. I. Manning has measured and described the extent to which the population of Sydney lives in different suburbs according to the attributes of income and wealth, and age and ethnicity.[53] Stretton has put the matter more graphically by noting that (according to 1964 figures) Ku-ring-gai's citizens occupied $4800 worth of real estate per head compared with Liverpool's about $2000—for a family of five, $24 000 and $10 000 respectively. 'On the rateable part of this—the 'unimproved' land only—Ku-ring-gai needed a rate of 1·18 per cent to raise $37 per head. As a fine example of regressive taxation Liverpool had to nearly double that rate, to 2·19, to raise $29 per head.'[54] In other words, the poor pay more than the rich, in terms of proportion of income, and get less in return.

Clearly, in this present situation of inequality of resources, to increase local council's powers, especially in an area of social policy like urban planning, without first redistributing the resources available to each local government area, would simply aggravate existing inequalities.

What then of those 'democratic' arguments in favour of increased local government planning powers on the grounds that people should be given the maximum opportunities to participate in decisions vitally affecting the quality of their daily lives, that power should remain at all times with or as near as possible to the people, and that local government is the best safeguard against excessive centralization and bureaucratization of government.

It may be that individuals value their power to influence decision-making at the local government level. But this power is not always exercised in the best interests of metropolitan planning concerns. Painter's study shows that most of the pressures applied to local government by individuals or groups, whether developers or residents' groups, are based on local self-interest, be it of the profit-motive or environmental variety, and have shown scant consideration either for neighbouring areas, other social classes or metropolitan-wide welfare. Property owners act to defend or enhance the value of their properties. Residents want a particular standard of amenity in their areas in the form of good roads, other sorts of council services, or the sort of land use they want to see next door. This applies to occupants of industrial, commercial and residential property alike. Expressions of political involvement by owners or tenants tend to occur not when the council makes policy decisions such as how much to allocate to kerb and gutter construction but when a decision is made as to whether kerb and gutter is to be provided to their particular street; not when council formulates a zoning scheme for a municipality but when a developer lodges an application to build a multi-storey block of flats on the neighbouring property. *No one* wants freeways or rubbish dumps or factories or high-rise housing or flats located near them. But *everyone* drives cars, dumps rubbish, and needs a place to work and live.

Thus while the purely *local* impact of the recent residents' action groups' concern with protecting the amenity of their areas may be beneficial, the metropolitan and national implications have scarcely been thought about. The impasse in metropolitan growth and change, which is the logical culmination of the current reluctance of most local areas to see industry, high-density housing, airports and so on located in their vicinity, may well be desirable. This would be true if it had the effect of persuading the government to pursue an energetic decentralization policy. But in the absence of decisive government policies on such things as transport, the role of the private car in the context of accelerating resource shortages, and decentralization (and these strong policies have to date been lacking), the overall effect of the current spate of environmental protection may be to penalize still further those people at the bottom of the socio-economic scale. In other words there is a potential conflict between environmental concerns and redistributive or equity objectives. In Sydney, for example, the 'drawbridge' or defensive actions by the middle class in the inner, eastern and north-shore suburbs in protecting their areas from further growth or intrusion by undesirable land uses enhances the advantages of those who already have considerable resources at their disposal. The likely effect of their drawbridge tactics will be to send industries, low-cost government housing and so on to those outer suburbs, like Blacktown and beyond, which welcome growth yet have less amenity and accessibility advantages to offer their poorer inhabitants.

In short, the reluctance of most individuals to give up their cars, single-family dwellings and attendant property rights and values or to go and live in the country, combined with the ability of the rich to pay on the open market for the choicest residential areas and then to protect their choices politically from what they regard to be undesirable environmental intrusion, in the long run and in the absence of decisive government action to reverse the trend, will continue to exacerbate existing inequalities between rich and poor in Sydney.

Given the limited scope of present local council functions and powers, it is often the case that the issues affecting broad categories of people are resolved elsewhere than at the local level. Thus real estate interests and business groups seek to influence the administration of local planning schemes to further their interests by approaching members, ministers and the SPA. Major decisions about development at the urban fringe, sitings of new industries, the location of expressways, the installation of sewerage and water services are made by state government or by semi-government authorities. Although some of these decisions vitally affect the quality of people's lives and their futures, they are not as amenable to direct political pressure as are those issues which are resolved at the local level. The realization by many individuals that they are powerless in such important issues as freeway location and desirability and inner-city redevelopment has led in recent years to new forms of political action, the most effective of which have been the green bans placed on particular projects, areas or buildings by the Builders Labourers Federation (BLF).

Residents' Action and Union Green Bans

Resident and union stands for the environment and against mindless destruction for profit . . . demonstrate a refusal any longer to concede that the rich and powerful and entrenched interests have any unchallengeable right to make all the decisions—decisions which affect the lives of people on the job and in their homes and communities. It is a recognition that, if qualities are to be preserved, then responsibility cannot be left to those whose obsession is with profits, amassed by exploitation regardless of the irreparable destruction and the long-term costs to the community.[55]

The face of local political action in Australia, and especially in New South Wales, has been undergoing considerable changes in the past five years or so. The recent (since 1971) alliance between some middle-class environmental groups and the radical BLF marks perhaps a third stage in the evolution of the 'new politics'.[56] The first stage was the emergence in the old inner suburbs of local 'associations', the best known of which is the Paddington Society. Paddington was the first area to attract 'the new middle class',[57] with a cosmopolitan and essentially aesthetic concern for the quality of its residential environment. The Paddington Society has tried to have its area zoned as an historic precinct, freed from the uncontrollable inroads of demolishers and the possibly, in their view, unholy pastel paints of the southern European migrants. Their behaviour has been demonstrably that of a special interest group concerned to preserve the special environment of the area and to protect their property values. Membership and participation in the running of the society included few of the older residents and migrants.

The local associations were originally set up as local amenity groups and prided themselves on not being 'political'. This tended to hobble them when they were caught in local political situations, and the Paddington, Balmain and Glebe Societies have all resorted to political action when their special interests were directly threatened. The Jersey Road affair, when the Department of Main Roads attempted to demolish a row of terrace houses for a distributor road, was a good example of this. The Paddington Society linked professional expertise and access to decision-makers with the organizational ability to bring out a large number of people over a single issue. Presumably it was their status that forced the state government to set up a special inquiry, which duly advised against the proposal. It was then quietly shelved. Similarly in Glebe the academics and other professionals in the Glebe Society have been successful in having the proposed western freeway driven into an underground tunnel beneath the high status Toxteth Estate.

These exclusively middle-class societies were precursors to the more politically oriented residents' action groups which made their presence felt in the local council elections of 1971. Concerned with pollution and amenity these groups have emerged in suburbs of varied class character, from upper north-shore to inner-city working-class, on a variety of environmental issues. Perhaps the most common issues have been opposition to flat development, expressways and high-rise inner-city redevelopment projects. Until 1971 the main political resource available to these groups was access to professional skills and ability to win local council positions. Middle-class groups on the north shore and the gentrified inner suburbs of Paddington, Balmain and Glebe worked always through existing political channels. Working-class communities in the historic Rocks area and in Wool-loomooloo, more distrustful of these processes, engaged in less conventional forms of protest, like the Victoria Street (Kings Cross) squatters.[58]

But the realization by many middle- and upper-class 'greenies' that some environmental matters of great concern to them, like the preservation of old buildings and parklands from developers and freeway builders, were not susceptible to political influence at the local level led over the past three years to an unusual alliance, which constitutes a third stage in 'the new politics'. This was the working/middle-class 'popular front' between 'Establishment greenies' and the radical Builders Labourers Federation, led by communist Jack Mundey. Mundey grew up in the Queensland bush, left school early, and left the bush at twenty to try his luck at professional football in Sydney. In the big city he drifted into the union movement as a builders' labourer, and the grim conditions in the building industry gradually politicized him. These days he gets almost as much press coverage as the prime minister. This is partly because he is talkative, articulate and personally charming. It is also because of his capacity, rare in our society, of being able to think about the long run—a subject unfashionable since Keynes pronounced that in the long run we will all be dead. That is precisely what worries Mundey: not just that *we* will be dead, but that the human race may well be unless we begin to do something about resource consumption, overpopulation, pollution and conservation.

The unusual alliance between the BLF with a comprehensive socialist critique and those members of the middle class who have passed beyond the fight for economic survival and are concerned with the quality of their living environment emerged in June 1971 when some residents of upper-class Hunters Hill, as a last resort, sought union aid to protect Kellys Bush from the home-unit plans of A. V. Jennings. It has since been cemented by BLF green bans on a multitude of development projects from the Parkes Developments home-unit proposals for Eastlakes to the Australian Mutual Provident Society's $4 million car-park plans beneath the Botanic Gardens, the Askin government's plans to build an Olympic Games sports complex in the Moore Park-Centennial Park area, the Sydney Cove Redevelopment Authority's $500 million redevelopment proposals to dismember Sydney's historic Rocks area and Londish's $400 million redevelopment plans for Woolloomooloo. By mid-1973, development projects worth $3000 million had been halted by green bans because those projects would have torn down historic buildings or violated metropolitan parks.

This paradoxical alliance of groups of basically conflicting political philosophy in a common environmental cause bears a certain resemblance to the 'Radical Chic'[59] of New York society a few years ago— the brief espousal by the social and economic elite of east-side Manhattan of the Black Panther movement, a movement aimed at the revolutionary overthrow of American capitalism. That flirtation was abandoned as soon as the real threat to the Establishment was perceived. Is the fate of the BLF environmental activism destined for similar 'betrayal'?

The BLF is in fact vulnerable on several fronts. The October–November 1973 confrontation between it and the Sydney Cove Redevelopment Authority illustrates some of these. Mundey himself has admitted that the leadership of the BLF is ideologically far in advance of the rank and file and that probably only 30 per cent of the union fully understand and support his philosophy.[60] Given this, rank-and-file support of the green bans may well be undermined if the eventual outcome of the green-ban actions is to put large numbers of builders' labourers out of work, which could easily happen in less buoyant economic conditions. It is also true that the leadership of the BLF is far in advance of the political awareness of the working class generally. It has already been the case that some working-class residents of Woolloomooloo and the Rocks have been quite content to sell out to developers or, in the case of tenants, to move out to more modern dwellings offered them, even when these houses are twenty-five miles away.

More serious problems arose in 1973 from the conflict between the New South Wales leader Jack Mundey, president of the Communist Party of Australia (non-aligned), and the federal and Victorian secretary of the BLF Norm Gallagher, a member of the Peking-oriented CPA. (There are three 'communist parties' in Australia: the non-aligned C.P.A., the Marxist-Leninist C.P.A. and the Moscow-oriented Socialist Party of Australia.) Gallagher's group has never supported the green-ban line, and following the deregistration of the New South Wales branch early in 1974 for their 'lawlessness', the federal branch of the BLF launched a campaign aimed at taking over the New South Wales branch.

This move did not succeed initially, ironically because the bourgeois legal process in the shape of the New South Wales Equity Court told Gallagher to pack up and go back to Victoria. But that was not to be the end of this internecine struggle. Those involved knew that the federal branch might still succeed if worsening economic conditions affected the building industry and enabled Gallagher to recruit the support of the migrants in the union who have always been indifferent about or opposed to the environmental concerns of their leaders. These migrants, mostly poor southern Europeans, comprise 60 per cent of the New South Wales membership and have been more concerned with bread-and-butter issues like house mortgages and hire purchase payments than with the nation's heritage or the global ecological crisis.

But the BLF stand on social issues has been subject to erosion not only from within but by the joint action of the Master Builders Association (MBA) and the state government. In October 1973 the Sydney Cove Redevelopment Authority tried to use scab labour to break the ban in the Rocks area. The green-ban policy was obviously fraught with difficulties that were enhanced by the close links between the state government, the MBA and big developers and further complicated by the suspected alliance between the federal BLF and the MBA. This suspicion was confirmed and the green bans put in greater jeopardy in March 1975.

In the context of a tight employment situation in the building industry which put increasing pressure on the New South Wales leadership, Gallagher persuaded the MBA to lock out New South Wales builders' labourers from job sites after Easter unless they joined the federal branch. The New South Wales leaders had no alternative but to recommend to their members that they register with the federal branch. An editorial in the *Australian* on 25 March commenting on this 'surrender' observed that it 'is the end for the Jack Mundey style of social issue . . . While the Federal leadership of the BLF publicly agrees with the concept of environmental bans, its support has always been qualified and unenthusiastic. The most likely result of the Federal victory will be that most of the bans will be reviewed and lifted.' The tone of regret evident in the editorial was indicative of the degree of support that the green bans had sustained. 'Green bans were an inevitable result of official attitudes which regarded people as irrelevant factors to development. The demise of the New South Wales branch will at least leave the legacy that the human consequences of build, build, build cannot be ignored.' At the time of writing, it is difficult to predict the future of green bans, but it does seem highly unlikely that the policy will be extended, and quite likely that existing bans will be lifted.

The BLF-residents alliance has effectively delayed major development and redevelopment proposals and brought the issues involved, issues basic to the welfare of the metropolis, to the attention of state and federal governments and the general public. If the green-ban policy succeeds eventually in changing state government priorities in development matters which have metropolitan-wide consequences, the BLF will be judged favourably by future historians and future residents of Sydney. If on the other hand, as seems more likely, the Liberal government continues to be more receptive to the growth/ free-enterprise ideology, the continued drawbridge tactics by environmentalists may have the regressive effects on the distribution of wealth that were outlined in the previous section. That is, in the absence of decisive government action to curb and provide alternatives to the continuing expansion of the Sydney region, and given the political and economic powers of the rich to protect their immediate environments, the only place for 'undesirable' elements of urban growth (like polluting industries, low-income housing estates) to go will be out west where they will further increase the disadvantages already suffered there by the poor.

Summary

After World War II New South Wales, and Sydney at the heart of it, grew faster than anyone foresaw—in wealth, population and city size. Between 1947 and 1971, overseas migrants and their Australian-born children accounted for more than half the population increase in Sydney.[61] The same was true of Melbourne. The ideology of a predominantly working-class immigrant culture with bitter memories of the depression, plus Australian nationalism and New South Wales rivalry with other states, powerfully supported this growth. So too did capitalism.

For a while tentative attempts were made to contain and regulate this growth. But these efforts were based on ideas about town planning imported from the very different environment of Britain, a slow-growing, traditional, crowded and class-dominated society. They were quite radical ideas but they were doomed to failure, lacking any roots in popular feeling or in the immediate economic interests of any major group. So the whole planning programme was watered down and failed to sustain political support.

Meanwhile Sydney grew, inexorably and massively, and at the very low density of eight persons per acre, covering 500 square miles by 1971. A city one-third the size of London in population had come to fill an equal area. Local government remained miniscule and often corrupt. State government concentrated on providing services—housing, hospitals, schools—and on general growth of its capital city. No one perceived what was happening, the inequalities that were being generated by this single-centred city growth. There was no comprehensive urban vision. Inevitably Sydney, with its centre on the coast and half its circumference interlaced by the harbour which restricted movement, spread rapidly and thinly north, south and west in increasingly segregated communities of different social classes. Its centre *had* to grow upwards. If it grew outwards it would *have* to be at the expense of inner-city working-class housing. Its communication system *had* to be enormously expanded or the city would strangle itself in traffic jams and inaccessibility.

The question was, what would blow up first? There were several pressure points. Lack of space for central-area functions called for massive inner-area redevelopment, tearing down homes and ruining a beautiful old city. More and more people had to reach this centre to keep the ever-growing urban 'machine' going, and that meant more roads or rail extensions. More people wanted to live more centrally, and that meant capturing more parkland or other open space for housing, or richer people buying out and crowding up or sending out poorer people. The house-building programme, public and private, was largely for families, not for old people, or for young single people— flat-dwellers who wanted good accessibility since all members of their household were travelling to work each day. Sooner or later these needs would have to be met too.

Inevitably therefore the uproar would, and did, begin around high-rise inner-area redevelopment (in the Rocks and in Woolloomooloo), freeway extensions (in inner-city Glebe), parkland sites bought up for housing (Kellys Bush), building of flats, and 'gentrification'. When these threats arose, people reacted with whatever instruments lay to hand, sometimes in surprising alliances: residents' action groups, BLF green bans, conservationist groups—coalitions with common negative aims but few shared positive aims. Builders' labourers needed work but conservationists feared growth: they needed homes, but middle-class residents' action groups sought to keep the *hoi polloi* out of *their* neighbourhoods. Currently planners despair that they can get nothing done because some people object to every decision they make. Citizens despair that they have no way of making the 'technical experts' listen to their preferences except by crude, direct action such as sitting down in front of bulldozers.

There *are* comprehensive and effective ways of tackling these problems, but they have to be long-range (in time) and large-scale (in powers and spending, and space). The kinds of things we must consider urgently are city shape and city size, suitable population densities and ways of moving people around the city. Should cities be linear or round; single-centred or multi-centred? Should there be one large city in each state, sprawling along the coast, or should growth be diverted well away from Sydney to new cities or existing 'growth centres'? How should people move about in cities? Should we build more Canberras—low-density cities planned for the private car? Or should we invest massively in public transport? If we want to do that, it is only feasible if planned as an integral part of strategies concerning city shape and size. Low residential densities are not *necessarily* incompatible with an efficient public transport system, but they are when the housing is scattered in every direction. Should we be trying to increase overall population densities or, less drastically, providing more choice in housing types and densities while still providing quarter-acre blocks for all those who still prefer them?[62]

To solve these problems we need resources, knowledge and power —that is, lots of money and trained staff over a long period; research leading to comprehension of urban problems, communication between experts and government and ordinary citizens; and regular, published monitoring of social conditions and urban development to keep an informed debate going. Above all we need more comprehensive powers—a metropolitan planning authority working in close co-operation with other state authorities and local government—and a closer liaison between different policies and programmes. It is no use operating only through traditional town planning authorities. It is essential to relate housing, transport, location of industry, education, health and recreation policies more effectively.

But these three—power, resources and knowledge—must go together. Alone, they are no use, and without all three, the 'disjointed incrementalism' of day-by-day political bargaining, conservative or radical, is all we can have. The task is obviously long and hard and calls for persistence. Meanwhile we must reject two dangerous misconceptions: firstly that the disjointed incrementalism of pluralistic politics is a *desirable* state rather than a sorry and often inevitable outcome of ignorance and powerlessness, and secondly that 'reformist' visions, like those of Hugh Stretton, or the Department of Urban and Regional Development, are irrelevant. We need visions that are accompanied by practical political programmes and we need the gritty, patient reforming impetus that worries away at administration and its effects but also keeps its eye on people and their needs and hopes—on people in cities, not just at smaller street scale or local-authority scale.

Conclusions

Planning in a Property-owning Democracy: Past, Present and Future

> A man with much property has great bargaining strength and a great sense of security, independence and freedom; and he enjoys these things not only vis-a-vis his property-less fellow citizens but also vis-a-vis the public authorities. An unequal distribution of property means an unequal distribution of power and status.
>
> J. E. Meade 1964[1]

> The wide distribution of house property is unquestionably a factor in Australia's social stability. Revolutions are seldom made by house owners.
>
> P. McGuire 1942[2]

Themes

This study began by outlining the redistributive possibilities of urban planning, then proceeded to analyze why in practice these possibilities have not been realized.

In exploring the ideas and social values of planning advocates it was found that there were certain inadequacies in their social theory. The town planning movement emerged from the social reform movements of the late nineteenth century and its rhetoric has traditionally supported the aim of improving social conditions. It has at different times even emphasized its mission to help the urban poor. It was concerned about social problems (crime, violence, delinquency, overcrowding, ill-health) but its solution to these problems was to improve *physical* conditions, to provide better and cheaper housing, parks, playgrounds and open spaces and to eradicate slums. This 'physical determinist' approach failed to come to terms with the real causes of the problems—the existence of poverty and the nature of the economic system.

Most of the planning advocates up to the late 1940s believed that garden suburbs and garden cities were the answer to urban problems. They had adopted the physical planning component of Ebenezer

Howard's garden city concept but had neglected the radical element of Howard's theory, that of municipal ownership of land. The notions of community and social integration were central to town planning ideology. So was the assumption that both could be achieved by physical arrangements. Both concepts looked backwards to the supposed organic solidarity of the social structure of a rural society while ignoring the inequalities in the distribution of land, wealth and power in such a society. This assumption that physical arrangements rather than economic and political change could bring about social reform has been a persistent weakness in the social theory of planning advocates.

Few participating in the early town planning movement perceived that in order to achieve their professed social aims, town planning must be allied with economic planning and with the political question of the distribution of resources. The Department of Post-war Reconstruction 'planners' did recognize that physical planning was only one of the policies needed to achieve national economic and social goals and to influence resource allocation. The most important reform of the forties, the Commonwealth-State Housing Agreement, originated in the Department of Post-war Reconstruction. Together with commonwealth reforms in welfare services, this did more for redistribution than anything before or since. Following this achievement, planners gave less emphasis to welfare considerations than they had done before the war, perhaps because they assumed that the poor were being taken care of by the state housing commissions.

While the post-war reconstruction 'planners' understood that physical planning was only part of the broader problem of resource allocation, they did not take the next logical step—the creation of an authority in which economic, social and physical planning were functionally integrated. The need for such an authority was made explicit for the first time in 1970 in Hugh Stretton's *Ideas for Australian Cities:*

> Big time metropolitan planning . . . must be integrated as the land-use and communications branch of central economic planning. The 'chief planner' will have to be the Premier. The chief 'planning document' will have to be his budget. His chief executants will probably include massive development corporations, directed by economists, and dealing in as much as a third of all new urban land.[3]

Since that was written, a new federal government has established a Department of Urban and Regional Development, with a redistributive philosophy which it is attempting to implement in most of the ways outlined by Stretton; capital budgeting for resource allocation and dealings in urban land using economists and development corporations.

These 'political planners' are a new breed compared with the apolitical advocates of the past seventy years. The men of yesterday were disturbed by what was happening to the cities aesthetically and by the living conditions of the urban working class whose slum life threatened both the physical health and political stability of the city, so their motives were both humane and expedient. Property was also a major consideration. The need to keep it inviolate imposed limitations on the reforms that might be attempted. Perhaps because of their middle-class backgrounds and their respect for property, these reformers sought to ameliorate harsh conditions and to avoid divisive social conflict. Town planning was presented as an issue that transcended class and party divisions and benefited all sections of the community from workers to middle-class residents and landowners (by safeguarding property values and protecting the character of particular neighbourhoods) and capitalists (by cultivating an efficient workforce).

Between 1900 and 1950, planning *ideas* were influenced by the economic and social circumstances of the time. Hence the emphasis on slum reclamation in the depressed thirties compared with the concern in the booming twenties with catering for business efficiency in a rapidly expanding city. But *action* on planning issues was dependent on the state of politics, and suffered accordingly. For, as a contemporary planner has explained, 'A development plan must be acceptable and workable; and to that end judgment must be based on what can or cannot be done in the prevailing economic, social and political situation.'[4]

Planners themselves, while not often espousing radical social values, have attempted to regulate through zoning and subdivision control the worst abuses of a free market and its consequences for urban growth. Their failure has been due in part to the inadequacies of their ideas, but more to the inadequate political support which planning has received.

This failure of political support stems from the nature of politics in a property-owning democracy. The structure of political power has been and is such as to protect property owners and to pamper rural interests. This business, rural and conservative bias has dominated the very political institutions through which efforts have been made to implement planning: lower houses in South Australia and Victoria dominated by coalitions of country and city rich; upper Houses in each state at the mercy of big property owners and rural conservatives; city councils whose members have vested interests in protecting existing property and privileges or in real estate and land speculation; local councils whose main aim has been to attract as much development as possible, preferably private rather than public because of ratable values; a Liberal Party dependent on the business and financial community and governing in its interest. Through these political institutions the class of owners has acted to protect encroachments on and threats to its property rights. Hence most efforts to introduce even the mildest forms of planning legislation have been met, especially in the states' upper houses, with a 'compulsive shudder of the property instinct'.

In New South Wales Greater Sydney bills proposing metropolitan government and incorporating town planning functions were defeated in the upper house in 1915 and 1931. Town planning bills were rejected in 1919 and 1922 and the 1945 Town and Country Planning Bill was amended in the upper house to place planning control in the hands of local government. The appearance in 1952, following the exhibition of the City of Sydney planning scheme, of the Pitt Street Property Owners Defence League to oppose any reduction in plot ratios (building densities) on city sites was further evidence of the resistance offered by property owners to any restrictions on development rights. The proposed restraints were never imposed.

In Victoria Greater Melbourne bills were rejected in the upper house in 1913, 1915, 1936, 1937 and 1951–2, and a town planning bill was shelved in 1930. Outside the legislative sphere Melbourne property owners, following the Sydney precedent, established a Building Owners and Managers Association to resist any reduction in allowable plot ratios in the city.

In South Australia the upper house rejected the Town Planning and Housing Bill in 1917 and heavily amended the Town Planning and Development Bill in 1920 after the Adelaide City Council and real estate agents had denounced it. In 1929 the conservative lower house reduced the mild 1920 act to an innocuous control of subdivision act. Again in 1954 and 1960 town planning bills were rejected by the upper house after protests from the Real Estate Agents Institute and the Chamber of Commerce, and in 1966 the upper house heavily amended the Labor government's Planning and Development Bill. In 1959 the South Australian Landowners Protection League was successful in persuading the government to censure town planner Stuart Hart for his deliberate delaying tactics in approving applications for subdivision of the hills face.

Whenever they have deemed it necessary, then, property owners have been able to use the political institutions of the state to prevent encroachments on their property rights by planning legislation or regulations. This form of action was used especially before World War II. Since then they have been able to manipulate the planning process itself to make gains from property ownership and to use the same political institutions to support the 'national hobby of land speculation'. Such planning as has been attempted has therefore been hampered at every level by private property interests exerting influence on public authorities and by the corruption of some public officers and politicians with foreknowledge of planning decisions. The land-use plans produced in each city have been subject to constant pressure as a result of the capital gains in land value that can accrue to individuals from changes in the plans. In Sydney and Melbourne the plans themselves have been described as 'speculators guides' indicating which areas are to be rezoned from rural to urban and at what time. Government service authorities have also been subject to pressure to change their programmes to provide services that would increase the value of particular areas of land.

These problems, and most of the difficulties of equity and compensation related to planning and servicing development, could be avoided if the land were in public ownership for a period prior to urban development.

The most important obstacle, then, to a redistributive approach to city planning has been lack of control over the fundamental resource —land. The effects of this have included land speculation, especially on the urban fringe, land shortages due to withholding by landowners, shortages of development funds because of the high prices public authorities must pay on the open market to acquire land, and the limitation of planning to the negative role of responding to planning applications by major private developers.

Consider what happens when a government decides on the comprehensive redevelopment of its central area, or some part of it, for example Woolloomooloo or the Rocks in Sydney. Because of shortage of capital, the scheme has to be made attractive to private developers. To ensure an adequate return, intensive development of retail and office space is necessary. This limits the role of the town centre as a focus for a wider variety of activities and imposes on the authorities the need to improve the transport system serving peak-period movements to the city centre. With rising car ownership this imposes a further problem of road congestion in central areas. More generally, commercial and industrial growth in and around a city centre and increasing central employment reduces the number of workers who can live within easy reach of the centre, while the public sector is called on to finance the additional demands on transport services.

The proposed industrial development of Westernport indicates the fate of environmental objectives in a society which universally accepts both the right to speculate in land and the sanctity of the growth ideology. The nation-wide worship of economic progress is perhaps best illustrated by the fact that there is agreement between all major political parties on the desirability of increasing gross national product. The Labor Party has seen the achievement of high growth rates as a way of supplying funds with which to finance its health, education and transport proposals. In 1961 and 1963 the party promised to achieve a national growth rate of 5·5 per cent a year. This growth-mindedness put the Liberal government on the defensive and forced Menzies to promise a growth rate programme during the 1963 election campaign. The Labor Party's priority of growth is also reflected in its poor record in city planning when it was in power in the City of Sydney from 1945 to 1965. State governments of all political complexions have been keen to attract private capital from abroad and to establish new industries within their territories. Thus governments have equated the interests of private enterprise with the national interest, and the political and administrative apparatus of the state has been used to promote the interests of business and industry with scant regard for equity and the environmental and social consequences. This class power in action in urban development has been evident in the unrestricted growth both of the central business areas of the capital cities and their metropolitan areas; in the transportation plans for massive freeway programmes; in schemes like the proposed industrial development of Westernport Bay; and in the failure so far of environmental authorities in New South Wales and Victoria to control pollution.

In Victoria the Environment Protection Authority launched only three prosecutions in twelve months. In New South Wales after two-and-a-half years the Department of the Environment and the State Pollution Control Commission (SPCC) had not sought the prosecution of a single company. Top business leaders in both states occupy positions on environment protection authorities. The director of the New South Wales Department of the Environment was a former manager of the Caltex refinery at Kurnell. The government's appointed conservation representative on the SPCC is New South Wales manager of Imperial Chemical Industries and a former president of the Chamber of Manufactures who was awarded the OBE in 1971 for services to industry. He told a meeting of the chamber in 1970 that to blame industry for environmental pollution was an 'emotional fallacy'.[5]

The aim of an improved planning system would be to remove these problems through a conscious overall strategy of redistributive social justice. The private initiation of development would be replaced by positive planning which allocated land to uses according to social need and economic efficiency rather than to maximize individual profits. The question that must finally be answered then is whether these changes can be wrought in a capitalist society?

The impact of the changing structure of power since World War II on the process of urban development and city planning has been especially noticeable in the influence of new industries like car manufacturing and in the rising influence of the technocrats, especially those working for state planning and highway authorities. Indeed, through the narrow technical criteria of their planning, government authorities staffed by these technocrats have become new sources of oppression and injustice closely rivalling the private sector in responsibility for post-war planning problems. But neither of these new sources of power has supplemented the enduring influence of that older source based on property ownership. Nor have they eroded the continuing influence of the Country Party.

In December 1972 a Labor government was elected to federal parliament for the first time since 1949. A major thrust of its election programme was its urban policy. This next section looks at its new approaches to old problems and old sources of opposition.

New Approaches to Old Problems: Department of Urban and Regional Development 1972–4

Keith Hancock wrote in 1930 that it was a weakness of democracies that, 'having willed an end, they try to shuffle out of willing the means'.[6] The federal Labor government of the forties displayed this weakness, especially in its urban policy. It failed to tackle the problem of the property rights attached to private ownership of land, although the *Commonwealth Housing Commission Report* had recommended an inquiry into land nationalization. It failed to devise means enabling citizens to participate in the planning process, although this was one of its most important aims in theory. And it failed to implement its programme of regional decentralization before it was defeated in 1949.

The federal Labor government that won office in 1972 after twenty-three years 'in the wilderness' established in its first glorious days of social democratic idealism the Department of Urban and Regional Development (inelegantly referred to as DURD) to tackle these old problems. Theory would educate government, while intellectual idealism would be forced to come to terms with political feasibility. Both would be tempered by the direct participation of those whom they served. DURD's objectives are explicitly redistributive. It is concerned above all with the equity effects of urban development and with improving the lot of that 20 per cent of the national population 'at the bottom'.[7] It has, its Marxist critics claim,[8] redefined the problem of inequality, which is no longer understood as a function of the ownership of the means of production but is simply a function of location—where people live and how accessible they are to the city's jobs, goods and services. This criticism may be true but it is not particularly useful since it merely states the obvious, that the Labor Party is not a socialist party but a social democratic one and as such chooses to tackle the consequences of the capitalist economy (like locational inequality) rather than to dismantle that economy. And this is in response to the preferences of the majority of Australian workers who want more say in and more of the benefits of the present system rather than its replacement by any socialist state.

The best indication of the degree of commitment of the government to urban problems is in the budget allocations of 1973/4 and 1974/5, especially the latter, since the economic situation began to deteriorate by mid-1974 and there was considerable pressure on the government to cut back on its social reform programme. The 1973/4 budget provided $136 million for the cities, raised the allocation for the states' public housing programmes by 25 per cent and provided $32 million of a proposed $700 million programme of improvements to urban public transport systems. It provided $30 million for the states to begin to tackle the backlog in urban sewerage services (a programme which needs an estimated $850 million to complete), and made special grants to local councils in the 'deprived west' of Sydney ($5 million) and of Melbourne ($3 million) to improve their services and amenities according to local preferences. Evidence of the government's wider ambitions in influencing urban development was the provision of $33 million for urban growth centres and $30 million for land commissions. It allocated $9 million of the $33 million for urban growth centres to Albury-Wodonga (which spans the New South Wales-Victorian border). The other $24 million was for the nominated growth centres of Bathurst-Orange (140 miles west of Sydney), Campbelltown (thirty-five miles southwest of Sydney) and Gosford-Wyong (thirty to fifty miles north of Sydney), and Melbourne's southeast sector and Geelong (forty miles southwest of Melbourne), Monarto (fifty miles east of Adelaide), and Salvado (north of Perth).

In 1974, budget expenditure in all these fields was increased: land commission allocations to $57 million, sewerage to $105 million, growth centres to $223 million, area improvement programmes to $14 million. Altogether the total outlay on DURD programmes in the 1974/5 budget was $433 million, an increase of $266 million on their first year's allocations, and a firm indication of the government's determination in this area of social policy.[9]

The purpose of the proposed land commissions is to purchase large areas of land in or near major urban areas suitable for urban development or redevelopment in order to provide land at low capital cost to the average citizen, to effectively plan and service the large areas involved and to retain for the community some of the equity in developed land. The funds for the land commissions are contingent upon the establishment by each state of a commission to acquire and develop land and on the introduction by each state of land price stabilization legislation to prevent land speculation in growth areas both on the metropolitan fringes and in growth centres. The intention was that land would be made available for building on long-term leases without the necessity for homebuyers to pay a capital sum for the grant of a lease. However, since the release of the *Report of the Commission of Inquiry into Land Tenures* the minister has indicated his willingness to accept a system of freehold (but with no development rights attached) rather than leasehold for *residential* land.

The prospective role of the commissions was accepted readily enough by the Labor government of South Australia and initially by Western Australia, until the Tonkin Labor government was defeated in March 1974. South Australia has established a land commission but the upper house amended the Land Commission Bill to prevent the *leasing* of land of less than one-fifth of a hectare (about half an acre) in area and to prevent compulsory acquisition of land on which there is a dwelling, factory, workshop, warehouse, shop or other commercial or industrial premise, an amendment which greatly reduces the redevelopment powers of the commission. The upper house has also rejected outright the bill to stabilize land prices.

In Western Australia the upper house shelved the Land Control Bill, the Land Commission Bill and the Salvado Development Bill in December 1973. All three bills had been under siege from real estate and business interests as represented by the Land Legislation Study Group, which published an elaborate *Report on Proposed Land Legislation to the Government of Western Australia* (August 1973) claiming, among other things, that the state and local governments would be bypassed, providing 'a major opportunity for the Federal Government to dominate the decisions of the state'. Similarly an Adelaide real estate developer described 'the whole thing as a Commonwealth plot',[10] and senior executives of the Master Builders Association, the Housing Industry Association, the Real Estate Institute and the Chamber of Commerce and Industry in South Australia formed a Land Use Advisory Committee to fight the land price stabilization legislation.

The Liberal-Country Party governments of Victoria, New South Wales and Queensland have been more reluctant to co-operate with the federal government. While quietly welcoming the extra money for sewerage, they resent the conditions attaching to the funds for growth centres, land commissions, local government and urban transport. The deputy premier of New South Wales, Sir Charles Cutler, expressing the views of the Country Party, has said that the budget 'while increasing allocations to the major cities, is robbing the country of its rightful share of finance. It is thus fertilising the Federal Government's idea of a centralist authority.'[11] The Country Party president in Queensland has similarly described the land commission proposals as 'contrary to Country Party philosophy'.[12]

The Victorian government introduced land price stabilization legislation in November 1973 but the act contained no new machinery and no powers of acquisition. In 1974 an Urban Land Council was established, in the words of the Victorian minister for local government 'to advise on and promote growth *outside* the metropolitan area and to assist in the provision of cheaper home sites, especially for lower income earners'. He went on to say that 'the prime objectives of government activity are *to aid private enterprise* to effect comprehensive and well planned development and to provide primary and sullage sewerage, and services, *rather than acting as a developer in competition with the private sector*' [my italics].[13] The federal government's aim in establishing land commissions however is precisely to compete with the private sector and thereby to reduce the price of land, as the Swedish government has been doing successfully for the past twenty-five years.[14] The governments of New South Wales and Queensland have not as yet been persuaded to co-operate with the federal government's new initiatives.

Yet again the influence of the Country Party and of big property owners on the states' political institutions threatens to undermine the ambitious plans for reform. Some aspects of the new urban policy can be achieved through federal government action, for example the recent decisions to purchase the Church of England's housing estate in Glebe (inner Sydney) and provide 700 new and renovated homes there in the next five years in a mixed income scheme and to move 30 000 of its own public service staff from the city centres of Sydney and Melbourne to outer suburban and country locations. But most of DURD's new initiatives, especially the roles proposed for the land commissions and development corporations and the recommendations of the Royal Commission of Inquiry into Land Tenures, which submitted its report in November 1973, require the exercise of state powers and therefore the close co-operation of the states.

The Commission of Inquiry into Land Tenures under the chairmanship of Mr Justice Else-Mitchell was set up in July 1973 to recommend appropriate policies and procedures for the administration of publicly owned land. The report submitted by the commission in fact went further than its initial terms of reference in recommending the public ownership of development rights—that is, the elimination of private gains from land-use changes. This, the report argued, would have five major advantages. The first was social equity:

Under the present system of land tenure the good fortune of holding land within an area for intensive development is a matter of chance for the individual landowners; millions of dollars are won or lost by a decision of an elected local council or by the stroke of a planner's pen. Those millions of dollars come from the collective pockets of the community.[15]

Secondly the reservation of development rights would improve the planning process by removing pressures for planning changes that are profitable to individual landowners rather than desirable in the public interest. Removal of speculation, the report argued, would also reduce costs and prices and benefit government finances and, finally, it would reduce pressures for premature development. The report does not advocate a freeze on the price of land. Rather it suggests a freeze on an owner's right to change the nature of its use and in so doing profit at the community's expense. The report thus attacks pure speculators, but not developers, who are encouraged to co-operate with the envisaged development corporations. As yet, developers have shown no great enthusiasm for these recommendations.

Bearing in mind 'the deep-seated psychological attachment which many people have to land',[16] the recommendations do not affect the right of individuals to buy and sell their blocks or their homes, provided the use of the land is not changed. In short, the report perpetuates the Australian tradition of a man owning his own land and building his own house on it. It rejects the ideal of all land being leasehold, recommending that residential land in the new metropolitan and regional growth centres should be made available on the basis of a title in fee simple but with restrictions limiting the use of the land to residential purposes. For commercial and industrial development in the new centres the report recommends leasehold tenure so that all such land remains in public ownership and is leased at economic rentals.[17]

The federal government can adopt these proposals for the Australian Capital Territory and Northern Territory. But since the basic objective of the recommendations is to remove the speculative element in land prices throughout Australia, the states must be persuaded to adopt similar measures. Therein lies the main difficulty in implementing the commission's recommendations. It is clear that the non-Labor state governments are reluctant to support the new urban policies, which they regard as inconsistent with their 'philosophies' and as an erosion of state sovereignty. Their opposition is likely to prove the most intractable of all difficulties facing DURD.

The next and final section examines some recent changes in public opinion which may provide the support necessary for DURD to overcome the opposition of the recalcitrant Liberal states and the political power of the big property owners.

Can Capitalism be Civilized?

Chapters 6, 7 and 8 outlined certain aspects of the structure of political power in Australian society that militate against a redistributive approach to city planning. But those chapters also noted complementary attitudes among the general public. For example the worship of economic growth as synonymous with 'progress' is reinforced by the Labor Party's belief that more growth means a bigger slice of the cake for the poor. The vested interest of insurance, development and finance companies and big property owners in speculative development is reinforced by an electorate consisting of property owners and their families all enjoying the appreciation of the value of their own homes, which is outpacing most other costs and prices. The Manhattan syndrome (the overdevelopment of the central city) not only makes profits for insurance companies and developers but is applauded by many citizens who find the rising, ever-changing skyline exhilarating. And pressure for freeways comes not only from automobile, oil, spare parts and hire purchase companies but also from the habit and expectation of every car owner of driving his own car when and where he pleases, and for governments to make this possible. We are dealing therefore not simply with a capitalist conspiracy but with a powerful set of cultural values and social habits. The strict Marxist reply is that these values are determined by the capitalist class, that the ideas of the ruling class are the ruling ideas. This seems to me to be only half true in the Australian situation in which, since World War II a majority of workers have been able to enjoy a degree of affluence sufficient to convince them of the acceptability of the capitalist system.

Capitalist societies, partly because of their productive capacities and partly because of regulation and the development of more sophisticated economic techniques, have proved capable of satisfying many of the most pressing working-class claims. This has been largely the result of a vast increase in goods rather than through redistribution, the extent of which has often been exaggerated. The spread of social services has also had a significant impact on the general standard of living and has reduced potential sources of conflict. So Australians, like the people in other liberal democracies, have voted pretty consistently for a market society rather than a socialist society. There has rarely been mass support for reformers' views; never for those of revolutionaries. This change or limitation of consciousness, which has brought so much anger and sorrow to Marxists, seems to be a result of more than economic improvements.

The modern worker can offer reasonable grounds for his present preferences and for his inactivity. He can point to his powerlessness, for drastic social change is simply not available to him. His own skills and organisations may have become more sophisticated, but the ruling class . . . has also gained in strength, skill and elusiveness. Meanwhile the worker becomes disillusioned about the possibility and the rewards of drastic social change—his own organisations are subject to bureaucratic and oligarchic tendencies, public economic enterprises suffer from 'the dead hand of government', and the actual performance of socialist states shows little of the spectacular productive advantages and the widespread liberation of men which were promised. The alternatives to capitalism thus seem greyer than they were painted and, while their shortcomings are exaggerated by much of the mass media, they are not simply invented by them.[18]

H. Marcuse may argue that capitalist society is intolerable and that only slaves would bear it voluntarily.[19] But the workers seem to be saying that it is unbeatable, that there seems nothing better and that the best course is to adapt to it. 'The mass of people do not embrace the system with the mindless, brainwashed, shallow complacency which Marcuse sometimes imputes to them.'[20] Middleclass intellectuals are often so little attracted by the consumer goods characteristic of modern society, the automobile or the television, 'to say nothing of the beer can and the packaged goods of the supermarket, that we greatly underestimate the degree to which they bring enjoyment to others.'[21] We may want to educate the next generation to enjoy different pleasures, but it would simply be arrogant and inconsiderate to impose these intellectual and middle-class preferences on people with different opportunities and life experiences.

I do not share the revolutionary vision of a harmonious conflict-free society if only the institution of private property and its consequence, class conflict, were abolished. I believe that such a state would still be characterized by different and competing values and visions of good and that inevitably some decisions would prove disturbing to some people and require rules and constraints.[22] Moreover writers like Parkin, Djilas and Dahrendorf[23] (all of whom share important radical values) have shown that profound social stratification and inequalities of power can and do exist in societies in which private property has been abolished. *Control* of the instruments of production, without ownership, has proved to be an effective new source of power. New classes may and have derived privileges from political power itself and may and have established economic inequalities without property ownership and inheritance. 'For power is a general category of which ownership is only one case. And class conflict is only a special, though crucial, case of group conflict, which is itself only one, though the crucial, case of social conflict.'[42]

The question then is, can capitalism be civilized? Can a conscious overall strategy of redistributive social justice be achieved? Can pollution be controlled? Can the environment be protected bearing in mind the tenacious hold on power by the capitalist class, the methodological weaknesses of democracies in implementing the brightest ideas, and especially bearing in mind the effect of the political preferences of the majority of Australians working through the established political system on factors determining for example the success or failure of urban planning? There is no doubt that much of what has occurred in the last thirty years has been the result of capitalist manipulation and corruption. But it would have been impossible if the general political climate had been adverse to such happenings, if the majority of Australians had not wanted precisely the sorts of things they thought a capitalist economy could deliver for them. Much of what happened and failed to happen in urban planning in the fifties and sixties can only be understood by keeping this in mind. Can these majority preferences be changed? Can 'progress' be put in its place? Can the values of redistributive social justice, environmental conservation and resource protection attain higher priority in the making of public policy?

Urban social reformers, conservationists, anti-pollution campaigners are themselves pressure groups; in a liberal democratic society they have an opportunity even if they are a small minority to obtain a hearing through the press and television to modify public opinion, to persuade governments to change their ways and to prefer long-term to short-term gains. Remember that a main reason for the failure of radical urban planning in the past has been lack of political support. It was only when some citizens began to organize and rebel against freeways, high-rise redevelopment, unlimited metropolitan growth, that previous inequitable urban policies began to be reconsidered. In Adelaide over the last five years there have been major changes in urban policy in the fields of transportation, redevelopment, decentralization, and public participation in the planning process. These have been brought about by persistent public pressure on a receptive government and by a changing pattern of interests among some sections of the business and property-owning communities.

The changing attitudes of some property developers are reflected in the ideas of G. J. Dusseldorp, chairman of Lend Lease Corporation and a member of the Commission of Inquiry into Land Tenures. He supports the public ownership of development rights, regional development, limitations on city size and some control on the overbuilding of the central city.[25] His ideas involve both a new environmental concern and a recognition that profits can still be made under the umbrella of state development planning. Sir Arthur Rymill's condemnation of the Adelaide transportation study is another example of environmental concern cutting across 'class loyalty', since the freeway programme was clearly in the interest of the capitalist class to which he belongs.

In Sydney, Melbourne and Adelaide over the last five years middle-class residents' action groups have protested against a variety of environmental issues precipitated by both government bureaucracies and private developers. Their protests on particular issues have led to a more general questioning of the supremacy of technology and profits over nature and human values, although in many cases their stands have been based on their own local self-interest with little awareness either of wider metropolitan concerns or of the conflict between their middle-class environmental objectives and the more welfare-oriented objectives of the working class.

Public opinion must be mobilized in such a way that elected representatives regard themselves as trustees for the quality of air, water and landscape and for a distributively just society. This assumes that opinion can be mobilized and has some prospect of influencing a majority of electors, and that elected representatives are responsive to the views of those who elect them. These assumptions are not, in a democracy, absurd. But can these movements of reformers using representative institutions outweigh entrenched power groups?

I have shown that property owners and polluting industries do exert a disproportionate influence on governments, especially on those local governments in relation to which they are major employers or taxpayers. They do not always stop at lobbying; bribery and black-mail have been used. They have large funds at their disposal with which to buy media space. They belong to a network of cross-connected institutions. *Reformers and large corporations do not therefore compete on equal terms.* The competition comes closer to being equal if the large corporations are suspect and the civil service is reasonably honest, and if the corporation is unable to base its case on a crucial issue like the risk of serious unemployment.[26] But corporations are powerful and permanent. Social reform, anti-pollution campaigns—in general, movements to make the world a better place—depend on the energy of a dedicated few who don't always have the patience to wage a long campaign. The prospects for radical change (which often now means *stopping* things happening) are least hopeful when trade unions share the intentions of corporations, as in the car industry where both bosses and workers want to sell cars irrespective of resource shortages and environmental consequences. But the attitudes of some other unions have been changing dramatically in the last few years.   •

Posterity has not been a fashionable concern for public men since Keynes dismissed the subject with the observation that in the long run we will all be dead. But that concern has been revived in Australia in the most unexpected quarters: in the persistent stands by the Builders Labourers Federation (BLF) in New South Wales and Queensland, and the Plumbers and Gasfitters Union in South Australia on issues ranging from preventing the construction of freeways and high-rise redevelopment projects to preventing the destruction of parks, trees and historic buildings; and in single-issue stands by some other unions, for example the black bans on oil drilling on the Great Barrier Reef and on the Newport power station proposal in Melbourne.

The BLF has been by far the most significant in the number and nature of its green bans and in its methods of co-operation with (mostly middle-class) residents' groups. Right-wing politicians have described the BLF's methods as the 'democracy of the lynch-gang'. That some middle-class residents have supported these methods illustrates the central problem. At present, nowhere within the existing administrative and political structures responsible for the development of our cities is there a place for the voice of their users to be directly heard and considered as an effective factor. History, especially the more recent history of the 1960s, has given rise to disillusion with the omniscience of the 'technical expert' and the omnipotence of government. This disillusion has generated the feeling among aware sections of the middle and working class that they must take matters into their own hands. They are forced to do this because to back up their convictions they have only moral rights, whereas the other party in these conflicts, whether private developers or public authorities, are backed with a full panoply of legal rights. It is this conflict of legal and moral rights, individual and community rights, that is at the heart of the problem. To resolve the conflict the moral rights of the community must be given a place within the legal and administrative framework. Only governments can solve this problem. 'They, and only they, can adjust the system to accommodate to the circumstances, and the first call upon them is for legislation which will give the people's wishes and the people's voice a proper and effective part in the total process of deciding future developments.'[27]

Can representative democracy handle these problems? What are the limits to the reformist reach of democratic institutions within the class-bound body of capitalist society? And will more participatory and redistributive policies in the end enhance overall human welfare?

Political resistance is inevitable. Its nature has been outlined. But this type of resistance may be overcome given a government subject to a variety of public pressures and not wholly corrupt. Political obstacles to reform derive not only from organizations, government or private, but from the established habits and expectations of the people. The myopia that confines the present vision of men to the short-term future is not likely to disappear overnight. But promising changes have already taken place in important areas; in some trade unions, some state governments, in the new federal government's urban and environmental legislation (though its powers are limited and conflict with the philosophies of some states), and even in the usually right-wing, free-enterprise defending press. If their editorials reflect responses to changing public attitudes, the redistributive approach to city planning is gaining ground and so too is the environmental movement.

Heading its editorial of 14 January 1974 'Social Equity an issue in society', the *National Times* argued that

> one of the more popular illusions in Australia is that Australians are an egalitarian lot who are not worried by class conflict . . . but it is economic success, not egalitarian attitudes, which has dulled class conflict . . . Urban changes can discriminate against working class people. It was perhaps the most encouraging fact about the election of the Whitlam government a year ago that a majority of Australians endorsed Labor's rhetoric for some redressing of priorities, so that the poor and the lower income groups in areas in the cities could be given a better deal . . . The reformism of the Whitlam government is likely to prove one of its significant long-term influences.

And in similar vein the *Australian* editorial of 29 January 1974 observed of DURD's special grants to the western suburbs of Melbourne and Sydney that

> these are projects which a civilised society should regard as part and parcel of its normal social welfare activities. No society should feel morally comfortable when large sections of its less affluent urban population are forced to live in barely-serviced, amenity-less wastelands which have the sole advantage of being dormitories more or less within reach of their places of work.

The same newspaper made an even more significant comment in its editorial of 25 November 1974 on the environmental legislation then before federal parliament. The editorial was headed 'Putting progress in its place'.

> Even as the fickle trendies and camp followers of '72 desert the Labor Party in droves because of the economic situation, many of the social attitudes which first attracted them to the Whitlam cause are being implemented, although the results are being overshadowed by the larger and more important problems of inflation and unemployment.

The editorial applauded the legislation for 'giving Federal Cabinet the power to overrule proposals which take more ecologically than they give economically', and for 'involving the people, especially those in areas affected by development plans ... Where local residents object they can ask the government to call for an environmental impact study'. It ended by warning us that 'if we want to enjoy the advantages of an affluent, industrialized society then we have to accept the costs as well'.

All of these events indicate the increasing popular pressures for more equitable and more secure access to a reasonable quality of life. They are I think now approaching such a strength that governments which still uphold the exclusive property rights of a capitalist society,

> yet which claim also that they are promoting a fully democratic society—one in which all people are able equally to use and develop their human capacities—will have to acknowledge that property can no longer be considered to consist solely of private property—an individual right to exclude others from some use or benefit of something—but must be stretched to cover the opposite kind of individual property—an individual right not to be excluded from the use or benefit of something. This means the creation, by law, either of more common property or of more guaranteed access to the means of labour and the means of life which remain privately owned, i.e. a diminution of the extent to which private property, especially in productive resources, is a right to exclude.[28]

I see no inherent reason why a social democratic society cannot effectively carry out a policy of redistributive social justice, act against environmental devastation and achieve a more truly democratic, participatory policy. To say it could not would be to contradict existing facts and examples of changes in this direction. But there is every reason to believe that public pressure for it to act in this way cannot be safely relaxed.

Radicals have never been much interested in practical reforms that fall short of revolutionary change. There is often even a tendency to oppose piecemeal reforms as mere props to the capitalist system.[29] But if it is true that the prospects for a socialist revolution are negligible anyway, and this does seem to be the case in Australia, we can hardly be doing much damage to those prospects by advocating reforms, and we might in the meantime be doing some good.

Some civilizing policies, desirable in themselves, capable of gaining popular support, and at the same time a step towards a society in which essential goods and services are allocated on the basis of need rather than ability to pay—in other words, a step towards the kind of community that the left aims to bring about—might look something like this. An expansion in the services of government (but with far more attention to the preferences of the users) in the administration and improvement of health, education, justice, urban and arts programmes would not only rescue our system from a fatal encounter with the natural environment but could also produce enough 'growth' to aid the income distribution problem. More specifically the urban programme would acquire land in advance for public and private development on terms that secure a share in, if not all of, betterment values for the community. It would acquire a larger public-sector stake in the housing market on terms that make access for deprived groups easy and upward mobility, to different places or to owner occupation, easy too. It would concentrate a richer mix of public services and enterprises—as employers and as service providers— in more attractive nodes of less attractive areas and provide better transport to them from surrounding neighbourhoods. It would 'positively discriminate' in public-service provision in favour of deprived areas: smaller classes, better libraries, better pay for teachers in poorer schools; more swimming pools for the poor areas farthest from the beaches (which are also the areas with the most youthful populations);[30] more suburban decentralization of cultural activities. It would selectively 'invade' richer areas with development for middle- and low-income people, ensuring access to jobs, and public transport. It would limit the process of indefinite urban growth around a single central business and commercial core, and within that metropolis it would redistribute local tax resources at local scale to match needs. It would also *invent methods*, as distinct from espousing the principle, of involving the public in the planning process. *At what stage* of the process should they be involved—before, during, after, or all three? *How* do we involve them? Questionnaires to everyone in the metropolis? Phone-in votes after television programmes and press advertisements explaining the choices—who chooses the choices? Citizens' representatives on planning authorities? *Which* 'public' will participate, if it's not compulsory—should it be compulsory? If the purpose of participation is to give 'ordinary people' more say in decisions affecting the quality of their environment and daily life, how do we guard against the possibility that those who already win in the economic market-place will also be the winners in the political market-place created by new participatory procedures. Will these procedures be an unwelcome burden to all but a few radical intellectuals and middle-class environmentalists?

If the left is to put its energy behind practical reforms of this kind, it will need to redirect its thinking away from grand schemes based on the premise that capitalism is about to collapse, and toward detailed fact-finding and rigorous argument on particular issues. This approach does not imply ideological sale of souls. Now that the prospect of a continued, unlimited increase in material wealth has faded, we need more than ever a worked out conception of the good society—that is, an ideological stand—if we are to discuss policies intelligently.

Appendixes: Cases of Land Speculation

1 Environment: Westernport

In 1960 a group of people living in the area between Springvale, Frankston and Portsea on the Mornington Peninsula decided to 'put Westernport on the map'. They called themselves the Westernport Development Committee and were supported, through overlapping memberships, by the Hastings Shire Council. Some of them had property which would be 'profoundly affected' by any boom that might result.[1] Investors began buying cheap rural land in the area, and on French Island. Broken Hill Proprietary Co. Ltd (BHP) acquired 2000 acres on the island's western shore.

In 1963 Premier Bolte made an agreement with British Petroleum (BP) for a refinery at Crib Point. The land was swiftly rezoned and the agreement ratified by parliament. The terms of the agreement required very little from the company and millions of dollars from the government, not only for supplying water, roads and power to the site but also in outright subsidies of company operations. The act gave BP the right to compulsorily acquire easements from private landholders, a power until that time reserved only for the government. (It was also the forerunner of a number of acts which gave the governor-in-council, at the behest of private companies, the power to overrule public authorities as to easements affecting their property and lines.) Other major terms of the act were that the state would pay up to $7 million towards construction of jetties, channels and tugs of the company's design; that the company would be permitted to dispose of all effluent waters into the bay without fee or penalty, negotiate its own water and power rates, and lay pipelines as it saw fit; that the state would reimburse the company for repairs to jetties, channels and tugs for twenty years; and that the state would pay for pilotage, navigational aids and channels beyond the company's jurisdiction, 600 yards offshore from BP's property. Only two major requirements were made of the company. It was expected to pay for its own pipelines and to build a refinery that would comply with 'modern refinery standards'. These standards were not specified.

Bolte and two officers of BP signed the agreement before it went to parliament. The act also stripped the Hastings Council of any authority in the matter. But criticism of this act as a 'rubber stamp job' did not prevent the subsequent passage of two similar acts—the

Westernport Development Act of 1967, an agreement between the government and Esso-Hematite, and the Westernport Steelworks Act of 1970, which authorized the $1000 million Lysaght's (a BHP subsidiary) project.

In 1969 Bolte forecast that Westernport would be 'Australia's Ruhr'. He had already made overseas trips to attract capital to the area. Also in 1969, several years *after* the government had decided to industrialize the area, the Westernport Regional Planning Authority (WRPA) was formed under an amendment to the Town and Country Planning Act of 1961 to prepare and submit for approval a planning scheme for the area. The WRPA is made up of two councillors from each of the six shires in the region—Bass, Cranbourne, Flinders, Hastings, Mornington, and Phillip Island. Of the twelve representatives on the authority in 1971, at least six were involved in land dealings in the area. The chairman, who was also president of the Mornington Shire Council, was general manager of and property adviser to Colortone Property Developments Pty Ltd, which owned land on Mornington Peninsula. During 1969 Colortone bought four 10-acre blocks for $25 000 each. During early 1970 the other Mornington representative on the WRPA moved that these lots be rezoned from rural to residential. Council approved this. The president of the shire recommended rezoning to residential of three lots of land, one owned by the wife of the shire secretary, one owned by Merri Wendi Woke Woke Pty Ltd, of which the other Mornington shire representative and his wife were sole directors, and the third owned jointly by the president's wife, a solicitor, and Merri Wendi Woke Woke Pty Ltd. When asked if there were a possibility of conflict of interest arising from his dual roles on the WRPA and his management of Colortone Property Developments, the president of the Mornington Council replied, 'It's fair to say there is.'[2]

One of the Flinders shire representatives on the WRPA was the director of a private land company which owned 412 acres north of Cape Schanck. In October 1970 this company offered to sell their land to the authority for $160 000 to give it the chance of buying it for conservation purposes. When notified that its price was too high, the councillor indicated to the Authority that if it did not go ahead with the purchase for $200 000, he would suggest to the Flinders Council that they rezone it for residential purposes and allow subdivision to proceed. That councillor became chairman of the WRPA in September 1971.

In 1970 the press revealed that a group of Hastings councillors stood to make more than $100 000 on land deals. The sales hinged on the increase in land prices sparked by proposals for Lysaght's steelworks. At least three councillors had subdivided land near Hastings and two more were real estate agents, press reports claimed.[3]

Other landholders in the area included BHP, Esso, BP, and the Gas
and Fuel Corporation. BHP and East Coast Development Pty Ltd
also owned land on French Island, in the middle of Westernport Bay.
The island is within the regional planning area but, being unincor-
porated, is not represented on the WRPA. In 1970 the WRPA
received a report from R. M. Buchanan, a Sydney chemist, on the
feasibility of using French Island for most of the industry to be located
at Westernport. Buchanan was also a director of East Coast Development Pty Ltd, which had a considerable area of the island under its
control through ownership and options. Buchanan's report recommended the provision of a major aerodrome on French Island on
land owned by East Coast Development Pty Ltd. Early in 1971 the
WRPA had asked the government to carry out a $100 000 investi-
gation into developing an international industrial complex on French
Island, a suggestion based on Buchanan's study. A number of industries were interested in the island, including BHP, Imperial Chemical
Industries, Dow Chemicals and DuPont. The investigation that the
WRPA recommended was to be financed by Esso, BHP and others.[4]

Meanwhile, in December 1970, a draft report on the feasibility of
rezoning certain land for industrial use had been presented to the
WRPA. It was prepared by Plant Location International and recommended the rezoning of thousands of acres of rural land around the
bay. This report was referred to the authority's Industrial Development Advisory Committee, which included representatives from the
Nylex Corporation (whose chairman, Sir Charles McGrath, also
chairman of Repco Ltd, was a close friend of Bolte), Dowd Associates, BHP, Lysaght's, BP, Esso and Commonwealth Industrial
Gases. These members all had financial interests in land and industrial
activities in the area.

By this time local residents were angered that the future of the
peninsula and bay was in the hands of 'American consultants, the
W.R.P.A. and a combine of industrial speculators'[5] and that they
were not allowed to see the consultants' reports. But the Save
Westernport Coalition (comprising the Port Phillip Conservation
Council, the Westernport and Peninsula Protection Council, the
Citizens' Environmental Action League and the Clean Air and
Environment Council of Victoria) did manage to see a copy of the
report done by Plant Location International and they published its
contents in a pamphlet in July 1971. They revealed that plans for
Westernport included reshaping of the coast by filling in many miles
of the bay; two causeways to French Island and later a tunnel; industrial development on all of French Island, which would be squared
off for wharves and cheap land; the disposing of chemical wastes
through a pipeline which would cross Phillip Island; wharves and com-

mercial enterprises to be developed along the northern shore of French Island; and other industries to include a gas centrifuge for enriching uranium, a cracking plant to provide power for the island, a large petrochemical plant and another refinery, aluminium smelters and processing plants for paper and zinc. The report decided the fate of the western shores of the bay by arguing that BP and Lysaght's had 'set the character' of the area and that the expensive infrastructure had been developed to cater for their needs. The report also forecast a wide commercial industrial corridor from Dandenong to Hastings. The most urgent study of all, the relationship of the scheme to the welfare of the city, was not undertaken or envisaged. As the Save Westernport Coalition put it, 'It is doubtful if . . . any large city anywhere has been asked to hand over such an enormous recreational area to so few people.'[6]

The director of the WRPA reported to the authority in June 1971 on the proposed designation of boundaries within which industries could locate. In July the WRPA voted to zone a 5000-acre belt of farmland near Hastings for industry. An angry Hastings Council meeting of 7 July accused the WRPA of plotting the 'industrial devastation' of the area. In the proposed industrial zone were large tracts of land owned by BHP (2000 acres), Ampol-Sleigh, and the Gas and Fuel Corporation.[7] Some local councillors, conservationists, local organizations and 1400 individuals decided to oppose the rezoning, and the Westernport Peninsula Protection Council raised several thousand dollars for a 'fighting fund'. Nevertheless Bolte still maintained that the industrial zone would be 'a big lift for Victoria. I can see it having the biggest tonnage of any port in Australia. I am confident that the character of the Mornington Peninsula will not be significantly altered by the Hastings industrial development'.[8] And later in the year the government overrode objections by the Hastings Council and granted large rate concessions to the $1000 million Lysaght's steelworks. As Hastings shire president W. Nabbs commented, 'It appears that the government is prepared to go to any lengths to satisfy the selfish demands of large industrialists'.[9] And in 1972 Bolte still described the plans for Westernport as 'the greatest proposed development ever entered upon by this state'.[10]

Was it, though? It was certainly good for big business and for smaller land speculators. Big companies found the state government very co-operative in assisting its plans. Smaller speculators found local councils and the WRPA very co-operative in their efforts to profit from the unearned increment produced by a simple zoning change. Who, then, stands to lose? Certainly the residents of Mornington Peninsula and Phillip and French Islands stand to lose in environmental amenity. But so too do the present and future residents of

Melbourne who use the area for weekend and holiday recreation. And not all of them are middle class. The industrial plans for the area will provide jobs for workers, but at the expense of destroying a rare natural environment in close proximity to a metropolis whose population is expected to reach five million by the year 2000. Whose interests should prevail? Local middle-class residents and Melbourne trippers? Future generations of workers who will need jobs and would probably prefer the Westernport area to, say, Portland, which is much farther from Melbourne? Local speculators? Big companies wanting expansions for more profits? A hard question to decide, like most concerning environmental issues, for it is never simply a question of stopping growth. Most conservation issues require more money and therefore more growth. But perhaps the worst aspect of the history of Westernport was that the question was never asked. The Bolte government's priorities were never in doubt. Growth was good by definition. Industry should be given all the help a government could offer. The environment, and the people who lived in or used the area, could take it or, quite literally, leave it.

2 Housing: Victorian Housing Commission

One reason for the recommendation of the *Commission of Inquiry into Land Tenures Report* that the development rights attaching to land should be publicly owned was to avoid situations where speculation on likely changes of land use force public authorities to pay highly inflated prices to acquire land for their various programmes. The following case of acquisition by the Victorian Housing Commission (VHC) of *rural* land at a price which had risen in previous months to include the possible change of use to urban, illustrates this important problem.

In March 1962 the VHC, after consultations with the State Electricity Commission (SEC) in mid-1961, moved to acquire 1500 acres near Morwell in the Latrobe Valley for a satellite town. It found that 500 acres of this land was the subject of options obtained by a private company which had indicated to the Morwell Shire Council its intention of building a satellite town. A local real estate agent had approached the Morwell Council on behalf of the company Parksun Pty Ltd late in 1961 seeking council approval. It was unlikely that Parksun, with a nominal share capital of $10 000 and a paid-up capital of $10, really intended to build a satellite town. Having received approval in principle, neither the agent nor Parksun took steps to have the land rezoned. The real estate agent who acted for Parksun was also the VHC's agent in the Latrobe Valley.

Next to step in was Milgar Rural Industries Pty Ltd, a company with a list of directors from the wealthy suburbs of St Kilda, Toorak and Brighton and from Collins Street.

The interest of these people in the Latrobe Valley was such that if they were told where it was they could not find their way there ... Overnight these gentlemen suddenly discovered the Latrobe Valley and all this lovely rural land for which the VHC was going to pay residential prices ... discussions took place between the SEC and the VHC in July 1961. The VHC moved to make its acquisition in March 1962, but in February 1962 the hucksters jumped the gun by a month ... The total purchase price paid [by Milgar] was $57,474, not cash, but as a terms sale ... when the piece of land was sold to the VHC eight months later for $98,000 the actual profit was $40,526.'[11]

W. Phelan, Labor member for Kara Kara remarked, 'I could not be persuaded to believe that a Collins Street institution would buy this land unless it knew that it would later be acquired by the VHC at enhanced values.'[12]

This case is one of the smaller examples of the land acquisition problems of housing authorities which are trying to provide cheap land and housing for the poor. Most of the larger cases have not found their way into parliamentary debates, and details about them are hard to obtain.

3 Public Transport: Melbourne Underground Railway

Like housing and education authorities, public transport authorities must acquire land for their programmes under a system in which it has been possible for private speculators to hold the authorities and thereby the taxpayers to ransom. This happens either when public authorities publish plans of proposed future routes, locations or zonings, and speculators then buy up that land ahead of the authority, or when individuals occupying some public office and in possession of information concerning the acquisition of land for public purposes not yet released to the public use that foreknowledge to enrich themselves.

On 8 December 1970, J. Walton, a Labor member of the Victorian Legislative Council, told the council that the activities of certain city councillors who seized on the opportunities given by their public office 'have become a matter of public notoriety'. Walton referred to transactions by Withalit Pty Ltd, whose directors were Sir Bernard Evans, Lady Evans and a solicitor. Evans, a former lord mayor, was, at the time of the allegations, chairman of the Melbourne City Council's building and town planning committee and vice-chairman of the Board of Works' planning and highways committee. In March 1958 he had been appointed as one of the two council representatives on an underground railway investigation committee set up by the government. Withalit Pty Ltd was registered as a company in May 1958 and soon afterwards paid $300 000 for the property at 453–5 Latrobe Street (Withalit House) in the city. At a later date the underground investigation committee decided that the city's underground loop should run along Latrobe Street instead of Lonsdale Street as was originally recommended by a parliamentary committee in 1954. Since then Withalit has bought two other properties, as well as the laneway (which the council bought from the state government, then sold to Withalit) near the proposed Flagstaff Gardens underground station in Latrobe Street. In 1965 Withalit paid $183 000 for the property next to Withalit House and in 1966 bought the burnt-out Salvation Army building next to its existing holdings for $150 000.[13] In 1973 Withalit was paid $4.3 million compensation for the Withalit House property, which the government acquired for the underground railway[14]—a profit of almost $4 million.

Abbreviations

ANU	Australian National University
MATS	Metropolitan Adelaide Transportation Study
MMBW	Melbourne and Metropolitan Board of Works
MTPC	Melbourne Town Planning Commission
NSWPD	*New South Wales Parliamentary Debates*
SAA	South Australian Archives
SAPD	*South Australian Parliamentary Debates*
SAPP	*South Australian Parliamentary Papers*
SMH	*Sydney Morning Herald*
SPA	New South Wales State Planning Authority
VPD	*Victorian Parliamentary Debates*
VPP	*Victorian Parliamentary Papers*

Notes

Introduction

1 *NSWPD*, 1945, pp. 1767-8.
2 Stretton, *Ideas for Australian Cities*, p. 310.
3 There is a paucity of research on urban politics and economics in Australia and no coherent urban, political or social histories of any of the three cities on which this work focuses. There is also a glaring lack of material on social class, residential location and comparative accessibility to the whole range of urban services, with the exception of Manning, An Economic Study of Location—specific Service and Regulations in Sydney (Ph.D. thesis), and Davis and Spearritt, *Sydney at the 1971 Census*. There are only two works on the social geography of our cities: Jones, *Dimensions of Urban Social Structure*, and R. J. Stimson, 'The social structure of large cities' in I. H. Burnley (ed.), *Urbanization in Australia* (Cambridge 1974). But these works cover only the present and recent past. There has been little historical analysis of these questions of location, social class and comparative accessibility or even on changing transport patterns, employment locations and occupational structures, with the exception of an article by F. Stilwell and J. Hardwick, 'Social inequality in Australian cities', *Australian Quarterly*, vol. 45, no. 4 (Dec. 1973), pp. 18-37, and Stilwell's recent work, *Australian Urban and Regional Development* (Sydney 1974).
4 W. R. Thompson, *A Preface to Urban Economics* (Baltimore 1965).

1 Emergence of the Town Planning Movement

1 *The Growth of Cities in the Nineteenth Century*, p. 138.
2 Butlin, *Investment in Australian Economic Development 1861-1900*, p. 6.
3 R. W. Connell, Notes and Speculations on Class and the Cities, unpublished paper, Flinders University, 1974, p. 8.
4 E. Fry, 'Growth of an Australian metropolis' in Parker and Troy (eds), *The Politics of Urban Growth*, p. 5.
5 Butlin, op. cit., p. 213.
6 J. W. McCarty, 'Australian capital cities in the nineteenth century' in C. B. Schedvin and J. W. McCarty (eds), *Urbanisation in Australia* (Sydney 1974), pp. 21-3.
7 Butlin, op. cit., p. 324.
8 Ashworth, *The Genesis of Modern British Town Planning*, p. 47.
9 Ibid., p. 54.
10 F. J. Osborn, 'Preface' to E. Howard, *Garden Cities of Tomorrow* (London 1965).
11 pp. 226-7.
12 In Sulman, *Town Planning in Australia*, appendix A, pp. 424-33.
13 'Foreword', *First Australasian Town Planning Conference Proceedings* (Adelaide 1917), pp. 84-8.
14 Sulman, *Improvement of the City of Sydney*, p. 221; Fitzgerald, *Greater Sydney and Greater Newcastle*, p. 109.
15 Taylor, *Town Planning for Australia*, pp. 112-14.
16 Ibid., pp. 78, 99.

17 Taylor, *Town Planning with Common-sense*, pp. 40, 122.
18 B. McFarlane, *Professor Irvine's Economics in Australian Labour History* (Canberra 1966).
19 M. J. Webb, 'Planning and development in metropolitan Perth to 1953' in *Perth City and Region* (Perth 1968), p. 4.
20 Morrell, *Town Planning*, p. 832.
21 Ibid., p. 888.
22 And not only in England. The historian C. M. H. Clark (*A Short History of Australia*, p. 140) has contrasted the opulence of the squatter's life with the 'abject poverty' of the working class in the cities. 'In Sydney, according to an observer in 1860, a block of twenty ... wretched hovels afforded shelter for perhaps a hundred human beings. The high rents caused over-crowding, so that in houses occupied by Europeans as many as seven men and seven women squeezed into two rooms, while in houses occupied by the Chinese as many as 315 crowded into one building ... In Melbourne, too, sweated labour, jerry-built houses, and overcrowding created a contrast of bourgeois opulence south of the Yarra and working class squalor in the industrial suburbs of Fitzroy, Collingwood and Carlton.'
23 In *First Australasian Town Planning Conference Proceedings* (Adelaide 1917), p. 60.
24 Sulman, *Town Planning in Australia*, pp. 35, 188-9, 206.
25 'Presidential address' in *Australasian Town Planning Conference Proceedings* (Brisbane 1918), p. 26.
26 E. C. Rigby and T. G. Ellery, 'Future of Australian cities' in *First Australasian Town Planning Conference Proceedings* (Adelaide 1917), pp. 52-7.
27 *Australasian Town Planning Conference Proceedings* (Brisbane 1918), p. 187.
28 Ibid., p. 187.
29 Sulman, *Town Planning in Australia*, p. 213.
30 McFarlane, op. cit., pp. 15-17.
31 Gans, *People and Plans*.

2 Adelaide: Property, Privilege and Power

1 *SAPD*, 1915, p. 275.
2 *Ideas for Australian Cities*, p. 143.
3 Hirst, *Adelaide and the Country 1870-1917*, p. 11.
4 Ibid., pp. 16, 37.
5 See J. L. Moss, *Monopoly Owns South Australia* (Adelaide 1961).
6 Blewett and Jaensch, *Playford to Dunstan*, pp. 8, 9.
7 Vol. 20, no. 2 (Nov. 1933).
8 C. Reade and W. Davidge, *Australasian Town Planning Tour: recommendations in regard to planning* (Adelaide 1915), pp. 1-2.
9 *Port Pirie Recorder*, 4 June 1919.
10 Town Planning and Housing Association of South Australia, untitled pamphlet on reorganized constitution (Adelaide 1916).
11 *Advertiser*, 2 Nov. 1916.
12 *Advertiser*, 13 Sept. 1919.
13 *Mail*, 28 Sept. 1919.
14 *SAPD*, 1916, p. 878.
15 *SAPD*, 1916, pp. 880-1.
16 *Advertiser*, 23 Aug. 1916.
17 *Register*, 12 Sept. 1916.
18 *Advertiser*, 14 Sept. 1916.
19 *Advertiser*, 6 Oct. 1916; *Register*, 30 June 1917.
20 *Daily Herald*, 14 Nov. 1917.
21 *SAPD*, 1919, pp. 970-82.

22 *Register,* 7 Oct. 1919.
23 *Advertiser,* 14 Oct. 1919.
24 *SAPD,* 1920, pp. 662-3, 1471.
25 Town Planning and Housing Association of South Australia, *Urgent Memorial to Members of the Legislative Council concerning the Town Planning and Development Bill* (Adelaide 1920), p. 2.
26 Reade to the minister, 9 Sept. 1920, Town Planning Department papers, SAA, GRG 73, 1920/51-97, no. 64.
27 *SAPP,* 1920, no. 69, pp. 67-8.
28 *Register,* 2 Nov. 1920.
29 Memo by Reade, Town Planning Department papers, SAA, GRG 73, 1920/51-97, no. 87.
30 30 Nov. 1920, Town Planning Department papers, SAA, GRG 73, 1920/51-97, no. 87.
31 *SAPP,* 1921, no. 67, p. 7.
32 *SAPP,* 1923, no. 20, p. 8.
33 *SAPP,* 1924, no. 20, p. 3.
34 Town Planning Department papers, SAA, GRG 73, 1925/1-119, no. 11. Similar fears are expressed in another letter by him dated 3 June 1925 to the mayor of Brisbane, no. 51.
35 *Register,* 7, 13 July 1922.
36 Town Planning Department papers, SAA, GRG 73, 1922/444-79, no. 479, contains all these letters of request.
37 *SAPD,* 1924, p. 1729.
38 *Register,* 29 Nov. 1923.
39 *SAPD,* 1925, p. 771.
40 *SAPD, 1929, p. 2355.*
41 27 Nov. 1929.
42 Stretton, *Ideas for Australian Cities,* pp. 142-54; see also R. F. I. Smith, The Butler Government in South Australia 1933-1938, M.A. thesis, Adelaide University, 1964, ch. 4.
43 Stretton, op. cit., pp. 147, 142.
44 Ibid., p. 142.
45 *SAPD,* 1936, p. 2313.
46 Stretton, op. cit., p. 154.

3 Melbourne: Bureaucracy Tempered by Anarchy

1 E. C. Rigby and T. G. Ellery, 'Future of Australian cities' in *First Australasian Town Planning Conference* (Adelaide 1917), p. 85.
2 Davies, 'The government of Victoria' in S. R. Davis (ed.), *The Government of the Australian States* (London 1960), p. 175.
3 Ibid., p. 217.
4 G. Serle, 'Victorian Legislative Council 1856-1890' in *Historical Studies,* vol. 6, no. 22 (May 1954), pp. 192, 202-3.
5 Davies, loc. cit., p. 226.
6 Ibid., p. 175.
7 Blazey, *Bolte,* p. 41.
8 Davies, loc. cit., p. 224.
9 Blazey, op. cit., p. 41.
10 Davies, loc. cit., p. 224.
11 Blazey, op. cit., p. 102.
12 Ibid., p. 103.
13 Rawson, The Organisation of the Australian Labor Party 1926-1941, Ph.D. thesis, Melbourne University, 1954.
14 M. Cannon, *The Land Boomers* (Melbourne 1966).

15 Briggs, *Victorian Cities* (Melbourne 1968), pp. 322-5.
16 *VPD*, 1915, pp. 845-7.
17 *Argus*, 22 Mar. 1915.
18 *Argus*, 24 Mar. 1915.
19 *Argus*, 9 Apr. 1915.
20 *Argus*, 17 June 1915.
21 *VPP*, 1918, vol. 2, no. 19.
22 Local Government Act 1921, no. 3167, section 10.
23 *Public Investment in Australia*, pp. 210, 211.
24 *A History of Brighton*, pp. 381-2.
25 p. 114.
26 *Argus*, 6 Oct. 1914.
27 *VPP*, 1915, vol. 2, no. 59, p. 1503.
28 *VPP*, 1917, vol. 2, nos 28 and 29, p. 163.
29 Ibid., p. 200.
30 Ibid., pp. 300-2.
31 *VPP*, 1918, vol. 2, no. 19, p. 314.
32 MMBW, *Melbourne Metropolitan Planning Scheme*, vol. 2, pp. 10-12.
33 MTPC, *Plan for Melbourne*, p. 7.
34 Ibid.
35 MMBW, op. cit., p. 12.
36 *Argus*, 12 Apr. 1930.
37 *Argus*, 6 Aug. 1931.
38 MTPC, op. cit., pp. 19-20.
39 Ibid., pp. 155, 170, 241.
40 Ibid., pp. 187, 233.
41 Housing Investigation and Slum Abolition Board, First (Progress) Report, *VPP*, 1937, vol. 2, no. 4, pp. 93-8.
42 Ibid., p. 128.
43 Ibid., p. 44.
44 *VPD*, 1937, p. 1173.
45 *VPD*, 1936, pp. 1128-42.
46 Ibid., pp. 1159-61.
47 Ibid., pp. 3023-4, 3220, 3250.
48 Lieutenant-colonel Knox, member for Upper Yarra, *VPD*, 1936, p. 3330; letter from Prahran City Council, cited by Ellis, *VPD*, 1936, p. 3319; letter from Malvern Council, cited by Sir Stanley Argyle, *VPD*, 1936, p. 3268.
49 *VPD*, 1936, p. 3326.
50 Ibid., p. 3743.
51 *VPD*, 1937, pp. 92-102.
52 Ibid., p. 476.
53 *Argus*, 11 Aug. 1937.
54 5 Aug. 1937.

4 Sydney: National Hobby of Land Speculation

1 *The Australian People* (Sydney 1972), p. 198.
2 *Australia's Home*, p. 258.
3 R. S. Parker, 'The government of New South Wales' in S. R. Davis (ed.), *The Government of the Australian States* (London 1960), p. 115.
4 D. Aitkin, *The Colonel: a political biography of Sir Michael Bruxner* (Canberra 1969), p. 104.
5 Ibid., pp. 199-200.
6 Ibid., p. 225.
7 *SMH*, 22 Feb. 1930.
8 Parker, loc. cit., p. 89.

9 See P. Spearritt, A Social History of Sydney 1920-1950, forthcoming Ph.D. thesis, ANU, Canberra, 1976.

10 *NSWPD*, 1927, pp. 319-20.

11 Spearritt, op. cit.

12 *SMH*, 1 Apr. 1937.

13 *Daily News*, 15 Dec. 1939.

14 *NSWPD*, 1919, p. 137.

15 *New South Wales Statistical Register*, 1930-1, pp. 513-15.

16 Spearritt, op. cit.

17 C. B. Schedvin, Building and the Trade Cycle in Australia between the Wars, unpublished paper given at the 35th Anzaas Conference, Brisbane, 1961, p. 4.

18 *Evening News*, 25 Aug. 1920.

19 *The Australian Home Builder*, Aug. 1922, pp. 50-2.

20 *SMH*, 12 Mar. 1925.

21 *SMH*, 26 Aug. 1925.

22 Sydney, 1948, p. 27.

23 3 July 1928.

24 See my Ph.D. thesis (ANU, Canberra, 1974) for issues and evidence to support these and the following generalizations.

25 Spearritt, op. cit.

26 Schedvin, op. cit., p. 4.

27 *SMH*, 22 May 1931.

28 *NSWPD*, 1934, p. 657.

29 6 June 1934.

30 23 Feb. 1934.

31 *SMH*, 12 July 1935.

32 *SMH*, 16 Dec. 1936.

33 Ibid.

34 *NSWPD*, 1937, pp. 2392-4.

35 4 Feb. 1937.

36 *SMH*, 26 Apr. 1938.

37 *SMH*, 21 Apr. 1938.

38 *SMH*, 18 Sept. 1937.

39 28 Jan. 1939.

40 *Architecture* (Sydney), Nov. 1938, pp. 267-8.

41 G. R. Searle, *The Quest for National Efficiency* (Los Angeles 1971), p. 63.

42 Private correspondence from Sherrard to the author, 6 Oct. 1972, commenting on the first draft of this chapter.

5 Limits of Reform

1 Bean, *War Aims of a Plain Australian* (Sydney 1943), p. 81.

2 *SMH*, 5 Aug. 1943.

3 Goodman, *Communitas*.

4 See Davis and Spearritt, *Sydney at the 1971 Census*.

5 Bean, op. cit., p. 17.

6 Hancock, *Australia*, p. 105.

7 L. F. Crisp, *Ben Chifley* (London 1960), p. 183.

8 Ibid., p. 188.

9 e.g. Bean, op. cit.; B. Penton, *Think—or Be Damned* (Sydney 1941), *Advance Australia—Where?* (Melbourne 1943); A. J. Marshall, *Australia Limited* (Sydney 1942); Barnett and Burt, *Housing the Australian Nation*; Bunning, *Homes in the Sun* (Sydney, 1945).

10 Coombs, 'The economic aftermath of war' in Campbell (ed.), *Post-war Reconstruction in Australia*, pp. 98-9.

11 'A new social order' in Campbell (ed.), op. cit., pp. 208-9, 22-7.
12 Quoted by J. Playford, 'Who rules Australia?' in Playford and Kirsner (eds), *Australian Capitalism*, p. 128.
13 Bean, op. cit., pp. 120-1.
14 Ibid., p. 20.
15 Barnett and Burt, op. cit., pp. 10, 76, 86.
16 Crisp, op. cit., p. 196.
17 Department of Post-war Reconstruction, *Commonwealth Housing Commission Final Report*, 1944, p. 35.
18 Ibid., p. 29.
19 Ibid., p. 26.
20 Ibid., p. 27.
21 Ibid., pp. 43-4.
22 *Housing and Poverty in Australia*, p. 6.
23 Crisp, op. cit., p. 306.
24 Quoted in Crisp, ibid., p. 337.
25 Clark, *A Short History of Australia*, p. 237.
26 Crisp, op. cit., pp. 371-2, 373.
27 See A. L. May, *The Battle of the Banks* (Sydney 1968).

6 Adelaide: Conservatives, Technocrats and Citizens

1 *Advertiser*, 21 July 1950. Vaughan had introduced the state's first town planning bill in 1916.
2 Quoted in Playford, *Neo-capitalism in Australia*, p. 14.
3 Ibid., p. 7.
4 Blewett and Jaensch, *Playford to Dunstan*, p. 3.
5 Miliband, *The State in Capitalist Society*, p. 168.
6 Blewett and Jaensch, op. cit., p. 10.
7 *Advertiser*, 5 Dec. 1952.
8 South Australian Town Planning Committee, *Report on the Metropolitan Area of Adelaide 1962*.
9 *SAPD*, 1954, p. 12.
10 *SAPD*, 1954, pp. 1760, 1691, 1047.
11 *Advertiser*, 31 Aug. 1954.
12 A. Ramsay, 'Factors affecting the site and design of Elizabeth', *Royal Geographical Society of Australasia*, vol. 57 (Dec. 1955), p. 14.
13 Stretton, *Ideas for Australian Cities*, p. 159.
14 Ibid., p. 162.
15 Interview with Stuart Hart, 12 Jan. 1973.
16 *Advertiser*, 22 Aug. 1957, 1 Mar. 1958.
17 *Advertiser*, 17 Sept. 1959.
18 S. B. Hart, 'The South Australian State Planning Authority: the task ahead' in *Australian Town Planning Jubilee Conference* (Adelaide 1967), p. 60.
19 N. Platten, unpublished paper on MATS and the Future Development of Adelaide conference, Adelaide, 1969, p. 118.
20 South Australian Town Planning Committee, op. cit., p. 230.
21 S. B. Hart, 'Regional planning in South Australia', *Royal Australian Planners Institute Journal*, vol. 10, no. 1 (Jan. 1972), pp. 18-24.
22 Stretton, op. cit., p. 176.
23 *SAPD*, 1965, p. 74.
24 Buchanan, *Traffic in Towns*, p. 245.
25 *South Australian Year Book and Statistical Register* (Adelaide 1968).
26 *Advertiser*, 7 Feb. 1969.
27 Unpublished paper on MATS and the Future Development of Adelaide conference, p. 46.

28 *SAPD*, 1966, pp. 2870-1.
29 *Advertiser*, 26 May 1970.
30 *SAPD*, 1966, p. 2874.
31 Planning in the U.S.A., unpublished report to South Australian State Planning Authority, Adelaide, 1964, p. 102.
32 Altshuler, *The City Planning Process*, p. 317.
33 Op. cit., p. 273.
34 Town and Country Planning Association, *Planning S.A.*, no. 15, (June 1970), p. 2.
35 Commonwealth Bureau of Roads, *Report on Commonwealth Financial Assistance to the States for Roads.*
36 D. A. Hester, *Advertiser*, 22 July 1970.
37 *SAPD*, 1969.
38 Adelaide City Council, *Annual Report*, 1969-70, p. 20.
39 *S.A. Motor*, Jan. 1969.
40 *Advertiser*, 13 Feb. 1969.
41 M. Duigan, The Politics of Urban Transportation, B.A. thesis, Politics Department, Adelaide University, 1970, pp. 63-6.
42 Stretton, op. cit., p. 186.
43 Quoted in Duigan, op. cit., p. 69.
44 *High Density Living* (London 1966), p. 1.
45 Dunstan, 'Government in planning' in *Governments and Planning*, report of proceedings of the Royal Australian Planners Institute Congress (Brisbane 1972), pp. 13-15.
46 Ibid., pp. 15-16.
47 Ibid., p. 22.
48 *Hackney Project News*, no. 1 (Nov. 1972), p. 3.

7 Melbourne: Capitalism, Crude and Uncivilized

1 *Plans for Melbourne*, pt 1, p. 21.
2 *Age*, 28 Feb. 1972.
3 D. V. Donnison, *Social Policy and Administration Revisited* (London 1975), ch. 1.
4 See appendixes 1-3.
5 *VPD*, 1951, p. 4586.
6 Blazey, *Bolte*, p. 54.
7 Ibid., p. 85.
8 *Age*, 12 Mar. 1970.
9 MMBW, *Report on Amending Planning Scheme No. 1.*
10 Urban Research Unit, *Urban Development in Melbourne*, p. 175.
11 Stretton, *Ideas for Australian Cities*, p. 200.
12 Crow, *Plan for Melbourne*, pt 3, p. 7.
13 *Melbourne Metropolitan Planning Scheme*, vol. 1, p. 49.
14 Industry, Employment and Transport, unpublished paper, Melbourne, May 1972.
15 *Age*, 28 Feb. 1972.
16 *Age*, 10 Nov. 1972.
17 *Age*, 16 Oct. 1972.
18 *Age*, 24 Feb. 1973.
19 Urban Research Unit, op. cit., p. 171.
20 *Deschooling Society*, p. 63.
21 *Age*, 15 Sept. 1971.
22 *Age*, 8 July 1971.
23 *Age*, 25 Aug. 1971.

24 5 Oct. 1971.
25 Quoted in A. G. Austin (ed.), *The Webbs' Australian Diary 1898.* (Melbourne 1965), p. 72.
26 Barry Jones, Labor member of the Legislative Assembly for Melbourne, interview, June 1973.
27 *Age,* 27 May 1971.
28 *Age,* 20 June 1973.
29 *National Times,* 26 Aug. 1974.
30 *Australian,* 7 Sept. 1973.
31 *Age,* 8 Mar. 1972.
32 *Age,* 30 July 1970.
33 *Age,* 1 Aug. 1970.
34 *Herald,* 20 Jan. 1971.
35 *Age,* 17 July 1972.
36 See M. Jones's excellent account of this in *Housing and Poverty,* pp. 87-8.
37 'Some of the politics of redevelopment in Melbourne' in Troy (ed.), *Urban Redevelopment in Australia,* p. 119.
38 See City Development Association, *Redevelopment of Near-city Areas: three proposals for private enterprise participation* (Melbourne 1958); and M. Gold, *Your City and Heart Trouble: a review of a problem that concerns every person who earns his living in the inner City of Melbourne* (Melbourne 1964).
39 See Crow, *Plan for Melbourne,* pt 2, p. 79.
40 Stretton, op. cit., pp. 123-4, 197.
41 See maps in the forthcoming *Social Atlas of Melbourne* by the Cities Commission.
42 *Age,* 6 Jan. 1971.
43 Stretton, op. cit., p. 124.
44 *Age,* 8 May, 30 Oct. 1972.
45 Hanover Holdings Ltd, submission to state government, Nov. 1972, p. 14.
46 Ibid., p. 16.
47 *Age,* 19 Jan. 1973.
48 *Age,* 3 Apr. 1971.
49 *Age,* 9 July 1971.
50 R. Rivett, *Canberra Times,* 11 May 1973.
51 J. Floyd, Citizen Participation, town planning thesis, Melbourne University, 1972.
52 R. Rivett, *Canberra Times,* 3 Apr. 1973.
53 R. Bunker, 'Town planning and politics: a Melbourne case study', *Public Administration,* vol. 30, no. 4 (Dec. 1971), pp. 371-84.
54 *Canberra Times,* 7 Dec. 1971.

8 Sydney: Development without Improvement

1 Winston, *Sydney's Great Experiment,* p. 79.
2 W. R. Thompson, *A Preface to Urban Economics* (Baltimore 1965), p. 117.
3 Quoted in McKell, *Five Critical Years,* p. 52.
4 Ibid., p. 5.
5 Ibid., pp. 50-2.
6 'Planning in N.S.W.' in *Australian Town Planning Jubilee Conference* (Adelaide 1967), p. 96.
7 Planning and Government: N.S.W. 1945-63, M.A. thesis, Sydney University, 1968.
8 R. D. Fraser, 'Planning and government in the metropolis', *Public Administration,* vol. 31, no. 2 (June 1972), pp. 123-38.

9 Winston, op. cit., p. 73.

10 P. Harrison, 'Planning the metropolis: a case study' in Parker and Troy (eds), *The Politics of Urban Growth*, p. 67.

11 Ibid., p. 68.

12 Stretton, *Ideas for Australian Cities*, p. 240.

13 Fraser, loc. cit.

14 Harrison, op. cit., pp. 70-1.

15 The most recent example is Bunker, *Town and Country or City and Region?*

16 Stretton, op. cit., p. 242.

17 Harrison, op. cit., p. 76.

18 Stretton, op. cit.

19 Ibid., p. 246.

20 SPA *Sydney Region Outline Plan 1970-2000 A.D.*, p. 11. Other statements of this Sydney patriotism recur on pp. 1, 10, 12, 27, 33.

21 Stretton, op. cit., p. 258.

22 SPA, op. cit., p. 34.

23 Ibid., p. 98.

24 Department of Urban and Regional Development, *Urban Land Prices 1968-1974* (Canberra 1974), p. 21.

25 8 Aug. 1972.

26 J. O'hara, *SMH*, 16 June 1972.

27 *NSWPD*, 1970, pp. 4361-2.

28 Neutze, *Economic Policy and the Size of Cities*, P.V.

29 Quoted in Harrison, op. cit., p. 83.

30 J. O'hara, *SMH*, 11 June 1969.

31 Ibid., 12 May 1971.

32 Ibid., 13 May 1971.

33 SPA, op cit., p. 101.

34 6 Apr. 1972.

35 Winston, op. cit., p. 84.

36 Stretton, op. cit., p. 246.

37 'Market factors in the redevelopment of the central business area of Sydney 1957-66' in Troy (ed.), *Urban Redevelopment in Australia*.

38 Quoted in Harrison, op. cit., p. 72.

39 Stretton, op. cit., p. 263.

40 Quoted in H. Meares, City of Sydney Strategic Plan: planning in a political environment, B.A. thesis, Sydney University, 1972, ch. 3, p. 1.

41 Ibid., ch. 3, p. 4.

42 P. Loveday, 'Citizen participation in urban planning' in Parker and Troy (eds), *The Politics of Urban Growth*, p. 142.

43 Urban Systems Corporation et al., *City of Sydney Strategic Plan*, p. 93.

44 Ibid., p. 5.

45 Quoted in Meares, op. cit., ch. 5, p. 15.

46 Seidler, *Australian*, 27 July 1971; Gruzman, *SMH*, 22 June 1972; Mortlock, *SMH*, 2 Dec. 1971; Paterson, *Financial Review*, 22 Mar. 1972.

47 Sydney City Council, City Planning and Building Department Statistics, July 1973.

48 Calculated from details of building in the six sectors set out in 4D Planning and Design Pty Ltd, *Woolloomooloo Redevelopment Project*.

49 Harrison, op. cit., p. 98.

50 Painter, Local Council Decision Making in Sydney, Ph.D. thesis, ANU, Canberra, 1973.

51 Ibid., p. 45; E. Vandermark and P. Harrison, *Development Activities in Four Sydney Suburban Areas* (Canberra 1972), pp. 125-8.

[52] Painter, op. cit., pp. 235-6; Vandermark and Harrison, op. cit., pp. 104-8.
[53] An Economic Study of Location-specific Service and Regulations in Sydney (Ph.D. thesis).
[54] Stretton, op. cit., p. 259.
[55] Thomas, *Taming the Concrete Jungle*, pp. 131-2.
[56] A term first used by J. Power in 'The new politics in the old suburbs', *Quadrant*, no. 13 (Dec. 1969).
[57] Defined by A. Jakubowicz in 'Towards a sociology of the city: or the city game', *Australian and New Zealand Journal of Sociology*, vol. 9, no. 2 (June 1973), p. 61, as 'looking for an alternative to the "suburban" life. They are mainly self-employed, are employees in corporations, the public service, the media, universities or in the professions. They tend to be well-educated, literate, articulate, and have middle class skills that make the mystifying process of government, if not comprehensible, then at least accessible. Freed from the day to day insecurity of the manual worker, and from the entrepreneurial responsibility of the traditional bourgeois middle class, they have the option of dealing with the wider questions that they feel affect them'.
[58] See 'Sydney street demolishers stymied by squatters', *Digger*, 28 July 1973.
[59] Title of a book by Tom Wolfe (1970) which satirizes this brief flirtation.
[60] Discussions with the author in September 1973.
[61] F. J. B. Stilwell, *Australian Urban and Regional Development* (Sydney 1974), p. 30.
[62] For an excellent discussion of this issue see Hugh Stretton's 1974 Boyer lectures, published in 1975 by the Australian Broadcasting Commission as *Housing and Government*.

Conclusions

[1] *Efficiency, Equality and the Ownership of Property* (London 1964), p. 38.
[2] *Australian Journey* (London 1942), p. 110.
[3] Stretton, *Ideas for Australian Cities*, p. 267.
[4] S. Hart, 'Regional planning in South Australia', *Royal Australian Planning Institute Journal*, vol. 10, no. 1 (Jan. 1972), pp. 18-24.
[5] See 'Why pollution laws don't work', *National Times*, 21-26 Jan. 1974.
[6] Hancock, *Australia*, p. 105.
[7] DURD's objectives were outlined by several of its top public servants at a Royal Australian Planning Institute conference, Terrigal, 21-23 Sept. 1973.
[8] Catley and McFarlane, *From Tweedledum to Tweedledee, the New Labor Government in Australia*.
[9] Australian Government, *Urban and Regional Development 1974-5*, Budget Paper no. 8, 1974-5.
[10] *Financial Review*, 24 May 1973.
[11] *SMH*, 28 Aug. 1973.
[12] *Courier Mail*, 23 June 1973.
[13] A. Hunt, 'Planning key to land price curbs', *Age*, 8 May 1974.
[14] See G. M. Neutze, Urban Land Policy in Sweden and the Netherlands *and* Land Prices and Land Use Controls, unpublished seminar papers, Urban Research Unit, Research School of Social Sciences, ANU, Canberra, 1974.
[15] Commission of Inquiry into Land Tenures, *Interim Report*, p. 42.
[16] Ibid., p. 28.
[17] Ibid., pp. 121-65.
[18] Duncan, *Marx and Mill*, p. 306.
[19] *One Dimensional Man* (Boston 1968).
[20] Duncan, op. cit.

21 Passmore, *Man's Responsibility for Nature*, p. 93.
22 This faith seems to be the main weakness in Macpherson's argument in *Democratic Theory*.
23 M. Djilas, *The New Class* (New York 1957); R. Dahrendorf, *Class and Class Conflict in Industrial Society* (London 1959); F. Parkin, *Class Inequality and Political Order* (London 1972).
24 Duncan, op. cit., p. 202.
25 *National Times*, 21-26 Jan. 1974.
26 Passmore, op. cit., p. 62.
27 J. M. Freeland, 'Moral rights must become legal rights', *University News*, Sydney University, Dec. 1973, p. 4.
28 Macpherson, op. cit., p. 134.
29 See Catley and McFarlane, op. cit.
30 See Davis and Spearritt, *Sydney at the 1971 Census*, maps 16-20.

Appendixes

1 J. Iggulden, et al. (eds), *The Shame of Western Port*, p. 7.
2 *Sunday Observer*, 21 Feb. 1971.
3 *Age*, 23 Apr. 1970.
4 *Sunday Observer*, 7 Mar. 1971.
5 *Age*, 3 Apr. 1971.
6 Iggulden, et al. (eds), op. cit., pp. 3-8.
7 *Age*, 8 July 1971.
8 *Age*, 9 July 1971.
9 *Age*, 26 Nov. 1971.
10 *Age*, 9 Mar. 1972.
11 C. Holding, *VPD*, 1967, p. 3816.
12 *VPD*, 1967, p. 3830.
13 J. Walton, *VPD*, 1970, pp. 3010-11.
14 *Australian*, 23 Nov. 1973.

Select Bibliography

Planning Documents

Australia

Commission of Inquiry into Land Tenures. *Interim Report.* Canberra, 1973.

Commonwealth Bureau of Roads. *Report on Commonwealth Financial Assistance to the States for Roads.* Canberra, 1969.

Department of Post-war Reconstruction. *The History of Progress and Review of Regional Planning Activities through the Commonwealth.* Canberra, 1949.

Department of Urban and Regional Development. *Urban and Regional Development 1973–74.* Second Annual Report. Canberra, 1974.

—— *Urban Land Prices 1968–1974.* Canberra, 1974.

Evatt, H. V. *Post-war Reconstruction: a case for greater commonwealth powers.* Canberra, 1942.

New South Wales

Cumberland County Council. *County of Cumberland Planning Scheme Report.* 1948.

Development Corporation of New South Wales. *Report on Selective Decentralisation.* 1969.

Irvine, R. F. *Investigations into the Housing of Workmen in England and America.* Sydney, 1913.

New South Wales Parliamentary Papers. Report of the Royal Commission for the Improvement of the City of Sydney and Its Suburbs. Vol. 5, 1909, pp. 379–703.

—— Interim Report of the Housing Investigations Committee. 1937–8.

New South Wales State Planning Authority. Annual Reports 1966–7, 1969–70.

—— *Sydney Region: growth and change.* 1967.

—— *Sydney Region Outline Plan 1970–2000 A.D.* 1968.

Urban Systems Corporation et al. *City of Sydney Strategic Plan.* 1971.

South Australia

De Leuw, Cather et al. *Report on Metropolitan Adelaide Transportation Study.* 1968.

South Australian Housing Trust. Annual Reports 1950–72.

South Australian Parliamentary Papers. Report of the Select Committee of the Legislative Council on the Town Planning and Development Bill, and Minutes of Evidence. No. 69, 1920.

South Australian State Planning Authority. Annual Reports 1968–72.

—— *Adelaide 2000: towards a Strategy*. 1972.

South Australian Town Planning Committee. Annual Reports 1956–65.

—— *Interim Report on the Metropolitan Area of Adelaide*. 1960.

—— *Report and Plan for the Development of the Metropolitan Area of Adelaide*. 1962.

—— *Report on the Metropolitan Area of Adelaide 1962: report on objections*. 1965.

Victoria

Housing Investigation and Slum Abolition Board, First (Progress) Report, *V.P.P.*, 1937, vol. 2, no. 4.

Melbourne and Metropolitan Board of Works. *Melbourne Metropolitan Planning Scheme*. Vol. 1, *Surveys and Analysis*, vol. 2, *Report*, 1954.

—— *The Problems of Urban Expansion in the Melbourne Metropolitan Area*. 1958.

—— *Report on Amending Planning Scheme No. 1*. 1962.

—— *The Future Growth of Melbourne*. 1967.

—— *Planning Policies for the Melbourne Region*. 1971.

Metropolitan Town Planning Commision. *Plan for Melbourne*. 1929.

Morrell, J. C. *Town Planning*. Report to Minister of Public Works. Government Printer, Melbourne, 1915.

Town and Country Planning Board. *Organisation for Strategic Planning*. 1967.

Victorian Parliamentary Papers. Progress Report of the Joint Select Committee on the Housing of the People in the Metropolis. 1913.

—— Royal Commission on the Housing Conditions of the People in the Metropolis: First Report, 1915, Second Report, 1917, Final Report, 1918.

—— Select Committee on the Drift of Population from the Country to the City. 1918.

Wilbur Smith and Associates. *Melbourne Transportation Study*. Vol. 1, *Survey*, vol. 2, *Parking*, vol. 3, *The Transportation Plan*. 1969.

Other Sources

Altshuler, A. *The City Planning Process*. Cornell University Press, New York, 1966.

Ashworth, W. *The Genesis of Modern British Town Planning*. Routledge Kegan Paul, London, 1954.

Australian Institute of Political Science. *Australian Cities: chaos or planned growth?* Angus and Robertson, Sydney, 1966.

Australian Town Planning Conference and Exhibition. *Official Volume of Proceedings.* Vardon and Sons Ltd, Adelaide, 1917.

Barnett, F. O. *The Unsuspected Slums.* Herald Press, Melbourne, 1933.

Barnett, F. O. and Burt, W. O. *Housing the Australian Nation.* Left Book Club, Melbourne, 1942.

Barrett, B. *The Inner Suburbs: the evolution of an industrial era.* Melbourne University Press, 1971.

Bate, W. *A History of Brighton.* Melbourne University Press, 1962.

Birch, A. and Macmillan, D. S. *The Sydney Scene 1788–1960.* Melbourne University Press, 1962.

Blazey, P. B. *Bolte: a political biography.* Jacaranda, Melbourne, 1972.

Blewett, N. and Jaensch, D. *Playford to Dunstan: the politics of transition.* Cheshire, Melbourne, 1971.

Boyd, R. *Australia's Home: its origins, builders and occupiers.* Penguin, Melbourne, 1968. First published 1952.

Bryson, L. and Thompson, F. *An Australian New town: life and leadership in a working-class suburb.* Penguin, Melbourne, 1972.

Buchanan, C. D. *Traffic in Towns.* Penguin, London, 1964.

Bunker, R. *Town and Country or City and Region?* Melbourne University Press, 1971.

Bunning, W. *Homes in the Sun: the past, present and future of Australian housing.* Nesbitt, Sydney, 1945.

Butlin, N. G. *Investment in Australian Economic Development 1861–1900.* Cambridge University Press, 1964.

Campbell, D. A. S. (ed.). *Post-war Reconstruction in Australia.* Australasian Publishing Co., Sydney, 1944.

Catley, R. and McFarlane, B. *From Tweedledum to Tweedledee, the New Labor Government in Australia: a critique of its social model.* Australia and New Zealand Book Publishing Co., Sydney, 1974.

Clark, C. M. H. *A Short History of Australia.* New York, 1963.

Crow, R. and M. *Plan for Melbourne.* Pts 1–3. Victorian State Committee of the Communist Party of Australia, Melbourne, 1969, 1970, 1972.

Davis, J. R. and Spearritt, P. *Sydney at the 1971 Census: a social atlas.* Urban Research Unit, Research School of Social Sciences, ANU, Canberra, 1974.

Duncan, G. *Marx and Mill: two views of social conflict and social harmony.* Cambridge University Press, 1973.

Fitzgerald, J. D. *Greater Sydney and Greater Newcastle.* New South Wales Bookstall Co., Sydney, 1906.

4D Planning and Design Pty Ltd. *Woolloomooloo Redevelopment Project.* Sydney, 1971.

Galbraith, J. K. *The New Industrial State.* Hamish Hamilton, London, 1967.

Gans, H. J. *People and Plans: essays on urban problems and solutions.* Basic Books, New York, 1968.

Gibson, R. S. *Socialist Melbourne.* International Bookshop, Melbourne, 1951.

Glynn, S. *Urbanisation in Australian History 1788–1900.* Nelson, Melbourne, 1970.

Goodman, P. and P. *Communitas: means of livelihood and ways of life.* University of Chicago Press, 1947.

Goodman, R. *After the Planners.* Penguin, London, 1972.

Grant, J. and Serle, G. (eds). *The Melbourne Scene 1803–1956.* Melbourne University Press, 1957.

Hancock, W. K. *Australia.* Benn, London, 1930.

Henderson, R. et al. *People in Poverty: a Melbourne survey.* Cheshire, 1970.

Hirst, J. B. *Adelaide and the Country 1870–1917: their social and political relationship.* Melbourne University Press, 1973.

Hollingworth, P. J. *The Powerless Poor: a comprehensive guide to poverty in Australia.* Stockland Press, Melbourne, 1972.

Iggulden, J. et al. (eds). *The Shame of Western Port: speculator's dream, environmental nightmare.* Westernport and Peninsula Protection Council, Melbourne, 1971.

Illich, I. *Deschooling Society. Penguin,* London, 1973.

Jacobs, J. *The Death and Life of Great American Cities.* Random House, New York, 1961.

Jones, F. L. *Dimensions of Urban Social Structure: the social areas of Melbourne, Australia.* Australian National University Press, Canberra, 1969.

Jones, M. A. *Housing and Poverty in Australia.* Melbourne University Press, 1972.

McFarlane, B. *Economic Policy in Australia: a case for reform.* Cheshire, Melbourne, 1968.

McKell, W. J. *Five Critical Years.* Australian Labor Party, Sydney, 1946.

Macpherson, C. B. *Democratic Theory: essays in retrieval.* Oxford University Press, 1973.

Manning, I. An Economic Study of Location-specific Service and Regulations in Sydney. Ph.D. thesis, ANU, Canberra, 1972.

——— *Municipal Finance and Income Distribution in Sydney.* Urban Research Unit, Research School of Social Sciences, ANU, Canberra, 1973.

Mathews, R. L. *Public Investment in Australia: a study of Australian public authority investment and development.* Cheshire, Melbourne, 1967.

Miliband, R. *The State in Capitalist Society.* Weidenfeld and Nicholson, London, 1969.

Mishan, E. J. *The Costs of Economic Growth.* Staples Press, London, 1967.

Mumford, L. *The City in History.* Secker and Warburg, London, 1961.

Neutze, G. M. *Economic Policy and the Size of Cities.* Australian National University Press, Canberra, 1965.

Parker, R. S. and Troy, P. N. (eds). *The Politics of Urban Growth.* Australian National University Press, Canberra, 1972.

Passmore, J. *Man's Responsibility for Nature.* Duckworth, London, 1974.

Playford, J. *Neo-capitalism in Australia.* Arena, Melbourne, 1969.

Playford, J. and Kirsner, D. (eds), *Australian Capitalism: towards a socialist critique.* Penguin, Melbourne, 1972.

Roe, J. *Marvellous Melbourne: the emergence of an Australian city.* Hicks Smith, Sydney, 1975.

Sandercock, L. 'Reform, property and power in the cities', *Australian and New Zealand Journal of Sociology,* vol. 10, no. 2 (June 1974), pp. 120–8.

—— 'Capitalism and the environment: the failure of success' in E. Wheelwright and K. Buckley (eds). *Essays in the Political Economy of Australian Capitalism,* vol. 1. A.N.Z. Co., Sydney, 1975.

Scott, M. *American City Planning Since 1890.* UCLA Press, Los Angeles, 1969.

Simmie, J. *Citizens in Conflict: the sociology of town planning.* Hutchinson Educational, London, 1974.

Spearritt, P. *Selected Writings of Sydney Planning Advocates 1900–1947.* Australasian Political Studies Association, monograph no. 13. Sydney, 1973.

—— "Sydney's 'Slums': middle class reformers and the Labor response", *Labour History,* no. 26 (May 1974), pp. 65-81.

Stilwell, F. *Australian Urban and Regional Development.* A.N.Z. Co., Sydney, 1974.

Stretton, H. *Ideas for Australian Cities.* Orphan Books, Adelaide, 1970.

Sulman, J. *Town Planning in Australia.* Government Printer, Sydney, 1921.

Taylor, G. *Town Planning for Australia.* Building Ltd, Sydney, 1914.

Taylor, G. *Town Planning with Common-sense.* Building Ltd, Sydney, 1918.

Thomas, P. *Taming the Concrete Jungle: the builders labourers' story.* Builders Labourers Federation, Sydney, 1973.

Titmuss, R. *Income Distribution and Social Change.* Allen and Unwin, London, 1962.

Troy, P. N. (ed.). *Urban Redevelopment in Australia.* Urban Research Unit, Research School of Social Sciences, ANU, Canberra, 1968.

Urban Research Unit, *Urban Development in Melbourne.* Australian Institute of Urban Studies, Canberra, 1973.

Weber, A. F. *The Growth of Cities in the Nineteenth Century: a study in statistics.* Cornell University Press, New York, 1963 (first published 1899).

Wheelright, E. and Buckley, K. (eds). *Essays in the Political Economy of Australian Capitalism.* Australia and New Zealand Book Publishing Co., Sydney, 1975.

Whitlam, E. G. 'Cities in a federation', *Royal Australian Planners Institute Journal,* vol. 3, no. 6, 1965.

Winston, D. *Sydney's Great Experiment: the progress of the Cumberland county plan.* Angus and Robertson, Sydney, 1957.

Wolfe, T. *Radical Chic.* Bantam Books, New York, 1970.

Wright Mills, C. *The Power Elite.* Oxford University Press, 1956.

Index